Emotional storm

OTHER WESLEYAN BOOKS BY MICHAEL EIGEN

Ecstasy (2001)

Rage (2002)

The Sensitive Self (2004)

Emotional Storm
Michael Eigen

Wesleyan University Press MIDDLETOWN, CONNECTICUT

Published by
Wesleyan University Press,
Middletown, CT 06459
www.wesleyan.edu/wespress
Copyright © 2005 by Michael Eigen
All rights reserved
Set in Scala by BW&A Books, Inc.
Manufactured in the United States of America

For permissions to reprint previously
published material, see pages 255–56.

5 4 3 2 1

Library of Congress Cataloging-in-Publication Data
Eigen, Michael.
    Emotional storm / Michael Eigen.
      p. cm.
    Includes bibliographical references.
    ISBN 0-8195-6753-1 (hardcover : alk. paper) —
    ISBN 0-8195-6754-x (pbk. : alk. paper)
      1. Emotions.   2. Psychoanalysis.   3. Psychotherapy.   I. Title.
    RC489.E45E37 2005
    616.89'17—dc22   2004061176

To

storm survivors,

storm transformers,

and those who

live and work in

storm's heart

CONTENTS

ACKNOWLEDGMENTS

Many thanks to the mental health field—there must be a better
name for it—for giving me a place in which to cultivate my particular passions and help people in the process. It is a field alive
with creative sparks, and I hope this book shines with some of
them.

I am indebted to the National Psychological Association for
Psychoanalysis, the New York Postdoctoral Program in Psychotherapy and Psychoanalysis, and the Institute for Expressive
Analysis, not only for enrichment by colleagues, but also for the
deep satisfaction I receive from seeing generations of students
grow into creative lives of their own and, in the process, become
fuller, better human beings.

This is my fourth book with Wesleyan University Press, and
I am grateful for its support of my work. Tom Radko, Leonora
Gibson, Leslie Starr, Susanna Tamminen, and Stephanie Elliott
are among those I've worked with, and they have always been
supportive and helpful. Ron Maner and Richard Hendel, respec-
tively, have edited and designed my books with Wesleyan, and
BW&A Books has produced them.

Thanks to Kathryn Madden (Blanton-Peale Institute and the
Journal of Religion and Health), Monique Savlin (*Voices*), Marla
Morris (*Journal of Curriculum Theorizing*), and Danielle Knafo
(*Living with Terror, Working with Trauma: A Clinician's Handbook*)
for inviting me to write papers that form the basis for several of
the chapters presented here.

A lot goes on for me on the internet. I'm especially grateful
to John Stone and Sylvio Merciao for their Bion sites, Cheryl
Martin (psychematters.com), and Robert Young, who mediates

many useful sites. Thanks to many good e-friends, too many to name, including Howard Covitz for two e-interviews of me that appeared in newsletters of the National Association for the Advancement of Psychoanalysis. To be able to contact and be contacted by people the world over so easily is mind-boggling.

My seminar on Winnicott, Bion, and Lacan, ongoing for nearly thirty years, is an important source of sustenance and stimulation, giving me an opportunity to work with a wonderful group of therapists—searching, imaginative, caring, relentless. Thanks to Professor Donald Levy for steering me to Wittgenstein readings I made use of—though, of course, he bears no responsibility for whatever use I made of them. My practice, my family, my writing make my life real.

My patients and I work all sorts of storms, in all sorts of ways: joy storms, grief storms, rage storms, guilt storms. Going dead is a kind of storm too, sometimes even more dangerous than explosive ones. What life there is in therapy is a great teacher. Therapy is part of the sea of life, not just an objective discipline.

I am thankful that my patients work with me. I would do better if I could. We are all we have to work with. If human beings can't work with each other, what then? This book taps emotions, dilemmas, crises, and testimonies of those who see me. I have done my best to disguise individual identities yet be true to the emotional realities at stake. The realities at stake, I believe, go far beyond the consulting room, to the heart of what challenges us as a human group. If you think you recognize someone in this book, you are mistaken—unless, of course, that someone is you.

Emotional storm

When two personalities meet,
an emotional storm is created.
—W. R. Bion,
"Making the Best of a Bad Job"

Inside the Storm

Emotional storm—a highly charged expression with many meanings and dimensions. A colorful term, mixing dark, light, danger, thrill, richness. Stormy night, stormy feelings. If there are such things as primal words, words that unify opposites, slide through contrasting realities, "storm" must be one of them.

Many years ago, I was taught that mind uses properties of physical things to express itself, its states, its feelings: first, perception of the outside world, then emotional use of what is perceived. One experiences a physical storm, then uses storm to express feelings: first outer, then inner. As if inner is some kind of analogical tail.

But what if psychic storms come first or howling storms of infancy do not distinguish between soma and emotion? The baby has a bad feeling and kicks or waves, trembles with fear, fury, tightening in the face of pain. The baby screams, a scream one feels. It pierces, rushes through one, strikes a direct hit. Most adults respond with care, but some respond with rage and try to close their ears and hide until the screaming stops. One way or another, disturbance is passed along and demands attention. Such screaming storms. I believe the scream of infancy never stops. It is part of our beings all life long. We never stop hearing, if only in whispers, a screaming self. A storm with infinite faces.

Perhaps how we respond to a baby's scream depends, in part, on the responses with which our baby screams met. Is anyone without unconscious memory of infant storm? Our shared background resonance includes stifled screams, screams that can't stop, storm areas in various stages of development.

Whatever gives rise to the word "storm" has inside and outside roots. Inside-outside realities inform and play off each other. A baby's scream, a hurricane—both contribute to the meaning of storm; both tap, add to, a common affective core. Events with certain commonalities attract each other, drawing on a variably resonant fit between inner-outer. Eugenio Montale writes of a "fierce thread" that weaves together dark and light, a seamless thread working beneath what we later call inner, outer, spiritual, physical. That a religious thread emphasizes incarnation, spirit made flesh (inspirited flesh, enfleshed spirit), points to intimacy between realms that mind distinguishes. Inner storm–outer storm give meaning to each other, fill each other out, although, at times, the outer can mask the inner.

Storms of pleasure, too, not just pain. Sexual intercourse, climax, orgasm are often expressed as storm: cries, screams, shrieks, murmurs of sex, counterparts to a baby's cry. The term "climax" finds its way through many realities—the climax of stories and other writing, musical climaxes, the climax of social events, political movements. Peaks of feeling, positive and negative.

In Montale's poems, storm means war, sex, flesh, flowers, nature, eyelids, hair—something awful, poignant, brutal, unbearably blissful, delicate (yes, there are delicate storms), tragic, cold. Sensitivity opens emotional, perceptual, sexual, social storms. "Your sweetness itself is a storm / whirling invisibly." Soft, sweet, devastating. One swoons, almost passes out in storms of joy, ineffably sublime, beautiful, the nearly incapacitating thrill of life.

In Montale's poetry, there are storms of laughter, thrills that pierce the heart. Stormy waves of hair, double meaning of lashes, lashes and lightning, a lover's look, vulnerable, uncompromising. An absent lover becomes an empty shattering breaker. Through love's vicissitudes, war casts its shadows. Storms of beauty, storms of war.

A storm already brews in Eden, in the middle of the garden, in the background. What happens to the garden, us, the snake of creativity? The snake that time can mar, not kill? Montale turns the serpent into a swamp eel, "siren of sleety seas," "to lash upcurrent" under sea pressure, under the weight "of the flood, sunk deep, from brook to brook." The flood of life, of our beings, the flood of destruction that always misses something, someone.

The eel of feeling and unfeeling soul, sensitivity and insensitivity: "more inner always, always more in the heart / of the rock, thrusting / through ruts of the mud." One thinks of the eel as underground, underwater, perhaps hibernating through winter, dead in spirit, waiting it out until in spring, springing to life, "explosion of splendor from the chestnut groves / kindles a flicker in deadwater sumps." A little like the theme of many psalms, soul dies out, comes alive. In Montale, the emphasis is on the natural, the human, and most of all on creativity. The creative spirit, bowled over by eyelashes, war, love, delicacies of touch and sight anywhere. I add the baby's cry, the baby's joy, hidden in the abyss of experience.

> Springtime soul that looks for
> life where only
> desolation stings
> the spark that says
> everything begins when everything seems
> to be charred, buried breath;

This language spans personal, social, religious, aesthetic dimensions. It expresses mood, spirit, emotional tone and texture, and has as cultural background an archetypal language of transformation. Spirit seeks transformation in the darkest places, as if transformation *must* be steeped in death.

By accident or design, the poet hits the kabbalistic, alchemical, gnostic spark, "la scintilla," the spark of aliveness. Aliveness, Kabbalah tells us, is shattered, sparks thrown in all directions. Wherever you find yourself, there are sparks waiting to be redeemed, waiting for your partnership, your work. To work with shattered sparks, the work of lifetimes. The poem speaks of rebirth, creative spirit alive once more in "edens of fertility" and

brief rainbow, twin
to that within your lashes' dazzle, that
you keep alive, inviolate, among
the sons of men, steeped in your mire . . .

Inviolate rainbow radiance in the mire. Storm radiance, swamp radiance, heavenly, hellish storms. The eel lives through them. The poet discovers eel power, eel wisdom. The eel in the mire, alive in spring, whipping through us, the new apple.

And the psychoanalytic eel, psychoanalytic wisdom? Psychoanalysis is the poet's partner. It is nothing if not a language of intensity and injury, a language of emotional storm. It develops a catalogue of assaults. Assaults of instinct, assaults of culture. As if our nature and what we create with it are too much for us.

It can be difficult even to bear the rise of sensation and feeling evoked by a work of art. How long can we stay with it, with what quality? We break off, start again, slant it this or that way, funnel it through biases, tone it down with praise or negativity. We partly push away and turn off, in order to take in what we can. To take in, really take in, places us at the mercy of transformational activity. An activity precious to us, but which borders on the unbearable.

A specialty of psychoanalysis is focusing on unbearable emotions. Emotions are not simply unbearable because of taboos, repression, conflict, important as these are. Emotions are unbearable, too, because we cannot take too much of ourselves. It is painful to act honestly and lovingly when we meet truths about ourselves. Deception is widespread in daily life because it is easier to lie a little or a lot in order to get one's way and make things go smoother. A lot of social life is based on lying. It is asocial to speak the truth about ourselves or others, deep truth, reserved for closest intimacy, for oneself, or no one.

We take for granted that social life requires hidden asocial aspects, hiding thoughts and feelings, rerouting them, perfuming communication, making self palatable, image over substance. We don't want to taste too bad to ourselves, although psychic taste buds need challenge in order to evolve. I'm not sure we have discovered adequate alternatives. To kill in order to kill falsehood and injustice cannot be a good long-term strategy. To kill for truth, to right wrongs, to be caught between lies and murder—can we do better?

What psychoanalysis offers pales before what world society and individuals need. But it does offer a place to talk about life, explore one's truth, to taste experience and perhaps build a capacity to let experience build. It recognizes, at least, like the poet, that creating language for the impact of events is never-ending, that we hunger for language responsive to impact, a language of impact and response.

Psychoanalytic imagination, psychoanalytic language deforms, mars, shapes experience too. Language is not free of violence. It creates, not only reflects, experience. Realities grow from it. This must be part of what old Jewish wisdom means when it says we create angels and demons with our words. What I write and how I write has real impact on you, creative impact, I hope, destructive impact, I fear. Of course, you can do what we normally do in much of life. Block it out, deflect it, blow it off—a protective reflex that aids survival to a point, while warding off the work of mutual self-giving.

Many things feed deformation of meaning, one of them the press of affect. Whether we know how to conceptualize it or not, our response to what happens to us—our feelings about things —impacts us. Emotional responsiveness—unconscious as well as conscious emotional sensitivity—exerts enormous force on personality. Affect affects what we call our sense of self or ego, our very beings.

"When two personalities meet, an emotional storm is created." This remark by W. R. Bion is the takeoff point, the core of this book: What we do with emotional storm and what it does with us is an open process. We need to begin to learn how to make room for and work with emotional storm. Hiding or enacting it is not enough. We are challenged to learn more about becoming partners with our capacities, with who we are. Such work will not solve social or global problems, but these problems will not be solved without it. Social programs fail because selfish gain and destruction take precedence over self-giving. This is natural enough, but the storm we are requires more.

The way we affect each other, traumatize each other, create and re-create each other, hide from each other, take flight, try again, outmaneuver ourselves, sink, break, come back—news of storms in progress. While psychoanalysis is part of the warp, it takes seriously the shaping impact of affective attitude and creates caring, imaginative encounters with emotional impacts one too often feels defeated by. If psychoanalysis is unconsciously deformed by unconscious emotional storm and blindly reaches for what cannot be seen or touched, at least it bears witness to a storm center that requires our most profound attention.

We learn from psychoanalysis that emotional storm does not just shatter; it spreads through experience, often unnoticed or misnamed. Sometimes outside storms are created, not simply in place of or to express inside ones, but because inside ones remain inchoate, beyond grasp, nameless, hungry. Wars and tragic events involving individuals and groups that might have been prevented give name and place to a storm hunger with roots going back at least to birth, if not before. The affective storms of infancy, acute agony or joy, provide a dim background that feeds a need for affective intensity. Individuals are driven to feel more than they can feel and groups they compose make it possible for them to do so.

That people have written about "balance" since antiquity indicates early and keen awareness that the tightrope of peace is uneasily strung between tendencies to stifle or explode. A cultural dialectic in response to our storm center threads through history:

Confucius/Lao Tzu, classical/romantic, Apollonian/Dionysian, ego/id. Freud's concepts are riddled with dualities, making them not simply vague or unscientific, but powerful and suggestive.

Ego/id, for example. On the one hand, ego is associated with the cerebral cortex, inhibition, selection, repression, mediation; id with passions, drives, the subcortex. On the other hand, ego deludes itself, hallucinates. Freud gives as examples, falling in love, overestimation of the loved one, devotion to a leader, identifying with causes good or bad. We speak of blind devotion to authority or love as blind, referring to our common self-deluding/ hallucinating ability. Psychoanalysis catalogues ways in which ego lies to itself, partly to handle, evade, control, or otherwise deal with psychic pain (abandonment, intrusion, humiliation, shame, deprivation, castration, blows to self-esteem, or, in that apt word, mortifications, where even slights are taken as death threats). Ego, mediator of common sense and compromise, is liar par excellence. It is also devoted to truth, which it idealizes, kills for, and learns about.

When we use words like "ego" or "id," we forget that we are talking about ourselves. Take these masks away, add social conditions to the catalogue of pains, and we can trace across societies, groups, individuals ways we respond to ills, partly of our own making.

My work is with individuals. That is my calling. I sometimes wish I were a social reformer. But that is not what I do, except indirectly. I like to think that helping individuals helps the group, but I would not bet on it. Nevertheless, I do feel that processes at work in individual therapy have relevance for world affairs—at least, ultimately, in the long run. Because—and this would be too stupid to say were it not for the fact that we have not assimilated it—we are all people. And what can be learned from working with any person may have value for others.

We. Our. When we bomb and shoot and exploit each other for one-sided gain, we as a human group are involved in self-wounding processes. Self-wounding problem-solving is wide-spread. How we respond to our self-wounding attempts at solution of difficulties is an evolutionary challenge.

In everyday life, storms are displaced, diffused, limn events far from a storm center. "Reasons," "causes," "justifications" for storm today trigger, draw on, gather force from storms long in progress. One storm may be confused with another. Long work has convinced me, for example, that from infancy on, fear of starvation and suffocation fuse, and that dread of emotional and physical suffocation/starvation meld boundlessly. When we can't process feeling, we are suffocating and starving. This affective impotence can activate horrible world scenarios that take their toll but do not result in affective potency.

An aim of this book is to help activate, to whatever extent possible, affective potency. An alternative trope is affective digestion. To say that we swell with power in response to emotional impotence is to say that we are plagued with widespread emotional indigestion or are psychically suffocating. Psychic reality is a seemingly unlocalizable chronic irritant. The need for food, education, civil rights seems more tangible. Emotional reality may be more elusive but no less real. How we affect each other, respond to each other and use these responses—what can be more important, more difficult?

Emotional storm is one dimension of mutual responsiveness or reactivity. The chapters ahead approach emotional storm in a variety of ways. Storm changes values, takes on meaning in different contexts. To parents, baby is a storm. An infant, subject to its own storms, is subject to the storms of parents, who bring bliss and tumult. As the book opens domains, lines between somatic, psychic, social, spiritual storms fade.

This book takes forward themes that were implicit in my book *The Sensitive Self.* Vicissitudes of sensitivity run through subtle person-to-person interweavings, from the most precious mutual enhancement to realities of child abuse, gross or subtle. The need to be cruel, to care, to tone things down, to blow things up taps unconscious memory of affective intensity that drive people toward destruction in order to feel filled. One imagines murder will enable one to breathe or the power of economic exploitation will make one free. Where there are victims, sensitivity suffers, and struggle between constructive and destructive storms await us.

Storms we create through outside pleasures and horrors, important as they are, mask the ineffable fact that psychic reality itself involves storm systems that require a responsiveness we barely sense but must grow into. The chapters ahead turn bits of these storm systems a variety of ways, getting alternate experiences, building a sense of emotional processing, wherein emotional potency, digestion, breathing go together.

Chapters 1 ("Emotional Storms") and 2 ("More Emotional Storms") connect the reality of emotional storm to human sensitivity from infancy on. Emotional storms of infancy come closest to being total, nothing held back, nothing to hold back. Such all-out, nearly complete psychosomatic expression remains a backdrop adding something tantalizing to everyday, partial experiencing, egging us on to achieve something fuller. We use aspects of Bion, Bowlby, and Buber and view interlacings between infantile and adult experiencing, their eternal interplay. What happens to affective storms of baby life? Why are ideologies of control so insufficient? What can we make of the dialectics of sensitivity and power? What is experience looking for? How does the feel of ourselves grow?

We wade more deeply into clinical work, delineate mixtures of psychic tendencies, cite tensions we reshape ourselves to meet. Complexity and difficulty, if they are not too toxic and overwhelming, are food for the spirit. Faith is always dealing with hints or outbursts of outer-inner catastrophe, and emotional digestion plays catch-up. My portrayals are concerned with letting feeling storms speak, letting them have their say, seeing where they lead. The kind of "read" I hope for, the kind of writing I do, is a kind of "training" or invitation to stay with experience without pressing the eject button too quickly. Somewhat analogous to the ability of animals to "smell" or sense danger and nourishment, we have a latent capacity to evolve psychic taste buds. At this point in our history it is critical to develop an ability to taste storm nuances before they flame and learn how to communicate within the storm's heart.

Chapter 3 ("Smile and Scream") pays homage to a core experience in life, our repeated sense of falling apart and coming together. One way or another, this is a nuclear moment that generates languages of transformation, religious and secular, from earliest history to the present. This nuclear experience may take the form of feeling dead, then coming alive, or of breakdown and recovery. We might call it rebirth with a thousand faces, although most of the time it is an aborted, even deformed, psychic birth. There is in us an urge to get this birth right, once and for all, an intimation tapping more total experiencing of infancy, when dying out and coming back, disintegrating and reforming underwrote a sense of lack and wholeness. In this chapter I give personal and clinical examples of attempts to go through reshaping experiences in hope of better outcomes. My models are movies by Kurosawa and Fellini, traditional writings and vision, as well as clinical experience. Freud takes us straight to the heart of how we react to wounding processes. Later psychoanalytic waves, literature, art, and history add to our sense of what we do with each other, dramas of mutual resonance, injury, recovery—phases of a basic rhythm that can misfire.

Chapter 4 ("No Amount of Suffering") takes us more deeply into the power of suffering, good or ill. Trauma often destroys, but can also stimulate the use of capacities that otherwise might not have been forced to develop. There is no final victory over destruction in this life, but successive attempts to work with destructive forces *can* make us better people and bring us to new places. In this chapter I focus on the dimensions of suffering of two individuals, branches of suffering that are dead ends, branches that support life. The lure of destructive radiance can be hideous, and, at times, the best we can do is become more open to a sense of helplessness. There are times when waiting and doing nothing opens more possibilities than storming ahead.

Chapter 5 ("Somatic Storms") connects emotional with somatic storms. The intimate interlacing of feelings and body would come as no surprise if we did not persistently disconnect them in our minds. Why do we keep separating them, in spite of all our lip service to mind-body unity? There is enormous gravitational pull to separate all our parts, to separate from ourselves, a part of how consciousness works in its differentiating mode. It is easy to forget in a life oriented toward tasks, business, achievement, that touching a body is touching a person. This kind of forgetting makes killing easier, a business kill or personal triumph at someone's expense. Yet it is obvious that when a mother touches a baby's body, she touches a person. And words or glances or tones that affect a person affect a body. What do we do with this basic permeability? Do we shut it out, rise above it, wound it, become partners with it? Somatic storms take us deep into a person. Emotional storms take us deep into a body.

In Chapter 6 ("Dream Images") I trace the work of emotional storm in dream images, using my own dreams and life as the principal point of entrée. Dreamwork is important in processing affects and often works with catastrophic dreads and traumatic impacts. There are creative as well as destructive storms. Dreamwork produces the former too, awakening us to possibilities, fresh ways of experiencing. One of the amazing things about dreams is how they can recirculate odd bits of psyche, bric-a-brac pieces with old roots, old nuclei, life springing out of lost corners. Storms of life, death, sex, trauma—truly a storm with changing faces.

Chapter 7 ("Killers in Dreams") studies one of the most common and frightening of dream images: the threat of murder, attack, or break-in. Killers in dreams take many forms and have many meanings. Death *is* scary, and murder is real. If dreams represent and help process emotions, what scares us in daily life will be part of them. Yet fears of aggression and lack of control take many turns. We fear dying when we come more alive as well as the reverse: infusions of aliveness *or* deadness can be threatening. The rise or fall of energy can appear as killers in dreams and spill into the outside world. Separation between dreaming activity and reality is not what we once thought it to be.

A psychoanalyst's hope: if we can work with our night killers, maybe our day killers will diminish. The fact that killing threatens us day and night says something about the sort of beings we are. Whatever or whoever else we are, we have a psyche that kills, and we need to study and oppose it. We need to struggle with ourselves and see what more we can do with our makeup. A new dimension of struggle perhaps, becoming better dreamworkers, better processors of affect and emotional storm. How do we open ourselves to this task if destructive surges threaten our attempt to work with the latter? This chapter is a detailed attempt to do such work.

Chapter 8 ("Training Wheels") portrays affect shifts in therapy with a woman I call Eva. The focus is on two particular people, Eva and myself, but the chapter is meant to give a sense of how thoroughly, if often unconsciously, affect fields underlay, pervade, influence what goes on between people in general. The very texture of contact and lack of contact is at stake. Therapy tries to absorb and work with storm currents it evokes, as well as those that spring outside it. A lot happens between therapist and patient that may or may not reach words, that may not even enter awareness. Some comes to the fore, but there is much dense underpacking that gives the relationship its power. Rather than tie up loose ends, therapy pulls some threads that take the patient deeper into life.

Chapter 9 ("The Binding") focuses on the biblical story of Abraham almost killing Isaac. Without derogating a traditional emphasis on faith—this tale often is seen as a paradigm of Israel's great faith—I use depth psychology to search out difficulties we have in relationships, particularly, our struggle with destructive urges and attitudes. Familial violence is endemic, and many are the parents I've seen who struggle with fury toward each other and their children. Child abuse is a world problem. Suicide another. We are not very good with our emotional storms, but most of us try our best.

That God tells Abraham to kill Isaac as a test of faith is madness. But madness in relationships is not unusual. The urge to kill one's children, to kill those close as well as far, the horrible fact that violence is part of intimate bonds as well as part of fights for external territory and power, is dramatized by God's order to Abraham. Indeed, in Christianity God sacrifices his son, Jesus, for the redemption of sin. Guilt and murder go together on either end, guilt because of murderous wishes or acts, and murder to cleanse guilt. Emotional storms that religion organizes and unleashes continue to gather force today. Lines between affective attitudes in individuals, groups, and nations are slim indeed.

The story of Abraham and Isaac is called "The Binding" in Judaism, and it is striking that "binding" is a term in psychoanalysis, referring to the binding of affect, drives, impulse—a term used to refer to rerouting, sublimating, transforming, or simply controlling. To control destructive urges, attitudes, tendencies— no small order. We succeed only partly. And from the perspective of police blotters and world conflict, our success is fragile and questionable.

What is needed is not simply control, but a sense of the human full enough to undertake the affective work that needs to be done, that we don't yet know how to do, that we make forays into. The opposition sanity-madness is not very helpful. Often we cannot tell the difference. Claims to sanity frequently turn out to be mad. Rather than claim a point outside madness, we may need to learn how to work within it.

The final chapter ("Guilt") takes up one of the nuclear themes in human life, a great storm of storms: the press or absence of guilt. Guilt is present in variable ways, with variable functions, sometimes in excess, sometimes seemingly not at all. I have long been struck by intersections in the writings on guilt by Wittgenstein, Levinas, and Bion, and I try to bring this out in this chapter. Often we find ourselves *in* guilt, rather than finding guilt in us, as if guilt precedes us, awaits us. We may have to go some to discover what awaits us, to begin the adventure of relating to what is already there, to help it evolve, to evolve with it.

What we learn from our encounter with guilt is very much open-ended, a journey in progress. Guilt is an enormous force. Politicians try to manipulate it. It fuses with hate, with love, with dread, with caring. It sensitizes us, makes us more responsive. It suffocates us, makes us mad. It is a capacity we are grappling with, learning about, growing with.

What role can guilt play in an Age of Psychopathy? Is it passé, beside the point, laughable in a triumph-oriented world? Guilt plays a role in adaptive, affiliative behavior, social bonding, interpersonal regulation, the connection between people, but rolls off the drive to succeed, survive and win (perhaps another kind of "connection"). We can dissociate guilt, have contempt for it, ignore it, pay lip service to it, as we do what we have to do to make it in the real world. The still, small voice of the prophet—a scandal or a joke?

Paul Krugman tells us that in the United States the robber baron is more rule than aberration. Walter A. McDougall says something similar, documenting the "creative corruption" of the hustler in our rise to power. The importance of power, money, and ideology slants our sense of the human. Ambition helps make us strong, gets us places, and I wouldn't minimize its contribution to vitality and well-being. But it also leaves us truncated, suspicious, resentful, angry, ready for battle.

Psychotherapy battles for another kind of voice, another concern. Its contribution may appear marginal, but is no less important. It struggles to point to a realm of feelings and attitudes that mark our existence, that make for better or worse living beyond the fact of capital acquisition or religious certitude, a broader feeling context for our lives.

These chapters end on a ledge, with the challenge that guilt brings. Guilt as an index not of oppression but of sensitivity, of caring. In this, psychological portrayals in the Bible are as relevant as ever. The battle of caring with all other attitudes—no smug grin, no easy words, no fabricated image to cover a slick will. Quite a ledge, quite a fall.

I want this book to end with loose threads. Threads for readers to pull, to take their own ways. There are failings, pockets of excess, gaps, deficits, narcissistic outcries, gut howls, moments of extravagant modesty. But a lot of life is in these pages too, a lot of problems of life, a lot of hope, goodness, faith. I am more moved than ever by the work individuals do together in the privacy of a room, a work where the currency of exchange is mainly something felt, ineffable, attitudinal. I am proud to share this with the public world, in the belief that feelings count and the ways they are structured by attitudes count. And in the belief that the importance of everything else in life—its great and crucial importance—is permeated by affective attitudinal contexts. Quality of life includes emotional quality, personal quality, quality of character. Materiality is judged in terms of what it adds or takes away from the quality of felt existence, the good we put it to.

1 Emotional Storms

"When two personalities meet, an emotional storm is created." So begins the last essay W. R. Bion wrote, "Making the Best of a Bad Job," written in 1979, the year he died at the age of eighty-two. In 1978 he wrote appreciatively of Martin Buber's *I and Thou*, with reference to what happens when people meet with an open attitude. It was one of the last entries in his journal, *Cogitations*. I think of Buber's words, "All real living is meeting." Bion's emotional storm is part of meeting. Bion and Buber, two octogenarians, tell us it is not a storm that goes away with age, not something we get used to. It is part of experience all life long, a central fact of what it is to be a human being.

At a talk I attended many years ago, John Bowlby remarked that the same basic emotions are with us from infancy to old age, among them grief, anger, joy, fear—feelings we never outgrow. Bowlby spoke of a young child's reaction to separation from his mother, his rage at her return, his freezing up—explosion and shutdown following each other. Growth requires a good deal of interactive pleasures, pains, joys. Withdrawal is part of interacting: we rarely, if ever, are *all* there. We cajole each other out of corners of self, find each other in odd places, sensing and making sense of ins and outs of attachment.

Bowlby showed research pictures—photos of children and mothers at various phases of connection/disconnection—but let on that he was speaking about his own feelings too. He joked about following his grown children to the United States because he did not like being far from them, not too far, too long. His talk communicated acceptance, not merely tolerance, of feelings we share or undergo alone.

Bion's statement focuses less on separation than on presence, what it feels like to be together. We impact on each other and look the other way, unable to handle what we evoke. If we pay attention, emotional intensity mounts. We fear increasing turbulence and try to play it down. What do we do with emotional waves set off in one another? Bion's eye falls on what feelings do to us, our insufficiency in the face of emotions.

We are creatures who do not know what to do with ourselves. In the Bowlby example above, there is a rhythm of breakdown and repair. The sense of trauma-recovery and breakdown-repair is a basic emotional sequence that informs and colors our lives. It is part of basic faith and trust that meets many challenges. Nevertheless, even when the sequence comes out well—on the side of repair, recovery, reconciliation—something in us does not altogether let go of the breakdown. We keep one of our many inner eyes on it. The fact that we are beings subject to emotional breakdown does not go away. To one degree or another, we are plagued by undercurrents of anxiety, haunted by awareness that catastrophe is around the corner. As in old comic movies, disaster and mishap take one by surprise, though one is always anticipating them.

Part of everyday sensitivity involves nursing ourselves past transient breakdowns. We get better at helping each other along. Still, there is a residue, a question. Sometimes helping and being helped means giving up—at least, for a time—areas not open to immediate help. For example, someone sees a therapist, senses the latter's limitations, and brings forth aspects of problems *this* therapy *might* handle. One sets aside areas exceeding the current situation. Help we give each other is limited to help we *can* give, although personality problems ask for more.

Like a baby adapting to a feed, we adapt to help at hand. But some of us are cranky or colicky about it, depressed over the outcome, desperate, anxious, demanding, hidden. If pressed enough, we break into a rash or a cough or digestive woe. We could not fit into the feed. We could not slip into a self that worked.

Being with each other sets into motion stuff that does not fit in. So many subcurrents, hints, feels, bits of nameless life spread and undulate and bounce in noncategorized ways. Mixtures of things that fit and don't fit interlock, bombard, melt, mount, rush through cracks of self when we're together. How much we look away from when we say what we almost mean. Evasion enables experience to survive.

Emotional storm is something basic—like grief, anger, fear, joy, any of which can be stormlike. It is not just that we are born more physically immature than other animals. It is more a matter of emotional immaturity. Our bodies grow up faster than our ability to digest feelings. One of the oddities of adult life is the robust, grown-up bodies we see about us without psyches to match. Emotional immaturity far outstrips our physically immature beginnings. As a human group, we are still awaiting an ability to work with our emotional life, although we may take some credit for starting to try.

It is not just about feelings, but about the "feel" of feelings, how feelings feel, including how life feels. We impact on each other as a matter of course but screen out much of the impact. For example, we brush off anxiety that is part of social contact, unless it forces us to pay attention. Ignoring unpleasant states helps us to get through things, but "getting through" is not always what is most important. A man recently complained that he is good at getting through things, not living them. He has the doomed sense of rushing through life, while waiting for it to be over. It has begun to disturb him, this hidden sense that beneath his busyness, he is waiting life out. Turning away from our emotional sensitivity can put in danger our very sense of what it feels like to be alive.

Emotional storm is not pathology. It is part of reactivity, permeability, responsiveness—part of what happens when people meet. We are not sick because we are sensitive or sensitive because we are sick, unless we want to view human sensitivity itself as a kind of dis-ease (i.e., we are not comfortable with our sensitive natures). Too often we pathologize our extreme nature in order to escape it. We normalize a certain everyday insensitivity and put down emergent sensitivity, stigmatizing it when it is troublesome. "Did anyone ever tell you, you are just too sensitive?" How is that as a self-justificatory gambit to stay on top of things? We are good at dismissing what we cannot handle.

Bion does not call our sensitivity and reactivity ill or normal, just difficult. We create storms in each other. We *are* emotional. Emotions quicken when we come together. He states the obvious. Emotional reality is. An ability to stay and work with it needs to evolve. What happens to primary emotionality, emotional storm? How do we respond to feelings? What transformations do they undergo? To what extent can we stick with them? What happens when we do?

Notions of control, mastery, regulation are not much help. They may be of practical concern in certain instances ("Control yourself—don't kill, rape, injure"). But notions of control and mastery have been around a long time without doing very much to build feeling capacity. Too often "control" substitutes for feeling, covering over ignorance of the latter. We stop rather than undergo important life processes. It is one of the conundrums of living that we find it difficult to sustain what makes us feel alive. The fact that we are not up to our emotional life is part of who we are.

If Socrates confessed ignorance in the face of problems related to thinking, we might begin by confessing ignorance when it comes to problems of feeling. Confession of ignorance is part of self-knowledge. Ideologies of regulation and control tend to jump the gun, since we aren't sure what it is we are trying to control and regulate or how to go about doing it. Understanding doesn't do the trick if we don't know what it is we are trying to understand. We are not sure what use to make of understanding or what to expect of it. We do not understand very much about understanding and often miscalculate what it can do.

We rationalize emotions in order to tone down their ability to disturb. It is not surprising that control breaks down, oscillating with explosive outbursts and freezing up. If feeling life is sat on, it does not have a chance to evolve. Mental maps are useful but no substitute for the thing itself. There is need to build emotional muscles through exercise of feelings. Overuse of medication in the service of control can contribute to a deterioration of our capacity to tolerate emotional states. Insofar as we are ill-equipped to engage emotional reality, a rise of feelings may be experienced as an attack, responded to in kind. A typical, resulting bind is depression in response to emotional violence, followed by emotional violence in response to depression, a spiral signaling a block of affect flow and a failure of attention to value parts of the emotional field.

What is my immediate prescription? Return again and again to the point of mutual impact. Emotional storm is real and ought not to be obliterated because we don't know what to do with it. Emotional sensitivity is precious. It is important to stay with impacts or, at least, discover that one is unable to. What happens when one can't endure another's impact? Where does one go when one tries to escape the storm? What happens if one tries to escape reactivity? If one succeeds?

We need to grow with impacts, or around them, and let a sense of what it feels like to be together develop. The sense of what it feels like to be together is what makes us—all of us—partners. To not cultivate the feel of another is a kind of soul-murder. The evolution of the human race depends on not aborting the feeling of another.

Primary emotional storm, vulnerability, permeability. The first thing to do is to acknowledge it. Grant it space, time, recognition, honor. Note it: we are in and part of emotional storm. It is us and we are it—partly. Don't pull the plug by violence or collapse. It is enough to begin with a sense that emotional storm is happening. The simple fact: impact is happening, impact is happening, impact is happening. No need to sanitize or soundproof it. We are struggling to build our capacity to bear being with another human being, to bear to build one's own responsiveness, reciprocal responsiveness.

Meaning arises from impacts; meanings keep arising. It is all right to draw the meanings out, learn from them if one can. Any impact gives rise to many meanings and to further impacts. Perhaps it is impossible to isolate impact from meaning. Fields of meaning try to circumscribe impacts. To write "felt impact" is tempting, but there are impacts that register first and are felt later, a little like discovering that one was shot by finding blood.

We do not have to know what an impact means, how to interpret it. It is enough to notice that it is, that it is happening. We rush to meaning to jump over what is happening. We do not let happening happen. Meaning puts the brakes on or provides insulation. In one attitude we rush to get past what is happening; in another we try to stay with it and linger a while. A kind of training, a discipline: to return to impact.

It may be impossible to identify "an" impact—there may be no such thing as "an" impact. Impacts are parts of impact fields. That a plurality of resonance inheres in "any" impact is suggested by the plurality of meanings impacts give rise to. Any impact is likely to be made up of sets of impacts with dominant tones and subtones manifesting in meaning as themes. However, do not view impact as multiplicity in order to skirt the fact that something is happening. Often something happens without being able to say exactly what.

Emotional storm is happening. Emotional storm is happening. How much injury might be avoided by staying with this fact? Contact generates emotional storms. What don't we do to tone down, divert, channel, avoid the responsiveness sensitivity is prey to? Diversionary pleasures of entertainment may be harmless enough. But often we cut off impending storms by creating other kinds of storms. Instead of sensitivity storms we create insensitivity storms. We turn to predatory addictions, menacing uses of power—rev up one set of feelings to blot out others. As a group, not just individually, we injure ourselves to stop responsiveness. We cut feeling off, other off, self off—cut life off.

Bion describes the baby as an "annihilating force." In doing so he is not only referring to the fact that his first wife died in childbirth. The association of death with childbirth once was stronger than it is today, but it will always be part of awareness. Bion's annihilating baby draws on a background of real danger attached to birth, but most pointedly refers to *psychic* annihilation.

Babies exert enormous pressure on parents, which the latter may *and* may not be able to handle. Pressures are handled *somewhat*, sometimes better, sometimes worse. Somewhat is the rule and often is good enough or will have to do. Nevertheless, pressures mount and push toward breakdown. Temporary breakdowns are an everyday part of parenting, although things can spiral and take a bad turn. Emotional storms produced by an infant's impact tend to be met *and* covered over with love and caring. Love, too, has stormy components. The baby's pressure for attention—indeed, devotion—can propel love toward a breaking point. All too often, the stress of child care—especially the demands of love—fragments couples, precipitates rage, sometimes violence, drags one into depression and chronic fatigue. Anxiety stings a well-meaning mother—am I good enough? will I hurt my baby? can I do it? She pushes herself in the face of doubt and weariness, at times to the point of collapse. Her inner screams blend with the baby's outer ones and go unheard. What starts as love turns into hate, what promises to be joyful becomes unbearably frustrating. A personality may not possess the resources to support the love conceived when a baby opens one's heart. The promise of love is one thing, what one has to do to back it up another.

On the other hand, the atom bomb (baby) that scores a direct hit can change life for the better. One can work with difficulties and discover the transformational thread that goes with putting another first. In a recent session, a man caught a glimpse of this thread through its negative. He manipulated a girlfriend to have an abortion and now has second thoughts, not about the abortion, but about himself. He sees that he loses out in purpose and richness of living, not just by putting himself first, but by failing to take the other's existence seriously.

His feelings went through phases. When he learned that his girlfriend was pregnant, he was overjoyed. They used no protection, knew what would happen. They were happy. Then he began thinking she manipulated him. He didn't know if he loved her. They were just having an affair. They liked being together. Then she asked him to pay off her debts and said she wanted to stop working to be a full-time mother. His fuses blew. What was he getting into? Was she using him? She had had previous abortions. Why should he be the sucker? Good feelings spiraled down into a twisted, "realistic" self.

He was not ready. This was not a good time. A baby would upset his life, be too much. He was his own baby. He did not want to displace his ego from the center of his universe. He would be rational. He would not be rushed. Why had he succumbed to the idea of fatherhood with a girl he had known only a few months? He had his life as a whole to consider. And now, after the abortion, he began to think his "reasonable self" did not understand much about life. Maybe religion was right about the importance of the other. Now he sees his mistrust, circumspection, his sapiens, as fear of life, holding back, lack of faith. "Faith is what babies are about. I try to solve life by being rational, by manipulating it, outsmarting it. There's another way in—and I'm missing it."

He has not found a way in. He finds ways to get out of it, to keep life at bay, to postpone. But he begins to wonder. The lost baby impacts, the life he cannot live begins to hit him. It is not guilt so much as seeing what he is missing, what he can't let himself be part of. Yet it was fear of what he would be missing— self-centered freedom—that compelled him to abort a different way of life. Whichever way, something is missing.

Never had he seen how thoroughly addicted to himself he was or how afraid, unwilling, unable to embrace another person. For the first time since I knew him, he saw that there was an issue, that the quality of his life and the kind of person he might be were at stake. It was precisely because he froze, pushed away potential impact of others, aborted feelings that could lift him beyond himself, that *not* having a baby brought home his predicament. He chose to maintain an illusion of control by pushing life away. In this case, the real baby he dared not have became a signifier for life he dares not feel.

On the other hand, there are those who shut a baby up with adoration. Bion applies this to Jesus: "All that they could do was to decide Jesus was God and shut him up under a tombstone of heavy, cold, religious adoration." Jesus, like baby, is new life threatening old order. When aliveness (Jesus, baby) comes alive, "the religious outfit and the scientific blackguards . . . try to keep the humanists and artists and poets under control by murder" or with "loving adoration" or try "to find out where the dangerous embryo is, so that they can worship it to death." Control becomes important as an ordering principle where responsiveness fails.

One takes the wind out of someone's sails by overpraising. A woman has an undiagnosed skin disease that comes and goes for "unknown" reasons. There seems to be some autonomic tie-in with dread and rage. She can't bear her mother's gooey looks, her mother's loving touch. They stop her from breathing. She breaks out in a rash. If her heart's desire is touched, she dies, falls ill. She is a danger to herself. Hate contains her. She thinks of her mother's adoring look when she takes a bite of food—and stops eating. A love that's too close, too much—claustrophobic love, suffocating love. Instead of merely sweating, she gets rashes. She breaks out, trying to break out of her skin, out of her mother's skin, away from that worshipful gaze.

Where can one go to escape that worshipful gaze? One solution is to destroy oneself partially, play one's life down. But my patient wanted to live. So she let herself live a little, making sure her life had enough bad stuff to give her room. Not that there wouldn't be enough bad stuff anyway—but she made sure. In part, she controlled her mother (inside) by attempting to control how much life she could have—less room for mother, less room for life. Many people protect "the dangerous embryo" by not letting it grow too much.

How to tone life down so that it is livable. Sensitivity to impact ripples through many dimensions. Impact of ideas, feelings, events, people—new growth processes of many sorts. Bion calls the creative function Messiah or Genius. James Hillman calls it Daimon. For William Blake, Jesus is Human Imagination. How to convey the rise of life that shatters, uplifts, reorients, gives one shivers, leaves one breathless, makes one work. So many suicides and so much madness left in its wake. Yet there is hunger for intuition, hunger for creativity. We lust for the storm we feel and wait on each nuance. If all earth's soil passes through worms, all the feelings in the world pass through us. Feelings seek, and stimulate, a new kind of digestion. How does one digest a storm? A little at a time. Art, poetry, dreaming are fragments of digestive work. Without this work, feelings turn against us. What is enlivening is endangering, if we cannot evolve with it.

This may not sound like much compared to the exercise of power. A path of vital aliveness—which may or may not care about people—is self-centered power. One need not feel one's oats, one's élan at the expense of others, but often one does. How easily one crosses over into cruelty. So much politics is the art of masking destructive power as the national good, the good of the people. Words like "compassion" become masks for power operations, as political enclaves practice the art of convincing masses of people to act against their own interests.

An antiphonal refrain relates power intoxication to a deeper sense of injury. Wounds are bandaged by winning. The injured injure. Address the wounds, and power madness diminishes.

Can striving for power be reduced to injury, overt or hidden? Isn't winning a thrill in its own right; isn't it addicting? Where can the legitimate, constructive use of power have its say?

The joys of power, competence, and striving for mastery have their own impetus, although they fuse with and can be co-opted by other motivational strands. It is often impossible to distinguish between constructive/destructive aspects of power. Blends of tendencies are the rule, the reality. It is not a matter of undoing or subduing our need to exercise power, the pleasurable power we feel in exercising ourselves. It is more a matter of situating our sense of power within a larger field of experience so that it is balanced by other factors (traditionally, justice, love, common sense, wisdom among them). In this context, power interacts with, and is distributed through, considerations beyond itself.

Power is a basic state. But not the only basic state. In order to become power mad our range of feelings must be constricted. Trauma certainly plays a role in constrictions. To note this is not to take the air out of power. It is to open a larger perspective through which power has a chance of finding legitimate use, qualified by and furthering values that arise from other areas of living.

The malleability of infancy is with us all life long. We do not outgrow being subject to influence. Influence helps us grow and go beyond ourselves, as well as opens us to exploitation. Malleability and power, twin capacities, contribute to our ability to survive, although they can become cancerous. That we are malleable beings capable of channeling great power calls for growth of respect and caring for our capacity to mold and be molded. It is not enough to break molds (they form as fast as we imagine we break them), but it is a beginning to realize we are always less or more or other than we think we are.

We swim in fields of experience no more subject to immediate thought and vision than the physical universe is delimited by what the naked eye can see. My bias as a particular kind of depth psychologist is to emphasize the importance of what it feels like to be together, a special part of what it feels like to be alive. What life feels like when you are with me and I am with you. This is, admittedly, a limited part of the larger world of experience, but I am tempted to grant it a privileged place. Here we have a chance of slowing things down enough to speak and listen in depth, without the need to rush. We can give ourselves time to feel and say all we can and wait for more. We can give ourselves time to learn how to be with each other, to explore sore spots and obstacles. We can dare to peel masks and discover nooks and crannies of life that turn out to be unimaginably valuable.

A place to begin is with sensitivity to storm on point of impact when we are together. Staying with how we feel with each other and staying with it some more. To stay with that, and keep on staying with that as it changes, unfolds, complicates without precise beginning or end. My naive contention is that if we did more of that, we would be less interested in entrapping, dominating, and slaughtering each other, more able to resist our compulsion to enact destructive storms. More interested in what life feels like for its own sake, including, but not pre-empted by, self-centered lust for power (individual or group). The will to power must have its say, not its way. It commands no more than a vote in psychic democracy. It is part of a larger emotional storm that people need to navigate. One starts by tasting, developing a psychic taste for storms. A taste we need to grow into.

2 More Emotional Storms

"When two personalities meet, an emotional storm is created." I tend to say, when two "people" meet. Bion writes "personalities." Bion's word is good because it opens psychoanalytic fantasies as to what constitutes an emotional storm. Given the history of psychoanalytic ideas, one can imagine storm involving various personality structures—id, ego, superego, and various components of these structures—aggression, destruction, creation, love, bad (including exciting-rejecting, abusive) and good objects, introjects of varied emotional valences (toxic-benevolent extremes and mixtures), transformational objects, true and false self organizations, ego structures (schizoid, psychopathic, autistic, paranoid, communal ego elements), complex relational patterns, and so on. Lots of personality ingredients make up storms, and storms impact on lots of personality ingredients. There are many psychoanalysts capable of shaking the pot and cooking tasty and useful brews.

"All real living is meeting," writes Martin Buber. Near the end of his life, Bion said that Buber comes "much closer to recognizing the realities of the situation when human speech is resorted to." Closer than whom? Closer than those who use words and concepts to close off or tidy up the living reality of mutual impact. Buber's I-Thou evokes the emotional storm of meeting that ordinary "rational" language plays down. Here Bion couches a basic reality in terms of mystical power or force that "cannot be measured or weighed or assessed" by the human mind. Yet human beings feel or sense or intuit it and speak and write and draw and pray and dance it. Buber's I-Thou meeting is one such expressive try. For Buber, like Bion, emotional storm is normative.

Bion finds in religion, as well as science, examples of language used to tone down, obscure, rationalize, and escape the moment of meeting. For example, the term "omnipotence" squeezes intimation of unknown force or power into a mold derived from conquest and rule. Many mystics and writers—like Ralph Waldo Emerson, William Blake, and Walt Whitman, in their specific ways—intuit a creative power that is not top-dog, king-of-the-mountain power. In Buber it is power of relationship, I-Thou power, power of impact and response, response and revelation. Even the watered-down term "omnipotence," meant to express ultimate power, is packed with multiple realities, relational possibilities. For one thing, omnipotence refers to its counterpart, impotence, so that position and counterposition contain each other, two sides of a coin. As a marker of power, omnipotence-impotence shrinks into a wealth of meanings growing out of a larger reality pressing for attention.

Bion speaks of a certain primacy of *relationship* (his italics), "an open-ended reality in which there is no termination." No termination as ordinarily understood or circumscribed by "rational" language. And, one might add, no exact beginning. Wherever we turn attention, things have already begun and go on after our attention turns away. We cannot locate the beginning and end of processes. We select areas to explore.

A man (M) locates going dead at the precise moment his father screamed at him twenty years earlier. They were at dinner and suddenly, without warning, rage came. In a micromoment, M died. His feelings died and he became numb. In the years ahead he felt tumults of emotion, glorious and horrible moments, floods of feeling and meaning. But the deadness never left. His feelings were like waves pounding against a dead core. A deadness inside made it impossible to commit to any relationship, any person, including himself. In work, he chose money over his daimon. To be fair, he anticipated giving his daimon its due, once he had enough money to support his creative urge. He was taking a realistic detour, after which—redemption. Was it the deadness that allowed him to do this to himself? As the years went on, deadness hollowed a place in which rage began to boil.

Where did this rage start? Before his father? The Bible is filled with God's rage. Rage has an ancient history, vanishes in prehistory. How do we get inserted into it? Rage and deadness and hunger for life. M hungered for life, drew back into his deadness, boiled with rage. Perhaps he was his father after all, in certain ways. And his father's father? We have not even said a word about his mother or what rage he felt at her, rage at her weakness, seductive control, manipulative fantasies, white lies that skew a life.

Yet he dated his emotional death to a certain moment, a certain gesture. Had he begun to die before that? Was it a death long in preparation? Did his father's spreading depressive state plant seeds, provide gravitational pull? We are speaking of threads that go through a life, intertwine with other lives, tapestries of grievance, intergenerational resentment, envy, spite, hardship. Not just external hardships, making a living, getting along—hardships of intimate pressures from those we live with, those feeding on us with desperation and hope for something better, feeding on us with despair. Is all of history part of a moment's storm? A story storm going on in many lives at this moment, one or another way? Where do we enter it? The moment we went dead? Where do we locate a point of entry? A weak spot in the floor of M's being was dealt one blow too many, one rage too many, and he fell through. What about those who arrive already dead, unaware when deadness started because it seemed always to be there, unnoticed? Deadness and fury. A coupling looking for souls to live it. A relationship hungry for subjects and objects.

Melissa and her husband go out for a holiday dinner—no friends, no relatives. Alone together. They like each other's company, have a good time. She gets sadder and sadder, more and more depressed. A migraine comes, stomach cramps, diarrhea. Anxiety spreads. She is very unhappy yet goes on with the good time.

The next day she is worse—anxious, depressed, with a head-ache and stomachache. She tells her mate, but he is helpless. At night they light Chanukah candles. He goes off to do some work, and she sits and stares at the lights in the darkness. She stares for a very long time. It seems like hours. She loses herself in the lights, and when she comes to feels well again. Migraine, cramps, depression, anxiety gone. "A miracle of lights," she says.

She tells me this four days afterward in our session, and while we are sitting, going back and forth, exchanging thoughts and feelings, she drops to another level and says, "I miss my children," then weeps. It was a different moment. She felt OK enough when she came in, telling me what happened, report-ing, satisfied that she had gone though a difficulty and recen-tered on her own. Suddenly the platform gave way, her chest heaved, belly heaved—you could see feeling rise like a wave through her body, unbroken, instantaneous. She'd gone to a deeper home, more at-one.

Her children were raising families in other parts of the world. Later, I couldn't help saying, "You know, you're in a position to— you can live with one for half the year, and with the other the other half." "No, no," she said, "I like my life here."

Here is a wonderful instance of how psychosomatically sensi-tive we are—exquisitely sensitive. Waves of feeling translate into physical and emotional responses. Melissa tells her husband what she is going through, but that does not do the trick. She refinds herself through the miracle lights (which she lit with her children when they were young!), yet only in session, where every-thing cushions and invites feelings, does she make the deeper self-connection. Different storms at different moments, yet, in this in-stance, the same emotional current is at work.

There is more than relief when Melissa connects with miss-ing her children. She refinds herself more fully or, more apt, self (emotional reality) finds her more fully. The change in the room is palpable. The presence of one person has made it possible for another to let emotional truth open.

A moment's impact involving Jesus. A woman (W), a therapist in training, speaks about her impending visit home over the Christmas holiday. How good to try to connect with family, the treasure of moments of openness, grateful for these. Yet so much time is guarded, even cutting, as if there exists a general fear of feeling, as if emotion were dangerous, attached to loss of self or fear of loss. Was it easier to be in her classes, talk about patients, psychoanalytic thinking? What is psychoanalysis about if not about loss? Yet here too was defensiveness, cutting off, fear. Classmates and teacher jumped quickly to ideas, telling each other what they'd do, who the patient was, marking psyche with identifiable dog tags, useful if found dead on the field of battle.

One case presented was especially cutting, and the room hushed for moments before the gathering up of pain into concepts rushed forward. After class, W's pain burnt into her, in contrast with the ensuing discussion of it. She brought the case to our session, seared by the pain of (a) life, drawing back in fear. She hems and haws a bit, as if not able to admit just how meaningful the patient's story is to her. I almost feel she is embarrassed by her sensitivity, tries to cover up, unable or unwilling to access herself more fully.

I try to leave things open and ask if such pain ever gets to her. W shakes her head no, and I realize I've placed her in a funny position. The "right" thing for her to say is that the pain of patients cuts her to the quick. But what if she really doesn't care that much? What if their complaints and demands piss her off? Maybe she doesn't want them to get through to her *too* much. What if their therapy is more a place for her to practice a performance art? What about being guarded, self-protective, keeping a safe and useful distance? Maybe she was double-souled, caring/uncaring. After all, it is frustrating being a therapist, staying close to persistent pain, working with demands that do not let up. She wanted out and she wanted in. She was calling attention to how cut off and defensive all of us are and asking for help to make contact with the pain we fear.

She spoke a bit about Christmas coming, mixed feelings, looking forward to good family moments but knowing there would be uneasiness too, disappointment—there would be a pain that runs through family life, an unfulfillment. She almost didn't aver to problems with religion, lost religious feeling that is still there somewhere, pent up, confused, with nowhere to go, inhibited by disbelief and disillusionment.

In an almost half-dazed state, not exactly trance, but a kind of blank, mesmerized "feel," I opened my mouth and let the words make their way from the feeling. "It's the beginning of Christmas season and, in a way, maybe the birth of Jesus is the birth of a part of our soul that feels all the pain in the world. Maybe Jesus was someone who felt all the pain of the world in his or her heart. Then religious systems, belief, ideologies, fighting, persecution got hold of this heart and nearly ate it up. Maybe Jesus is the part of our heart that feels all the pain in the world and still feels joy."

By this time, W was weeping quietly, tasting a deeper self.

What can be more important than how a baby is received? Will a baby save the world? That is too much to ask, too much to place on a new soul. But that is the way it feels. The radiance of new life makes one's own heart new, makes one's own heart shine with radiance.

Then why all the child abuse? Because babies are helpless, the bottom of the pecking order, unable to defend against adult (or sibling) meanness, cruelty, injury, frustration, weakness, rage? Because people are unable to endure the pressures of living and take it out on whomever they can? Because victims victimize? Because people are traumatized traumatizers?

Because the innocence of children brings out vengeance, lust, sadism? The need to pierce innocence in others in order to mirror the innocence others pierced? To despoil in others what has been despoiled in oneself? To somehow taste lost innocence, lost nakedness by ravaging it, dirtying it, wiping it out!?

A man, sick of soul, tormented, injured, sullied, sticks his penis in a baby's mouth in the unconscious hope he will be clean, new, fresh again. The fresh-as-snow baby will make him fresh as snow. The sins, the decay of living will be wiped clean. He longs to feel the purity, the wholeness once more. For a moment's mad longing and pure hope, guilt has never left him. He regrets this moment into old age. Such is the demented human mind and its demented fantasy and hope that contact with a pure soul will make one pure. Instead, trauma mediates trauma. One ruins oneself and others in misguided attempts to heal. Yet the baby grows up and lives a decent enough life, and the man goes into old age filled with torment, missed possibilities, a savaged, savaging self, with a wish to do better. A man whose good moments and deeds almost justify existence, who sometimes lets himself feel them. There is a smile inside his heart for his life. There is horror, chagrin, a devil's grin and cackle inside his heart. A soul game of Russian roulette that never stops.

One takes in the power of an animal one kills and eats. One takes in the purity of a baby one sullies.

The baby is a storm threatening to dissolve, break down, drown barriers. It breaks the windows of one's house. It seeps in like an underground stream slowly rising through basement cracks. It burns the wood with its sunlight.

A baby threatens to open one's heart.

There are those who open their hearts and grow. And there are those who open their hearts but are broken by the hardships of life, fatigue, the demands of livelihood and child care and relationships, the demands and pressures of their own personalities. There are those for whom it is too much and those who can't get enough, those for whom it is infinitely enriching—the more one gives, the more one gets—and those for whom every bit of giving breaks another bone.

The moment-to-moment interplay of feelings between mother and baby has begun to be charted by professionals. Often with great sensitivity. We interpret these interplays. We give them meaning and have to give them meaning. They feel meaningful. Interlapping feelings are a basic emotional reality. The meanings that arise from them should be considered carefully. Other meanings may be possible. The feeling pool we touch with psychic tendrils subtends and succeeds attempts to bind or release it with meaning. It is to the interlapping we need to return, over and over. Return to the feeling that threads new eyes of meaning.

Why does Bion describe the "helpless infant" as a "growing annihilating force"? He means to point to an unknown feeling base, a kind of emotional background radiation, which presses for formulation and living. We tend to mistake our formulations for the basic emotional realities they subserve, represent, misrepresent, guide, structure. An emotion surges. I interpret it as an assault, and I fight back. An emotion surges. I interpret it as an invitation, and I look for an appropriate red carpet to roll out. There is no absolute necessity that binds me to one or the other possibility. At one point in life, I fight the rise of feeling; at another, I welcome it. I become interested and begin to catch on to typical sorts of meaning I give emotional currents. I could think otherwise and rather than focus on the thinking begin to get interested in emotional reality as such.

Bion speaks of "an experience that is emotional and nothing else." An emotional experience is what dreams are about or grow from or around or through. The dream's "origin is an emotional experience." Subject and object are like reversible head and tail. A narrative distributes itself around an emotional navel. If the emotion is experienced as a violent attack, the dream may express attack: I am attacked by an unknown intruder—my emotional life. Or I may attack someone—defending myself against the other within, unconscious aliveness, emotional surges and urges, or just emotion as such. If I cannot stretch around and accommodate emotional pressures, subject and object are permanent threats. That is, threatening feelings work their way out via threatening subjects and objects. Who does what to whom or what varies, but the emotional link remains the same.

To pick up a thread from the preceding chapter—the annihilating baby can be psychoanalysis, an idea, a feeling, a work of art exerting pressure to be born. A rough beast slouching toward Bethlehem takes many forms: any new birth that stretches personality, that stretches self or culture. The storm of meeting, a crossroads, a crisis can involve meeting a thought, an emotion, an attitude. In this regard, Bion speaks of the analyst as introducing the patient to himself and taking a more positive, at least tolerant, outlook toward storms of meeting and their transformations.

Bion uses the big-bang image to express incessant birth of consciousness and flow of ideas, sensations, memories, feelings, images, predatory and meditative will. He also uses it to express psychotic catastrophe, the breaking apart of personality into bits that rush away from each other with increasing velocity. In the latter instance, what seems a thought or feeling might turn out to be flotsam and jetsam from an explosion long ago, bits of psychic life estranged from their point of origin, racing mindlessly to oblivion. An explosion that seems to go on forever, an ongoing catastrophic process expressed in the butchered meat, wastelands and bleeding flowers of schizophrenic dreams. Paradoxically, trenchantly, Bion writes that the sense of catastrophe can link personality together—the very falling apart forever, racing toward oblivion, the shattering and disconnection, can be the glue that holds a self together.

Catastrophe as link, catastrophe we look away from. Small things take on life-and-death importance, while big things are scarcely noticed. Worry gets attached to nothings, while consequential somethings work out of sight. Little things magnified, big things minimized. Traumas made trivial, trivia made traumatic. What is the minimum a soul must take seriously before it disappears?

There is another meaning of the helpless infant as a growing annihilating force. The notion comes up in Bion's discussion of how creatures, including ourselves, autodestruct. Tool-making is an example of how good turns into bad. Tools we make take on a life of their own, proliferate, turn against us. Planes crash or are used as weapons. Technological advances turn us into targets of lethal gadgets or poison our air and water. Communication media deform consciousness, creating information addicts, cogs in the machine of marketing mania and greed. What seems an expansion of possibilities has unforeseen consequences (or are they really as unforeseen as we like to believe?).

Bion gives as example the stegosaurus in relation to the ty-rannosaurus: the buildup of armor in response to weaponry. "The tyrannosaurus provokes intrinsically an equal + opposite reaction—the stegosaurus." The latter ends up sinking under its own weight; its strength becomes its weakness. The analogy is to the tool of tools, the most amazing gadget of all—the human mind, "superior organ of discrimination."

How does one set about learning to use "mind"? It opens worlds, viewpoints, new fields of battle, along with fields of discovery. New fertile fields, new killing fields. What once we were so proud of becomes the most dangerous medium of all.

What kind of minds do we have? Our minds think up fantastic ways to destroy each other. *They* call us evil; *we* call them evil. *We* are good. *We mean well. We* and *they* use goodness to mask destruction, as a paranoid psychotic uses destruction to mask goodness. In this regard, we and they are interchangeable, growing around similar affect nuclei, like reversible opposing thumbs or ego heads and legs or tails. Mind has many opposing thumbs, like a Buddha has teats. Mind thumbs its thumbs at each other, and sometimes renegade thumbs break loose and shake hands. Shaking hands is an attempt to tame violent, shaking minds, an attempt to find another form of gripping, another form of touching. Mind touches mind in many ways. *Give peace a chance.* Not possible without seeing and feeling *our* violent minds, the violence of mind as such. Peace—an annihilating infant.

To learn to use mind is more difficult than learning to build and fly planes or operate computers or perform brain scans and operations or titrate mental states with medication. It is easier to organize thought around something external than to work with mind constructively. "While [our] gaze physiological is directed to observation and 'detoxification' of the menace *represented* by the atomic bomb, it will, by the same token, be directed away from the growing annihilating force, the 'helpless infant.'" We point to instruments of destruction rather than focus on the source of these instruments: mind and its use. Mind, the growing annihilating force, the 'helpless infant.'

Atom bomb—signifier of mental menace, the menace we are. If explosive force is instrumental in creation, and we are part of creative evolution, there is no escaping the fact that we are carriers of explosive force. We are explosive force—but not only. There are other tendencies—cooling, stabilizing—reciprocally adjusting one another. We are junctures of shalom, and rage, and much else that adds plasticity, variety. We are, too, an embryonic being with alternative possibilities.

Do we always remain embryonic with alternative possibilities?

A woman with many years of therapy (nearly five years with me, many more with others) recently had the first moment in her life in which she found herself saying, "I'm glad I'm alive." When I asked about the last time she felt that, she searched a while, then replied, "Never." A moment of feeling happy? Is that enough? Not enough, perhaps, but real. Something that did not appear before. It must be hard for many to imagine a life without that feeling. But there are people who find it impossible to believe they might feel alive. Such moments, I believe, justify existence, certainly justify therapy. A moment like this proves that, for some individuals, in some instances, the capacity to feel alive is regenerative. If you lose your limb or heart or brain, it won't regenerate. Once it's gone, it's gone. But if you lose your soul sense, psyche, spirit, emotional being, or never quite have it—the dead can rise, the lame walk, the heartless can have a beating heart, the mindless can discover a thinking mind.

We are creative beings capable of rediscovering, refinding, recreating ourselves and contributing to the lives of others. Some take this for granted. Some overuse, exploit and abuse it. Some do not rise to the struggle. Still, we do not denigrate what we are capable of when we say, too, that we are atom bombs or terrifying infectious agents. What we produce reflects who we are, creates who we are in multifarious ways. Atom bombs and infectious agents provide mirror images we dare not cover.

"Atom bomb," for example, is a term that takes on many values depending on viewpoint and concerns: Saddam Hussein, right wing of the Republican Party, liberals, the omnivorous rich, the omnivorous poor, George W. Bush, Osama bin Laden, the "Supreme" Court, economic rape of the world by corporate greed and power, violent fundamentalism of every sort. Dealing with external problems is necessary, but how do we deal with one of the most potent forces of all, mind, attitude, lust for power and control that feeds the external forms many problems take? As we push our agendas—yours, mine—the "helpless infant" will be searching out its next manger, new ways to house and succor the growing annihilating force.

The magnificent mind we do not know how to use. A complicated toy that keeps slipping out of our hands and causing damage. With the odd property that often we don't know where the damage comes from. With the odd property that instead of stopping or dying out, the more mind gets damaged, the more damaging it becomes. We look outside to jiggle this or that lever or inside to jiggle a component part we can locate. We hope for the best, make adjustments as we go. We hold our breath as configurations set in motion work their way out or open places we'd rather not be. If only our minds were as easy to manipulate as video games. There are masters of games but no masters of mind or life. When it comes to the real thing, we are beginners, novices.

As Ecclesiastes asks, what is the end of all this analysis? What good is harping on the point Bion makes: "all biological living constructs have an inborn mechanism for self-disposal" and a life form, including mind, "is blind to the quality which is to lead to its own destruction"? We read that the character making these remarks is Alpha in a work with many characters expressing aspects of Bion's sense of life. We know from other parts of Bion's work that alpha function is his term for unknown processes involved in initiating and carrying on digestion of affects, digestion of life's impacts. Whatever these processes are, they are involved in making experience part of our beings, working life over, feeding impacts into growth processes. Bion likens alpha function to primary process or dreamwork, attempts to work with emotional nuclei.

What we have here is a dramatic statement of the importance of trying to process the impact of destructive experience. Alpha function nibbles on traumatic globs, wounds of all sorts, and, to whatever extent possible, turns them into something useable. The use may simply be a more accurate, fuller, truer picture of life. A good portion of life is hurtful, and, in the long run, ignoring or pushing past injury is not enough. We need more alpha function in the storm.

There would be no Shakespeare without abiding injury. Shakespeare's is the art of depicting injury and vicissitudes of tormenting emotional storms. Shakespeare functions as part of a human digestive system, a tendril of emotional sensitivity fused with intellectual acuity, passing permutations of wounds and wounding activities through literary alpha function, mixing dream, hallucination, and analysis. Art, writing, mysticism, even forms of political and scientific mastication: parts of mind's attempts to digest, elaborate, discover what is possible.

Will it do us good to chew on, and begin long digestive work on, what makes us self-destructive? Bion's oeuvre is a kind of dark feast. One of his conclusions runs contrary to our culture's current emphasis on action. He advises a certain passivity in the face of evil. A waiting.

In more general terms, a waiting on experience. It takes time to experience, more time to digest experience. We are partial digesters, and, if we are lucky, partial digestion feeds further partial digestion, intermittently extended over time. It is good to realize actions grow from and feed partially digested experience. This is more than incomplete information. Undigested experience leads to emotional indigestion, which hurts. Chronic irritability of human creatures partly grows from chronic states of emotional indigestion. To realize we are in a chronic state of emotional indigestion *might* go some way toward engendering a gentler approach to one another. We might give each other time, sometimes quality time.

It takes time even to perceive each other, and perceive each other again, and again, and again. Perception grows. Experience is subject to development, processes over time. To learn to give each other time—nothing is more important. Yet much of our social and political and personal life is organized around speed and a show of strength and action—action that largely grows from emotional indigestion. It is no wonder the world suffers from widespread bellyaches, always potentially explosive, often devastating.

It is dangerous to put the brakes on and try to do something better because there are always those ready to take advantage. One will appear a fool to say, "I don't know. I'm waiting." The flood of events will carry the fool away and wash him ashore in another world.

Nevertheless, for some, perhaps for many, the issue is joined, and one responds to the invitation, life's reflux in one's throat.

One of Bion's last entries in his intellectual diary: "Mathematics, science as known hitherto, can provide no model. Religion, music, painting, as these terms are understood, fail me. Sooner or later we reach a point where there is nothing to be done except—if there is any exception—to wait."

What about the bright side of life? The good a baby brings, the challenge, the opening of heart and life, expansion, growth? Why all this emphasis on darkness?

The bright is real too, more real perhaps. It is no accident religions call attention to the pain of life and, in one or another form, affirm joy. Emotional storms can be positive. There are subtle storms, quiverings, delicate fluctuations of feeling stream-ing back and forth between souls and bodies, exquisite, too much to take, wanting more as one's capacity to suffer joy brings one to the point of fainting. There is growth from the hard work of creating nests where life can flourish, places from which new life can branch out, fly.

We conceive the goal of working with the full scope of feel-ings but scoop out what we can. Joy and wounding, emotional honesty/lying, plenitude/lack limn each other. We are made of double nuclei and the fusions/contrasts ripple, as feelings slide from one gradient to another. Put two beings together, lack and plenitude ignite, just as meldings and frictions of God's void/fullness ignite big bangs.

Shakespeare set the task by envisioning a magical tempest that heals rather than harms, an emotional storm in which no one is hurt. An ideal vision perhaps, but one worth striving for. An evo-lutionary task—learning to work with our stormy beings, learning to prosper and create with them and minimize destruction.

I don't think an emphasis on darkness is simply gloomy. It is also a weeping for the pain we feel and inflict on ourselves and each other, a cry for something better, taking up the impossible challenge of more honest and kindly growth. Are we doomed to cruelty and power madness? Some of us refuse to bow down to our neural and chemical programs. We do want something more, better, and are willing to try to work for it, as best we can.

Heinz Werner depicts development as moving from less to more differentiation. It is a notion many (including myself) crit-icize, but it is a trope useful for certain purposes.

Let us start with an emotional moment. Baby feels agony or joy. Let us say agony. Agony arises. There is no frame of refer-ence for it. It just is. Perhaps it is felt as an attack, an agon, too much. Perhaps it is just felt and undergone as something awful one can't do anything about. Screams. Screams.

There may be no ideas about it at all—just the state itself and pain happening to someone, to me, to sensitivity, to whatever or whoever feels pain. The feeler of pain. We do not have to affix an artificial identity to the feeler of pain. But sooner or later, probably sooner, I's and you's arise around or grow out of the pain and the Primordial Feeler of Pain gradually grows into an I-you story or scene or narrative (e.g., I am in pain, you are my pain, I am my pain, you caused my pain, and later, I caused your pain and possibly my pain too). Some of these I-you stories become fixed and function as a casing for the pain nucleus. It is as if the emotion grows heads and legs or tails.

Part of therapy is to awaken awareness of the emotional nucleus itself, the emotion in the subject-object casing. To jump into the emotion as such is transformative. To remain in the casing is ossifying and injurious to self and others. The casing repeats the same old scripts and patterns. To encounter and enter the emotion itself opens fields of experiencing.

Kurt Goldstein wrote of a catastrophic reaction that brain-damaged people have to frustration when functioning fails them. They might be overwhelmed by helplessness and enraged at inability. Deficit and fury meld.

Bion tends to see such catastrophic reaction, melding deficit and rage, as widespread. In a covert way it inheres in communication. Often, without clear awareness, we are frustrated by our inability to communicate emotional states in ways that are satisfactory. We may fail to connect either with ourselves or others, and what we are feeling slides away. We may pretend such slippage is unimportant or a normal part of living, something everyone experiences, and so nullify it or play it down. But somewhere we are left with frustration and perhaps loss, as feelings that carry our most intimate facts and selves remain unborn or undeveloped.

We handle what we *can* handle and consign the rest to oblivion.

Often we are haunted by the intimation that what is in oblivion is more important than the bit we work with and manage to salvage or try to master. Some of us seek oblivion to find a missing X.

Frustrations attendant upon communicative processes press buttons and seek catastrophic reactions. This is easily seen on the internet when perfect strangers instantaneously inflame each other when communication fails. These flare-ups are not simply the result of distance between the participants. There is more at work than distance and difference between subjects, important as these are. After participating in and observing internet rages for many years, I've concluded that this reactivity is also a measure of estrangement from oneself. Or, rather, too great investment in a narrow band of being or identity, and too little appreciation of what beckons beyond well-worn, rigid boundaries.

Catastrophic reactivity is never far from the surface. In most exchanges on the internet, hurtful as they can become, people are immediately protected by the possibility of getting offline or surfing somewhere else. They cannot electrocute each other, give each other lethal injections, or pull a trigger that actually kills (not yet). This protection does not eliminate some form of emotional shock or injury, but it does afford a modicum of control. The internet provides a potentially important experimental playground in human relations, where people try to modulate emotions and impacts so that discussion can be furthered.

Of course, every group faces challenges of mutual modulation, but the range and breadth of internet access to ongoing fields of interplay bring conflicts between democratic, autarchic, and despotic tendencies to the fore with special speed and clarity. Such experiences heighten awareness of how important it is for those in positions of global power to have safeguards built into communication systems in order to offset what appears to be a spontaneous gradient toward catastrophic blowup. We are highly combustible beings. Real communication may be highly satisfying and promote genuine growth but is excruciatingly difficult.

Clea tells me she has been tasting and feeling pure panic. This is not the same as a panic attack, which she is all too familiar with. It is, rather, an apperception of pure panic. She sees the panic. It goes on reverberating, writhing, alive, chaotic, electric, pulsing, shivering. But it is as if it is just there, as if no one has claimed it, no one has grown around it to be thrown by it or go under. It is as close as she has ever come to a pure emotional state. She does not possess it, and it does not possess her. Clea gets a taste of ongoing emotional being that has its own momentum and rhythm.

It is an epiphany. For one thing, she suddenly sees the panic in the middle of her father's being and feels sad as he tries to insulate himself from it with distance and fury. She often was injured by his aloofness, which fused and oscillated with explosiveness. Clea never understood how he could be so far away emotionally and suddenly throw a fit over a small thing she scarcely noticed. How could something so unimportant to her be so big for him? Seeing his panic does not make his reactive style comprehensible, but she sees that there is a core emotional state he cannot handle.

"This panic ran through my family," Clea says. "A kind of constant, always there. My mother turned everything into a catastrophe. For her, everything I did was disastrous. My father would go away, die out. I'd get close to him and be happy if I made him come back. There were times I could make him feel warmly toward me, and I warmed myself for moments. But I was trying to make him come back in a way that would avoid an explosion."

He encased core panic with distance and rage. Clea realized how much she, too, encased herself. Her panic attacks broke out with an explosive capacity akin to her father's fury. Her fury was silent, drawn out, a bitter attitude that poisoned experience. She couldn't believe how freeing it was to see and feel the panic and feel the bitter edge fade.

"Pure panic," she says. "I can go through it, ride it out. It builds, climaxes, subsides. It has always been in the family. Now it has a rhythm."

There is an enormous difference between feeling fueling subject-object reactivity and feeling feeding capacity to undergo experiencing. Feeling becomes something to savor, part of the mystery of being, appreciative awakening to possibility. In this mode, even panic opens doors.

The Primary Feeler of Feelings grows heads and legs, subject-object scenarios, which lose the mystery of processes that give rise to these appendages. For the moment, Clea sees past I-vs.-you catastrophes that block and taint her life and gets a breath of affect as such. Enemies are real. They won't go away. One needs to protect oneself. But to free core feeling from painful contraction is a breath of air.

When I was young, I used to ask, why does this happen now? We were taught in therapy school that everything has a reason and timing tells tales. If Clea relates to panic in a new way, there must be a reason why this is happening now. Through such training I became quite good at finding reasons.

I'm less inclined to pursue this line of research now (except for fun outside of sessions, like crossword puzzles or in an emergency) than to give myself over to simple appreciation and regard. When Clea is sad, I'm sad. When she is happy, I'm happy. My emotional being, when I am not too tired and grumpy or preoccupied, goes with hers. This happens of its own accord simply because inside myself I wish her well. It is not anything I will, premeditate, or prevaricate. It just happens.

There were moments when Clea's anger frightened me.

Many, many moments when her bitterness ground my insides to pieces, made me choke on tears. For many years I felt, with her, extended states of crucifixion. Crucifixion by the simple agony of being, intensified by trauma.

At some point, outside awareness, something must have reached a critical mass, tipped the scales, and a new way of approaching feeling appeared. Many years of having someone in her corner, vibrating when she vibrated, had a cumulative effect. Cumulative resonance to offset cumulative trauma. It was not anything that could be rushed, this slow baking of emotional faith with a taste of emotional freedom.

Inside the heart there are different kinds of smiles. Simple, joyous heart smiles. Many were the times mine and Clea's touched each other off. We sat smiling at each other. Blankly smiling. Anguish comes again, acute stabs, hearts shake in shock, stiffen, close. And after going through something, opening begins again. A growing faith rhythm. This is the core of our work, the very core.

3 Smile and Scream

How is it possible that a moment of joy can offset years of suffering or emptiness? Religions hold the hope that salvation is possible at life's last instant. An extreme statement perhaps—but an accurate expression of something that happens at many moments throughout a lifetime.

Often we are pushed to a limit, a point of last resort, and sometimes we go under. A collapse that lasts an hour, a week, months or years. Rest may be enough for recovery. The self resets itself, starts anew. The psalmist writes of going to sleep weeping, awaking laughing.

One of my favorite portrayals of such a moment is Leo Tolstoy's story "The Death of Ivan Ilyitch," about a man whose life has been trivial but who, as he is dying, receives a godly illumination that makes it all worthwhile. An instant redeems a life. In Akira Kurosawa's movie *Ikiru*, this reversal is achieved through a loving work. A man learns that he is dying and in the time remaining tries to get the most out of life. Conventional attempts fail and, finally, he gives life meaning by humble persistence in overcoming bureaucratic indifference (worse than active resistance) to creating a neighborhood playground. In Federico Fellini's movie *Nights of Cabiria*, a street woman is conned out of her life savings by a promise of love. Near the end of the movie, she begins to smile again in the face of everything that has happened to her. For me, this smile is the defining moment of the human soul.

These works of art get to a similar place in different ways. They reach a point of affirmation, whether through revelation, labor, or relationship. A point where life is more or other than expected or where the same "just me" again opens and warms after living through traumatized hopes. Different nuances of rebirth or renewal, which make words seem crude and shallow. They are extended "linear" expressions of a "synchronic" event or dimension, a basic soul rhythm involving opening-closing, enlivening-deadening, going on throughout a lifetime.

W. R. Bion writes that he died during the First World War. I believe him. In his autobiography he portrays his immobility when his young daughter, Parthenope, tried to crawl across the yard to reach him. He sat in affectless paralysis as she struggled. The situation ended when the housekeeper, unable to bear it, picked the girl up and hugged her. Parthenope's mother died giving birth to her. A few years ago Parthenope, with one of her daughters, died in a car crash (Parthenope at the wheel). There are many deaths, many ways of dying in a lifetime. I don't believe that Bion's death in the war was his first, but it provided a significant knockout blow. His relationship with his second wife thawed him out, brought him back. He did not lose his chance at living, but damage was done and he always had an eye on it.

I recently saw the movie *War Photographer*, a depiction of James Nachtwey's life and photography, showing inhumanity, cruelty, and trauma across the globe. I feel Bion's writings do the same, provide pictures of psychic trauma taken in therapy sessions, soul deformations, hopes that feed on ruins. Variations of a scream that runs through life. We are that scream and much more. But when the smile comes, the scream does not stop. The smile that grows out of the scream is not the same as a screamless smile, one that makes believe no scream is there.

Psychoanalysis documents wounds to sensitivity and is, in a way, a language of wounds. It is a kind of Genesis, where God tells the new Adam, Freud, to name some things the old Adam left out. The original Adam, after all, named things before trauma hit. His language is, on the face of things, traumaless. Freud's is a trauma language, as Bion's is a posttraumatic stress language, to say the least. Psychoanalysis is an ongoing trauma language still evolving. Birth trauma, abandonment-intrusion anxiety, castration trauma, annihilation dreads—a growing glimpse of a trauma world, peppered by abusiveness and shocks that run through life. Bion's cases, sprinkled throughout his work, rotate around a nucleus of sudden shock coupled with deformations personality undergoes. One is persecuted by wounds one cannot process, tormented by ways one becomes monstrous. We have no scarcity of smiling monsters screaming around or within us.

Many try to soft-pedal the trauma world. We are told we can transcend or transform it, not get bogged down by it, emphasize the positive. You can choose between therapists who gravitate toward pain and those who deflect attention from it. But whether one makes too much or too little of traumatic impacts, stiffens against or molds around them, hardened trauma veins are there. We are caught in a vicious circle. Undigested trauma comes at us from the outside world. What we fail to make room for and work with persecutes us from within and without. Yet inside and outside reality precipitates trauma in the first place. Inner and outer life *are* wounding. We learn that we can adjust our sensitivity, turn it up or down, so as to modulate wounds. Some of us prefer it up high, some turn it down low, with the result that communication between people with different sensitivity levels becomes difficult. Habitual unconscious sensitivity preferences govern who feels real to us and who doesn't.

We learn from Bion's example that people who die go on functioning and may have full lives. Death in life often is partial, as H. Guntrip's self-portrayal shows. But precisely because one is not entirely dead, areas of deadness are intensely painful. So much of D. W. Winnicott's and Bion's clinical message, I believe, is the necessity of making room for not being, for dying, for oblivion, to let go the effort to keep oneself in life. Nothingness is an essential part of the rhythm of living.

I was in my thirties before I came upon the sense of being dead. Before that a mixture of joy and torment kept me alive. After the crash of my analysis (my analyst left the city as his own life hit a wall), I felt painfully empty, unreal, not there. It is difficult to describe how bad I felt, because these words don't fit. I've always been alive, interested, curious, engaged in something. I find life filled with wonders, and I love the world, sensation, being. I love experience. But something happened to my I that I never felt before. Maybe a numbing, like novocaine in the I-feeling. In my late teens and early twenties I knew depression, longing, suicidal despair. All my life consciousness has been riddled with painful fear, painful longing, since early childhood. Torments of trauma, rage, fear, longing. But the pain of deadness or some kind of anesthesia administered to the I itself— fun for my thirties.

It was ghastly. I thought it would never go away. But in time it lifted and other things happened, just as the earlier world of suicidal longing had run its course. This one-thing-following-another structure of experience, a little like fever after fever, gives one a somewhat spurious sense of reassurance. For while the current moment will lift or transform, the one coming may be fatal. I appreciate the loving, delusional optimism that greets the wild boar after saying good-bye to the wild ox, greets the fact that psychic life is our real currency of exchange as long as we breathe.

I have written of a patient who dated his death to a particular moment at the age of eighteen when his father broke into a sudden rage at him at dinner. It is hard to overestimate the harm done by rage in human life. Few things ravage the psyche so. Yet so often one's own rage keeps one alive. This patient spoke of his mother's emotional turmoil, madness, seductive need for control and his father's deadness and rage. He is drawn to jobs that deaden him and women who drive him mad. Nearly all of his adult life has been spent in deadening work that pays well and relationships with semipsychotic women. His vision of creative work and a loving relationship met the realities of a psyche unconsciously attracted to deadness and madness. In addition, his women tended to be rageful, combining his mother's labile emotionality and his father's depressed, self-absorbed rage. Little by little, he had to face the fact that the mad, dead, rageful, controlling people in his life were pertinent to his own makeup and carried messages about self.

We learn from Bion, Guntrip, and my patient that resilience works in partial ways. Something dies, collapses, undergoes deformation. Something stays alive, functions, gets through. Almost as if there are rings of self, second nature, third nature, going along with second, third, fourth tries. We die out, come back, wriggling like a bug to the last twitch. Life doesn't give up on itself no matter how much death it swallows. We keep coming back for more, no matter what we do to ourselves and each other.

I suspect the observation that we partly die in order to stay alive informed the rise of religion. Ancient mysteries were concerned with finding the immortal self, often by mimicking death and renewal. I think there is more to this than trying to outflank death. My guess is that human beings were always sensitive to changes of state, and that feeling more alive or dead at a given time was an impressive experience. We are sensitive to external impacts but also to internal changes. Sensitive to sensitivity.

The link Freud made between a certain discomfort or depression and group pressure has a long history. Sacrifice is part of group living, but there is no life at all outside groupings. Even if it were possible for an individual to be born and grow outside a group of any kind (which means outside of coupling!), Freud indicated that growth itself, the very development of self and character, has deadening and enlivening aspects. Character and personality can be burdensome, our human face too heavy to bear. Death comes when character wears us out.

Religions teach ways to transform or transcend character, the double pressure of group and self. An aim is to discover maximum aliveness, to die into the fullest aliveness possible. One tries to escape not just death but the sort of psyche we have, which oscillates between variable kinds and degrees of dead-ness/aliveness. A psyche that lives by being partly alive, with moments of epiphany. Religion is propelled not just by the conquest of death, but by the conquest of deadness. It is not enough to be alive. One must be fully alive, symbolized by total aliveness in life eternal, no trace of deadness at all.

A terrible tragedy in this life as we know it is that total aliveness is an ideal, an idea, an ideology. And that its "achievement" involves deception, making someone, often oneself, pay. I doubt that slaves were ever only an economic creation. They were, also, to bear the burden of death and misery, to free masters for higher things (to go up the scale toward total aliveness). I would not be surprised to learn that slaveowners unconsciously hallucinated themselves as immune to death, to the degree that the slaves were to fulfill that burden for them. Since some kind of hierarchical pecking order exists to this day, so that unconscious immunity (others die in my stead) is widespread, death is still largely a surprise. For many, deadness takes the place of death and ideologies of aliveness and deadness mirror each other. Hallucinated aliveness/deadness is pervasive enough to make moments of actual aliveness, with death on the horizon, startling ("O my God, I'm really alive, I'm really me, just plain me! I'm here! And here is really here!").

It is possible for patient and analyst to "totalize" analysis in different ways. Each may hallucinate a different analysis, and when the hallucinatory shell cracks, the sense of disaster reappears. Pam sought help when such a totalized, hallucinated analysis broke down. She was, finally, having the analysis she always hoped for, one which made her feel good. Her analyst gave her almost as many sessions as she wanted, with supplemental phone calls. He responded like a good father/mother to her desperate anxiety, and she felt better than she ever had. She could hardly believe her luck.

After several years, her "good" analyst began agitating for change. He said their analysis was a failure. She should use the couch, free associate, that what they had was merely supportive therapy, it was time to go further. His psychoanalytic superego reared its ugly head, a kind of psychoanalytic moralistic attitude substituting for reality. She insisted their work together had been what she needed, that she was getting better. She was feeling supported, nourished. Trust was beginning to grow. She tried to convince him that what she was getting was good for her and that they should continue.

He began missing sessions, became distracted, saying indiscreet and wounding things, at the same time insisting that their work become more analytic. His behavior made it difficult for her to stay, and she felt cut down by his pushing her out.

I won't pretend to know what happened but must share aspects of my vision, because the problems involved are important for who we are and the way we live our lives. You may have other points of entry, other modes of expression, methods of investigation—you might put what I say in very different ways. We add to, fill out, correct each other, take each other to different places. What I need to tell you, you may already know: we hallucinate a woundless state around a wounded core.

Pam and her analyst created their particular variation on this theme as their relationship gravitated toward a traumatic happening. It started so well, ended so badly, one more time. What is it that gets played out repeatedly? We can be morally outraged at the analyst, or at Pam, whatever their roles in fabricating a haven to be destroyed. One can always titrate deceptions that are part of a good feed.

Freud's fiction that a baby hallucinates a breast when hungry provides food for thought, a powerful imagining. In analogous fashion, it may be that Pam and her analyst hallucinated their relationship as a good feed, an oasis in distressed living. As Freud points out, hallucination fails after a time. Distress breaks through. The hallucinated analysis cracked and nothing took its place, just two people not knowing what to do with each other, each with his own ideas. They could not move past the trauma good feelings led to.

Wounded good feelings—precisely what the patient and analyst, without quite realizing it, move toward. The wounded core. One can't escape it, although one tries. Pam and her analyst tried by hallucinating a good analysis. Her analyst tried again by getting rid of Pam, making disturbance go away. Her presence in his life became a problem. He hallucinated her away by ending treatment. My guess is that his hallucinatory process went through phases, first hallucinating a good analysis, then hallucinating no analysis, then hallucinating the patient as not there (and she obliged). One might think the good-feed hallucination broke down because it wasn't providing the real nourishment of analysis. But the progression of events suggests that one hallucinatory scenario replaced another. The full breakdown of the hallucination fell on Pam. After the breakup, her life suffered. She did worse in work, got herself into dangerous situations, feared falling apart, began to feel "not there" and "out of it" in response to deepening depression, became erratically rageful. Worst of all, she felt her inside core, deprived of trust, wasting away, afraid of touching and being touched by others. Very much the screaming, then marasmic infant, when hallucinated trust breaks down.

The point where this therapy relationship failed is precisely a crux in analysis today. Part of what analysis does is open a situation where the patient can break down (partially) and recover over and over (partially) as part of sessions. The individual gets practice in falling apart and coming together, injury and recovery—part of what happens when two human beings are together. Pam and her analyst enacted feeling good and getting wounded, but did not bring the two together as part of the rhythm of their relationship. Rather than becoming a nucleus of work, each phase became a rigid totality. As alternate hallucinatory states, they did not modulate each other.

Winnicott writes about the personality becoming traumatized as it begins to form. I infer from this the possibility that, in such an instance, beginnings remain associated with possible traumatization. Whether beginning new work, a new relationship, coming upon a new feeling or thought or sensation, to start something, to come alive or to come together, means trauma. One cannot come together, because doing so risks the trauma that broke one to begin with. More precisely, because trauma hit as one began to form, one can neither come together nor fall apart, unable to "complete" a movement. To live between chaos and form is to be alive. What Winnicott depicts is akin to substituting hallucination for breakdown ↔ coming together. Trust in one's basic unconscious rhythm, the rhythm of recovery, is decimated.

Work with Pam becomes a process of enabling the basic rhythm of breakdown ↔ recovery to take hold, to become something one can trust, even if in jittery ways. Therapy, in effect, builds around letting resilience breathe. It is a rhythm that can take years to develop, discover, learn to work with, and it often happens in ways that surprise everyone concerned.

Nearly forty years ago, a young woman, Shula, started therapy with me, and almost instantaneously we developed an extraordinarily intense relationship. It was near the beginning of my practice, and it was tempting for a young therapist to have his head turned. I remember the intensity, the mixture of shock, fascination, hope for healing, fear of therapeutic megalomania, and caring I felt. I remember, too, the pressure of dependency, the need to make things work. Being with Shula was all-consuming, and something in me tasted the pull and pulled back. I was in it and out of it at the same time. The storm of "borderline" patients was on the horizon, moving in.

A maelstrom of emotions and changing states, rapidly oscillating between chaos and nothingness, not only smashed me, but acted like a giant magnet, sucking my thoughts and feelings into Shula's innards, as well as hers into mine. My approach to therapy became galvanized by such experiences: to stay open to the impact of the other, whatever gets set off, follow the impact through its transformations, stay with it, and stay with it some more. Impact (shock waves) gives rise to feelings, to images, to thoughts, to . . . an ever undulating series of states involving unconscious transmissions, imaginative visions, and reflective communications.

I felt an abysmal failure with Shula. After half a year of mounting and shifting intensity, a gripping bond, I left for a month's summer vacation. During that time Shula filled the gap with a destructive partner, and although we tried to work when I returned, her energies moved elsewhere. Although it sounds like I was at sea (I was), I also was on land throwing her a line, which she could not, would not grab and use. She became enveloped by her partner, who tyrannized her, a tyranny I could not compete with. Her partner offered a destructive intensity I could not match.

I felt awful. I was not up to the forces therapy may have triggered, emotional powers waiting for release. Shula became a drug addict (like her partner) who supported her habit by prostitution for many years. She felt pride at being good at what she did, good at degradation. Eventually, the low point began to shift. She entered recovery, got a decent job, and, after false starts, found a good partner. I was awed by her journey.

Why did she want to see me after all these years? I was fearful something bad would get stimulated by the intensity of our (real/hallucinated) bond, that she would destroy what she had built at the cost of such pain over so many years. Things were going well—why not leave well enough alone?

She said she came because she heard her voice with me. A deep inner voice that made her feel real. She thought of me often, during the worst of times, clung to whispers of the voice that began to speak in our sessions. It was a voice she always hoped to connect with. She came back to give it a try. She did not want her life to pass her by without giving it and herself a chance to be together.

Shula's case is extreme, but not as isolated as one might think. The other day I met someone on the street who I thought I failed with. I thought she left me because our bond became too painful. Many were the hours I went over our work and, although I did the best I could, experienced the limitations of my therapeutic ability. I apologized to her when we met and, to my surprise (and relief), she told me she got a lot from our time together, a very rich if painful time, that she let her worst out in sessions and outside them generally felt OK and lived her life. Our sessions helped her to go through things. I felt grateful for the hug we gave each other.

One of the great learnings of clinical work, pithily formulated by Bion and elaborated by Winnicott, is that for many individuals catastrophe links personality together. The very cement of personality is a sense of disaster. In such a situation, what feels most real to the individual is destructive intensity, an impending, pervasive intimation of disaster. For some, catastrophic dread is closer to the foreground, may steal the limelight and pre-empt conscious attention. For others, a vague fear of falling apart is part of the background and lends reality its tone and color. Fear of falling apart may even be what feels most real. Still others get used to not being there. Partly, this is defensive, but calling it defensive does not always do justice to it. It can be, simply, part of the sequence of catastrophe, a phase of shock akin to numbing, a sense that only the black winter after the meteor hits is real: my unreality, my not being there, my obliteration, is what is most real about living. To see these states as binding, holding, bonding self or personality makes the intense attachment and need for them a little more comprehensible.

Even when these states are less intense, they form part of a trauma world that goes on ticking in our personality, part of who we are, which, if unrecognized, can wreak havoc in relationships with ourselves and others. Part of psychic binocularity is to fuse or integrate images of health and trauma—one eye on injury, one on recovery and growth, although they work together, often seamlessly.

A vehicle that makes room for double-seeing is faith. Bion describes faith as an open attitude, open to O. It includes sensitive openness to impacts of reality and generative working with those impacts. The freedom (unbinding) of faith is, partly, a response to the binding of disaster. Faith meets catastrophe and supports personal resilience. Myths and religions echo this movement in terms of death and resurrection, transformation, rebirth, refinding and renewal. Movement through injury and recovery is part of our psychic pulse, a basic rhythm, more important than ever now, when there are mounting fears (again) that disaster has the last word.

4 No Amount of Suffering

The notion that suffering is redemptive has lost much of its appeal, although it is far from extinct. We bear witness to the cruelty of suffering, so much needless, pointless pain—resulting from disease (mental and physical), murder, torture, predatory actions, unwanted acts of nature. Terrorism from within or outside the systems and selves we inhabit. What good can come of it? Often precious little, as pain feeds pain, suffering begets suffering.

Yet there are individuals for whom suffering plays a role in opening, as well as closing, worlds. Perhaps it would be better if this were not so. But it is so, and we'd best pay attention. In our world, suffering is a fact of life, in every social system, in every human being. It will never be eliminated. But it can be addressed. It can be listened to. To some extent, we can speak with it, speak from it. We can cry, scream, touch, look into each other's eyes, feel one another. We can learn to breathe together.

There is suffering and there is suffering. Ordinary, everyday suffering is usually taken for granted. One gets through it, goes on with one's life. Indeed, one's life is premised on getting through it. One doesn't look too hard or long at pains that streak moments throughout a day or one could not get through the day. To sit and stare at injury and wonder what to make of it is, in most instances, a luxury.

To some, however, it is a necessity. Daily pains are not simply daily pains. They are world pains, soul pains, pains that streak lives, one's own life. They stop one short, floor one. They must be thought about. As Freud depicted, injury unites injury, spreading through psychic time dimensions, wounds linking together from early to late, late to early, symphonies of injury, creating vast seas of suffering drawn together in one insistent pain point. Trickles of pain unite with other trickles, forming networks of suffering through the psychic body and often in the body itself. Trauma hits soul and body in one blow, in many blows.

The person standing next to you may be dying. May be dead and gone for many years, waiting for life. She goes on speaking, dancing, laughing. You come closer and cannot find her. She was never there. Or she was there one moment, not the next. Invisible explosive waves made her a shell. No one noticed. You couldn't see it. An invisible suicide bomber exploded, and while your attention was riveted by torn bodies, blood everywhere, ghastly devastation for all to see, you did not realize that the intact woman standing next to you was nowhere to be found. She vacated her house before she lived in it.

"I remember the moment," she tells you. "Each time I remember the moment it could be any other moment. It is all moments. Like the report of an Israeli doctor who has to decide whether to treat someone or not. Who gets care in an emergency? The mutilated ones, of course. The bleeding bodies. They are obvious. Everyone knows they must be cared for if they have a chance of living. The aides were passing over a lady shaking, crying for help. She did not feel anything except something wrong. Something was wrong and she didn't know what. No visible wounds, no signs. The doctor took one look and said, 'Treat her!' She, too, must be included. No one could tell that the force of explosive waves knocked her lungs out. Quaking air passing through her destroyed her lungs."

My patient, Leila, paused to let her words sink in. I saw a child in a house of important (certainly, self-important) people. She looked alive. She looked like a person. How could they know she wasn't there? It would take a special doctor, a special person, to see insides blown away by invisible forces. She had become that special kind of person who can see feelings that are not there.

Almost as a response to deficit, she developed a very special psychic sensitivity. If you were dead, wounded, or hollowed out and standing next to her, she might notice. She knows the explosive force of invisible waves and has the touch a person sometimes needs.

It is difficult to notice or know what to do. She was sent to therapists as a child, but they tried to pressure her into life. They did not dwell on the fact that she was "gone." They built on her "thereness." Natural enough, but "gone" got left out. Perhaps they played for time, hoping she'd outgrow it. How could a house of love create an emotional vacuum? Perhaps the best thing to do if a child feels bad is pretend not to notice, let things slide, hoping they will change. But the vacuum settles into place, a gone place eating life's insides. It was a relief, long into adulthood, to find a therapy that didn't torment her into life, so that her special kind of sensitivity found breathing room.

Vance, too, was relentless in documenting emotional abuse. "My mother said I was somber. I felt a blackness in her pores, in her vagina, a poison." He could not get over the feeling of having sex with her, although there was little evidence this literally happened. The feeling was vivid—intense fantasy feeling that consumed his body, filled his pores, as if his cells fed on images of her sickness. She was beautiful in face and body but not there. Another bombed-out being, gone. Were corpses in beautiful bodies being invisibly warehoused and injected into mothers after they gave birth? Where are all these gone people coming from? Were they always there? We just didn't notice? We noticed but didn't want to see? Couldn't see because we dared not feel such helplessness?

"My father tried to hide my dysphoria. You could be filled with compassion but I have no feeling for it. It's too scary to be attached to you. You're too scary, not attentive enough. Do you know how to carry a person in your body?

"My mother stared with vacant eyes. Her emptiness did not rise to the level of contempt. Others had contempt when it came to emotional things. My father pretended to be interested, but he wanted things to be OK. He did not want to know or feel what I felt. My feelings were so much drama, window dressing, not serious enough to count. He dismissed them. His final judgment, 'You're too sensitive.' Implying I had it easy, he had it hard. *He* knew life and rose to meet it. He toughed it out. My pain was child's play. *He* had the feelings that counted."

There were broad, rough parallels between Vance's and Leila's backgrounds, holes in mothering, floods in fathering. Leila's mother was ill, dying slowly throughout her childhood. In a photo of her holding Leila in infancy, her eyes were glazed, not quite seeing, not merely self-referential or uncomfortable, as if somehow stopping at some invisible barrier before they met the infant's gaze. Her father filled the hole with emotional storms, intermittent morning rages, rushes of affect, love, sudden caring, erotic streamings, jokes—everything was funny. He tried to be related every moment he wasn't working. Everything was tears. Tears were funny too. He was as filled with life as her mother was with death. But it was the wrong kind of fullness, to match the wrong kind of emptiness. The baby and child was lost in a space that vanished and filled with noise. Emotional tumult blotted her out, couldn't find her in the dying. Her family was gifted. She was gifted too. Gifts filled with worms, and inside the worms creative treasures. For Vance and Leila everything was organized and collapsed around their mothers' illness and filled out, inflated around their fathers' energy, self-importance, self-centered outpourings, depressive exuberance. One balloon that never was fully inflated and another always about to pop.

Vance and Leila were galled by their fathers' lie-infested energy, as if lying made them strong or vitality gave them a right to lie. Lying was an ego thing but went deeper. Vance discovered that his father lied about everything, couldn't help it. He lied about the truth. Perhaps what galled Vance most was that his father's picture of himself was a ghastly lie, a lie that made living possible, in a life that made lying necessary. He talked as if life mattered, people mattered, feelings mattered. But what really mattered were *his* feelings, *his* use of life and people. He did as he liked and made believe he was thinking of others. Vance could not stomach this fundamental dishonesty. It made him a satellite of his father's ego. He could not stomach worshipping a god that did not see him, a god that insistently missed the mark, a nearly totally egocentric, self-excusing god. Whatever god did was right; what Vance did was wrong.

Yet Vance worshipped him with a love that tore Vance to pieces. His father was beautiful in his eyes. A beauty that ripped his heart out. Primal devotion—where can it go? In Leila it found its way to God. She had a lifelong love affair with God, a love-hate relation, to be sure. But it made her more forgiving of others, if not herself. No such luxury for Vance. He was stuck on his father and his father's betrayal of the god-image, an image both played roles in creating. What happens when you discover there is no difference between God and the golden calf? That neither exists or both are everywhere?

What happened to Vance was that he became a high achiever who swallowed the hook of severity. Not only was nothing good enough, goodness itself was a theory, a construct he knew but could not feel. He tried his best to be good, to live a good life. But what he felt most was being bad—the rage, the terror, the hate, the dread. The lie in everything scratched his eyes out. He could not let it go, and he did not know what use to make of it, except for self-torment. He knew he should take pleasure in life. Pleasure existed, joy existed (his father's overt message?). But what he actually felt was evil everywhere. His father lived by looking away from anything bad in himself, justifying it. Vance could not look away from the destroying, destroyed self. As if atoning for his father's psychopathy. As if he could not give in until all psychopathy in the world disappeared.

Any opening of his heart was intensely painful. It has taken years, but there *are* openings. They close fast enough, but cannot be denied. They are there (too). Moments of opening. And they are valued, even if devaluation catches up with them. "Heart feels," he says. "My heart—a little node on an organic, venous column, and it hurts so badly sometimes. Little moments of love." Five minutes later he spoke about the importance of integrity, how corruption kills, how integrity kills. Someone at a meeting told him he acted like "an incorruptible judge. Stainless steel." Immediately Vance saw corrosion behind the steel. He fell quiet, and in a little while a moment of recovery came. "I'm just learning to talk with people. It's the last part of my life, and I'm just learning to talk with someone who disagrees with me. To speak with someone who disagrees and not break off, not disconnect or try to win. To listen, to speak." Here is a moment that escaped the father's knife, escaped Abraham's blade, not soon enough to escape the posttraumatic shock that follows the sons of Isaac. A new kind of burning bush, corrosion eating good moments, which totally vanish yet endure. To listen, to speak—a new kind of life, a life of moments.

Leila lives a gifted spiritual life with friends, fellow seekers, family. Most of her hate is directed against herself. She is ill, like her mother; but unlike her mother, she is up and around, living as fully as her frame allows, living beyond her frame. Rich in life. But, like Vance, severe. There is a devil that accuses her, that gives no rest. Everything is a sign that something is wrong with her essentially, that she is miscreated. It is a drill that goes deeper and strikes no oil. She could be singing, praying, talking with her partner, and it tightens in the background, defeats her.

In their different ways, Leila and Vance share this severity, this drill, this devil. What is it? How does it work? In Flannery O'Connor's writings, destroyers aim at phoniness, especially phony goodness. Not just vices, but anything off, taints in virtues, any false move or tone or use of a function—a destroyer gets it. As I have suggested in an earlier work, her destroyers are like sharks cleaning psychic garbage. No end to psychic garbage, no end to destruction. This destructive force works in a seek-and-destroy mode, attracted to lies.

Isn't this different from the traditional devil, the father of lies? The devil, too, is a destructive force, whose work is not cleaning up goodness but destroying it. His force nourishes itself by destroying goodness. There are variations, substories. Satan was initially an accuser, like a prosecutor in a court of law. Satan, as a special kind of lawyer, served a legal function. He used law to prove fault. He exposed flaws, failings, hypocrisies—like O'Connor's destroyer, like Vance's, like Leila's, whether directed at others or self. He sought to prove souls unworthy of God's love. He sought to prove goodness spurious, no man good.

Christianity made Satan's job a little tougher, insofar as law no longer was a conclusive arbiter. A pivot point was grace. Accusation, destruction struck deeper. It was not enough to prove a soul guilty of sin or crime or black mark. The soul itself was sinful and dependent on God's grace for redemption. Satan cut into the heart of soul, and only faith in the mystery of God's free work at such a depth could make a difference. However, as time goes on, the destroyer makes inroads in each new playground.

As often happens in the mind of man, one age's villain becomes another's hero. Satan, the envious angel, brought low by prideful rebellion, began to be recognized as an important source of energy, linked with the power of his "faults." Pride, envy, ambition, cruelty, sexuality, the will to power, destructive force—signs of vitality, partly reworked by Blake, Nietzsche, and Freud. For Blake, reason became a tyrant, a force of severity, reducing reality to reason's limits, needing to be qualified by other dimensions, other worlds, other functions. The work of destruction continues, sliding through fashions.

In our present age of ambiguity, irony, equivocation, any tendency can function many ways, destructively, generatively, both. Alchemical and mystical models invite us to mix opposites, sublimate lower to higher (now also, higher to lower), and value the contributions that diverse capacities make in acts of transformation. Bringing together, mixing, transcending opposites, valuing capacities—sounds good, is important. But to the daily life of a

Leila or Vance caught in a destructive spin? A torment, perhaps a mockery. Good for those who can, sometimes good for moments for those who can't. But missing—a little like their parents and most of the adult world—where Vance and Leila live, where they must go.

Bion touches the substrate these people gravitate toward, dwell in, when he writes of a "force that continues after . . . it destroys existence, time, and space." This is an amplification or extension of Freud's "force against recovery," and Klein's "destructive force within." I think Bion pins the issue. He is stating point-blank what these people feel. He is describing exactly what they are up against, what they say they are subject to, what they report over and over with the greatest anguish and chagrin, because no one sees it, believes them, sees it as it is.

Vance and Leila may live full lives, although Vance does not connect with his and Leila is constantly under self-attack. Not just the externals are there. Leila and Vance are extremely sensitive beings, sensitivity filled with riches. They undergo experiences few are aware of or can take. They survive the worst repeatedly. They are taking medication, which provides some relief, but does not stop the process they must undergo. They know Bion's description inside their guts and fear it will never end.

Trauma plays a role in the initial shock. It gets things rolling, then destruction takes on a momentum of its own. The cardinal player now is their own natures. Will they ever recover from themselves? Vance holds on to the evil parents inflicted. Leila mainly annihilates herself, looking for proof of shame, degradation, banishment. She fears she is beyond the place where humanity lives, no one can find her. No matter how emotionally, spiritually full her life—she fears she is not seen or valued. She is not only invisible but somehow maimed, warped, beyond the human. She and Vance have discovered inner monstrosity, although to most people they look fine.

A sick, deranged id seeks a monstrous ego. Damage, warp,

something twisted runs through us. A trauma world is a permanent part of the psyche, and we do the best we can with it. It does not go away. We have an eye on it, and an eye on health, a special sort of binocularity. Images of health and illness fuse and split. We are stuck between being unable to distinguish between them, getting the distinctions wrong, or dividing them in so extreme a way that we further alienate ourselves, increasing a sense of exile.

Vance and Leila feel monstrous, feel monstrous things happened to them, feel they emerged from a family of monsters. Monsters they love, monsters they hate. The latter, more so Vance. Leila felt monstrous by contrast with the great people around her. An atmosphere of gifted, self-important people drove her into the ground. Abuse takes many forms, endless unseen variations of disaster. Leila felt grateful if someone noticed that she felt something, or, miracle (nearly never), came close to noticing with some precision (even in a generic way) what it might be. For Vance, feelings were something exploited by others. For Leila, they were a pipeline to God or an SOS to people who looked the other way.

Deranged ids seeking monstrous egos turned into psychopathic/depressive shells by omnivorously murderous superegos (a great "paradox"—superegos devoid of ethics). Destructive waves. The living soul breathes in an atmosphere made of annihilating forces, breathes in a sense of catastrophe. Catastrophe becomes part of the cement that binds personality, links it to others. Nothing is more binding than damaged bonds, more mesmerizing than toxic nourishment, especially when ecstasy merges with rage and terror.

One of the great secrets of trauma is that it trades in radiance. Not simply that radiance and black hole mirror, filter, mix with each other, which they do. Pain and something beatific inextricably fuse, creating a more intense, endurable bond than either alone. One becomes bonded to one's own deranged structures, self as one knows it, as well as to warps of others. Early writings on masochism and attachment to suffering are helpful but do not do the trick. Freud recognized a certain helplessness in the face of a destructive force he could not fathom. Blake recognized Satan's radiance. There are heavenly and hellish ecstasies and everything between. Radiance is not limited to goodness. Demonic glows captivate, enthrall. People come alive through demonic orgasms, even when intensity of aliveness reverses into agonizing deadness.

Proof of the power of a destructive force (Freud, Klein, Bion) is that it never lets go. There is no final victory over it, although it sometimes claims a final victory for itself. If you are a rager and fight your rage, you will have to continue fighting it your whole life long. Let down your guard and the flash takes you by surprise. In a blink you have traumatized someone and yourself once more. It takes less than a moment to become a terror, and recovery may take a lifetime. Reactive, incendiary rage is only one example. On the other side of the coin, if you are a self-decimator, your work is endless too. Again, no final victory. This tendency can run you into the ground, even make you ill in an instant. Either way (out or in) you place yourself or others in danger. Danger—disaster—is a constant in the background.

Destructive power is relentless. It never stops grinding one down. Vance and Leila have beautiful experiences, love moments, erotic breakthroughs, heart openings, love of learning, rich experiences with friends and loved ones. Leila has felt God many times. Vance has visions of goodness and love that he admits are authentic, even if destruction washes them away. He can't say he's never had these tastes—sometimes more than tastes—so it is all the more tormenting that hate and terror decimate them, an unknown annihilating force mocks them. Vance and Leila get through their days as best they can. They do not give in. They try to stay the course and undergo what must be undergone. They do their best and feel their best cannot be good enough. They struggle with themselves and may die in the struggle.

Freud made real inroads, inferring important consequences from the infant's period of dependence on parental might, goodwill, skill, kindliness, especially emphasizing paternal protection and maternal nourishment. Fusions of hostile pushing away, taking in, hostile and loving dependence, satisfaction, assertion form an affective background marked by a multiplicity of tendencies. The mother plays a special role in regulating distress.

Of special importance is the infant's sense of helplessness, which feeds the idealization of helpers. The other must do for the infant what the infant can't do for itself. There must be someone somewhere who can do it better. Helplessness fuses with rage, terror, idealization, love. Other researchers qualify infantile helplessness. After all, helplessness is an adult construction read into the infant. The infant does what it is able, plays a role in mutual adaptation, seeks the nipple, adjusts its body, helps regulate stimulation. It feels its oats its way, enjoying activity and the mutual play of energies. Again, the infant may seem to be helpless yet feel omnipotent, boundless, possibly identifying with the other's capacities. In clinical work, a sense of helplessness and being controlling go together.

Melanie Klein's formulations emphasize the use of good feelings to offset bad ones. Libido defends against the death drive. Life-affirming feelings play down destructive ones, especially difficult when destructive urges increase aliveness. Idealization is used as a defense against hostile anxiety, ultimately against the destructive urge within, yet often becoming part of it. The ego tries to save a sense of goodness in a psyche awash in annihilation dread. Idealizing goodness is one precarious, if often rigid, gambit. "Goodness" itself may become suffocating.

Helplessness tends to get lost in Klein's account, buried in drive or ego activity, warrior attempts to offset anxieties concerning destruction. Psyche is inherently active, as life is, but gains extra impetus defending against helplessness. Helplessness acts as a kind of rocket launcher, although it never is sloughed off. Helplessness may be helpful in generating cultural activity, but it remains a living undercurrent, an essential part of our reality we pay a price for. We propel ourselves away from feeling helpless, but we can't escape it in the end.

Our culture is phobic about helplessness. Helplessness is bad, associated with being a victim, getting poor health care, being poor in general, being subject to disasters one could protect against if one were more active. One should be proactive, fix things, work to make things better, redress injury and wrong, be an active agent of choice and desire. Emphasis on control spins out of control, as in the recent rash and crash of corporate greed, getting high on money, letting the rest of reality go to hell. Such heady greed runs through our world, a hypertrophy of "I can and will and have a right to." Why not milk the economy and political system for all they're worth? A sickly version of following one's dream, desire degraded to material terms. One feels shame and guilt at not being an inflated enough version of oneself. One feels shame and guilt if one is not a successful enough psychopath.

It is precisely psychopathic hypocrisy that Vance hated in his father. His father performed fatherly duties by initiating his son into the ways of the world. Vance found what he was expected to take in revolting and clung to the underside of life, yet he established a niche that worked. He did not lie down and die in the face of the lying nature of life, but the lie stuck in his gut and he could not digest it. The rape of goodness, pretense of goodness left him desolate. He saw the rage at helplessness everywhere, and helpless rage mounted.

Freud catalogued aspects of helplessness: birth anxiety, sexual and aggressive anxieties, intrusion, separation, abandonment anxieties, castration anxiety, death anxiety, mortifications associated with ambition and work and everyday interchanges. Wounds of all sorts. Wounds to sensitivity. Sensitivity in danger of being flooded, going under, going into shock, numbing, going dead, dreading the onset of aliveness again, baffled but trying to learn something about recovery. Freud wrote about our struggles to defend against anxieties associated with one or another form of helplessness that become imprisoned by our personality, the fortress we work so hard to maintain.

Vance rages at the prison, the crime of making believe personality is worth inhabiting, when it is really a killing machine. He hears that personality opens avenues of experience closed to him—not simply closed so much as not believable. He believes there are others who love, who are true, people who care. But he sees the lies of life like flies blanketing his eyes, stuffing his ears and insides. He cannot laugh or take it lightly. I have never heard Vance laugh. He is serious about pain. Every lie grows from, is attached to, bears witness to, promotes pain. Where he sees lies, he sees trauma. People should stop and look and listen, own that they are killing machines, own that they are helpless. He wants the world to care. If it did, he would not believe it, but he would long to believe.

Bion pulled on threads of Freud and Klein and made an art of helplessness. He saw that precocious activity often made matters worse and suggested that passivity in the face of evil could be more effective. This was not a matter of nonresistance but more a waiting on reality, letting impacts build and transform, becoming familiar with what one is up against, opening to unknown possibilities. In therapy, what one confronts is the disaster of personality, disaster that binds personality together, disaster that personality binds. What one confronts are ways personality responds to its traumatic plight. One finds ways to squeeze the sense of disaster into controllable packets, even if one creates simulacra of disaster to control. Very like the psychotic who thinks he can stop going crazy only to find out he can't—we try to control what we can't control and settle for what we can (usually another delusion).

Catastrophe plays a major role in Bion's picture. A new thought shakes, if not shatters, a person. New feelings make one tremble. Two people meeting create impacts neither is equipped to handle. Emotional big bangs are everywhere, and we keep growing to try to endure and process them. We grow or get worse but cannot stay the same. Bion calls the attitude of openness to experience faith. He calls the unknowable reality that impacts O. Openness to O-impacts, faith in the unknowable, catastrophic O. There is not much one can do except try to be available to the impact and the processing of impacts, and grow with the processing as it grows with you. This reaching toward openness, faith in O, is an ethics and a practice. It is unlike the self-aggrandizing practice of the dominant culture (Vance's and Leila's fathers), but a challenge to do right by experience.

Few authors express this kind of openness to sensitivity as fully as Rainer Maria Rilke. He seems wholly bent on letting experience speak, holding on to nothing, giving himself to the impact of the moment as it builds, transforms, opens, shatters. He stays close to terror. Even beauty is terrible when it does its work, when one cannot shut out the feel of things, insofar as one can bear, past what one can bear. Rilke opens the lid and speaks from the opening more than most. Every angel is terrible, he says, and one must open through this terror to find the place of poetry. The moment of helplessness when experience sears, stings, festers, ripples, vibrates. One lives for it. Without terror of opening, what sort of being could we be? Experience strikes us dumb, then poetry comes.

Is this one reason why Leila and Vance hold terror for us? Cling to terror as it clings to them? Adhesive terror that rips beyond pieces. They cling to traumatic impacts no one wants to know about, that no one can do anything about. Impacts that make one helpless, that reveal one's helplessness. Are they the failed poets of helplessness? Is the torment of their lives that poetry? Their torment is a revelation of what our successful world cannot leave behind. Our high-flying world cannot shake off the sense of catastrophe that marks us. Its solutions exacerbate the terror and rage, even as it makes living easier, better (longer life expectancy, higher educational level for many, more money, power, freedom, choice . . .). Annihilation creeps through good feelings meant to wipe it out. We use good feelings to annihilate annihilation and are surprised when good feelings explode. For a moment, helplessness is revealed, but only for a moment. Recovery begins, mastery regroups, but dread does not end. It is difficult to take in that good feelings are not always good, certainly not identical with goodness, and that hate can be more powerful. Are Vance and Leila ahead of us? They have no doubt that terror and hate are real. They will not be bought off by programs meant to enforce a sense of power.

Rilke opens to anguish, terror, beauty, to the trauma of sensitivity, to the impact of love/no love, the impact of time, presence/absence, the impact of sensitivity itself. He is so sensitive to sensitivity. He alerts us to give the world to itself by transforming it—precisely by letting it impact inside us, letting impact incubate, visible become invisible, swirling, dropping into dreamwork, poet-work, alpha function—passing through psychic digestive systems, tasting, transmuting experience, psychical beings working like new kinds of worms.

Bion is open to destruction, catastrophe, disaster, how life undoes life, how life frightens life. This is his faith discipline, his moment of transformation, his opening to the world. He does not let it go, anymore than Vance or Leila do. The mixtures of rapture, hate, terror, rage, rupture. He never budges. He stays and stays and lets the worst speak. He tells us this trauma world is real, it is part of the real world, the regular world. It is even part of the dominant culture, with its lust for mastery and confidence. Winning will not make it go away. Neither winning nor losing is decisive in this realm. He keeps sensitivity open to forces that make one insensitive, that make one scream, that make one stop screaming as one tries to shut everything out, especially the sound of one's life. He keeps sensitivity open to what happens as it begins to go under. He supports the individual's journey through being murdered and enduring a process of recovery, acknowledging helplessness as a dimension of repair. The work of helplessness—helplessness does work too.

I suspect Rilke's murder may be more exquisite than Bion's—no less dreadful, but more exquisite. Deliciousness is not too far away, if one stays with the trembling, the blackout, the resonance. His poetry opens places we've been too scared to believe in, precious places we need, where we live an inner life like bird wings fluttering, shaking sparks of water in the fiery air. Bion keeps his eye on desolation, explosiveness, how we attack the process Rilke discovers. We best not make believe we are not explosive, or that we know what to do with this part of our nature. A measure of acknowledged helplessness may aid the quality of our approach.

I'm not speaking against feeling one's oats, crowing, one's vital nature, active aliveness, ambition, power, social interchange, give and take—the stuff of life. I am saying, though, give helplessness a chance. Don't leave helplessness behind. Not just because Vance and Leila won't let us, although that is true enough. There are many kinds of Vances and Leilas in this world, many levels, qualities, tones, situations. Many sorts of abuse, the terror in families, in oneself, as well as between groups, nations, peoples, and the terrors of God.

There's a moment of helplessness that stops our breath, a quick shock, before we jump into action. I propose we do more tasting of that moment, sifting it, letting our faith muscle grow, as building tolerance for the fleeting shock begins to transform us. We are a race—the human race—of soul terrors. Righting economic, political, social, familial, military wrongs helps, helps a lot. But soul terrors, fragility, vulnerability do not end. It is a utopian fantasy to think they will. We ought not live our whole lives in terms of our fears, and certainly not our hates. But we cannot leave them behind. We need to open up and try to learn what we can do with them, with ourselves. Experts tell us all sorts of things. Sometimes they're helpful, sometimes not. Human nature is not something anyone is expert about, and medicine won't solve the problem, short of medicating much of humanity (which may be happening).

Society has not left Vance and Leila behind. They do well in life. They live the fullest lives they can, given their talents, abilities, disabilities. But they are caught by a downside they cannot shake out of, not with therapy or with medication. Seeking help has helped. They make richer, fuller use of themselves than they could without it. They have a wider range of experiences. I honestly think without help they could have died. Still, what feels most real, most true, to Vance is his terror and rage. He believes in love and truth, wants to believe in them. But his truth is trauma and emotional abuse. That's what he sees when he looks around, covered with goodwill, good feelings, and the will to power. He sees egos exploiting souls. He knows there is love in his home, the home he has built, his family, friends, colleagues, the world he has helped create. He acts as if he were loving, hoping the feeling will take. But his truth is elsewhere: in misery; in a suicidal sense of being a monster, a killer in a race of killers; in states of terror, helplessness, and rage. He wishes therapy would transform him, free him, but given that he is who he is, the next best thing is bearing witness, so the world knows that such things exist, and that normalizing ideas do not make them better.

Leila believes in radiance, the beauty in life. It is real for her. God is real. Spirit is real, the life of the senses deliciously real. Her crisis of faith is elsewhere. What kind of God permits the useless agonies people undergo, ghastly illness, a psyche subject to every nuance of fragility, every dreadful whisper and agony magnified? How has she endured such suffering and survived? How could she have been so unseen, dropped, empty, so stuffed with emotional noise and people's egos as a child? She could not help but feel ashamed. Her pain was a signal of failure. God must think she's awful. She is awful. Hate fills her pores, but she barely feels it. It seeps into her like poison. She pulls back, rigid, tries to hide, but she cannot make her insides go away. Hate is a judgment, a condemnation. She can never be a human being. To be merely wooden like Pinocchio would be a blessing.

Vances and Leilas will exist as long as traumatized sensitivity exists, as long as we wound each other and make believe we know what to do about it. To be helpless in the face of our predicament is no shame. To struggle with it is no shame either.

5 Somatic Storms

Those who work day in and day out with the intimate lives of people discover fields of experience largely unknown or neglected in ordinary daily life. A hazard of this strangely fulfilling work is becoming increasingly set apart, different, so that normal social intercourse becomes difficult, unsatisfying. A beauty is the sense of contact with mysterious areas of experience that make one feel compellingly close to deeper and truer realities, where emotional meaning holds sway.

In truth, someone like me was on the different side to begin with, and finding the consulting room as a way of life, or an important part of life, was a godsend. It enabled me to breathe, to find health, that is, my own way of being healthy. But there are no guarantees that psychic and bodily health go together. I say all this as a way of postponing getting into the work of this chapter. For I fear, after years of public education about psychosomatic connections, that drawing attention to intricacies of feeling and body will seem magical.

I feel apologetic, too, for perhaps reporting nothing new— perhaps not even anything not already known in the first quarter of last century. Nevertheless, it is difficult to suppress the wish to bear witness when, in daily practice, one sees somatic symptoms come and go or stay as a function (at least, partly) of an interplay of feelings, attitudes, and relationships. One feels impelled to bring to awareness still neglected, denied, or undervalued realms of being, on the chance that telling stories in one's own way will touch the lives of others. If I thought it would do any good, I'd shout: "These things are real. Find them. Feel them. They are important for how we live, perhaps if we live." Hidden springs of emotional meaning work our lives in surprising ways, shape and misshape us, add to the challenge of who we are, who we are becoming.

Some connections are obvious. A man suffers a defeat at work and can't eat at home. He loses fifteen pounds in two weeks. He is depressed. In reality this man will lose neither money nor his job, but he feels the defeat as an assault, an insult. He feels a loss of status, although his fellow workers or boss might not agree. Something he invested in, a project, a way of doing things, an opportunity to do something better, has been rejected, and it feels like the essence of his person has been trashed.

There is temptation to go to a psychiatrist for medication that will make him feel better. If that is necessary, fine. But with premature or promiscuous medication, chances are something will be missed or glossed over at great cost. If a defeat at work makes him fall through a hole in his being, a drama of self needs careful attention. The feel of a life is at stake. That a blow at work blows his physical-emotive digestive systems away, points to knots between areas of being he ordinarily separates. Whatever it is that connects him to living runs through body, emotions, attitudes, relationships. Learning about this connecting thread may get lost or downplayed by scurrying to feel better and get on top of things as quickly was possible.

It is a natural reflex, trying to right oneself as one falls or get up as soon as one can, if one is not too injured. But when injury comes from the emotional meaning of events, when the bruise or fall is to one's ego, vanity, image, getting on top as fast as possible may cause one to miss an opportunity to ponder and grow. Mastery is not always the best model when it comes to emotional meaning and transformational chances.

An example of the delicious magic (yes, magic, I admit it) of this work is the following. A woman, call her Stacey, tells me she had an awful weekend. At one point she could not swallow.

Whatever she swallowed did not go down. It stuck in her "food pipe" or in the language of her doctor, she suffered a painful esophagus spasm, possibly related to reflux. If she swallowed saliva it would sit there with the food pieces. She could breathe. Still, she was terrified. Something bad and uncontrollable was happening. She was stuck like this about six hours and, finally, vomited to clear herself, but still felt terrible. She did not feel as clear and OK as she used to.

She blamed her husband's anxiety. All weekend he was busy with obsessive paperwork that drove them crazy. She felt he was going overboard, doing work beyond the call of duty, ruining their weekend. Perhaps there were other anxieties he tried to offset with hyperactivity. Sometime over the weekend the thought occurred to her, "He was calm and confident when I married him. Now he's like my family I tried to get away from." The thought came and went over the weekend but came back as we were speaking.

Now Stacey remembers that she had missed her mother's call a few days earlier and was debating over the weekend whether or not to call her back. She has bad luck when she speaks with her mother. Invariably, she ends up depressed and weakened, as if poisoned. In fact, I have come to believe that she does get poisoned in contacts with her mother. Her mother is bad news. She lies and criticizes, spews negativity. Her mother love is tainted and dangerous.

With my encouragement, Stacey has experimented, during this past year, with not having contacts with her mother for long periods. During those periods, she feels better, is more alive, does more. When contact comes, she is done in. The evidence is clear. No mother, feel better; mother, feel worse. Maybe some day Stacey will enjoy or tolerate time with her mother. Meanwhile, these contacts go nowhere. From very early in Stacey's life, love and toxins were so fused that to get the former, she had to take in the latter. Driven by a need for support and love, the child drinks in cocktails of self-hate, confusion, depletion, depression, dread.

She gets addicted to poison blended with nourishment. Our therapy tries to give her time off from this addiction and give other states a chance.

It is not easy for Stacey to talk to her mother but also difficult for her not to. Stacey feels guilty about not calling her back. Should she or shouldn't she call, she agonized. What sort of person wouldn't call her mother—uncaring, unfeeling, cold, inhuman! She pictures a nice conversation. A warm, caring feeling spreads through her, a mother feeling in the core of her being. The contrast between this feeling and what she knows will happen jolts her. A real conversation will be awful. It *always* is. The loving mother within gets smashed by contact with the real person.

As she swings between the wish for a good call and the realization that it will be ghastly, Stacey's spasm comes back. Her saliva gets stuck, won't go down. She is dumbfounded. "It's back." She points to her throat and chest in disbelief.

"Your mother's stuck in your food pipe," I blurt out. The words just came, not a second lost, a kind of instantaneous communication. "She's indigestible."

Time stops for a moment. Stacey likes the word "indigestible" and says it a number of times. She wants to pause at this point. I feel a smile forming in my chest but mostly I wait in quiet startle, an odd form of peace. My mind takes off, picturing her mother stuck in her, unable to go in or out. If her mother can't get down through Stacey's mouth, maybe she'll try going up Stacey's asshole. Maybe she's a partly digestible mother, enough to animate some loving feeling, but largely indigestible and damaging. My mind goes on but I say nothing because Stacey signals not to talk. Don't ruin the caesura. Now and then she says the word "indigestible," a kind of mantra, but we are mostly quiet. While we sit, her symptom clears and she feels better. She looks forward to the rest of the day.

When she leaves, my smile comes out. This is beautiful work. I wish people knew about it, really knew how connected we are, how we affect each other, how subtle, full, and vibrant our connections are. We are called to care for our interconnectedness. One of our first jobs in Genesis is caring for the garden. How worth caring for this garden is!

Hardy is beset by asthma, colds, blocked sinuses. Some kind of low-grade illness always seems to be there, a chronic irritability. He has seen the doctors, has medication. But what most irritates him is his life. His body is part of his life, part of an irritating field of experience.

He is a healthy-looking guy. To me he seems outgoing, amiable, bright. If I were not an analyst, I might be a little surprised at his chronic complaints. From the outside, he seems to have a decent life, be a decent person. In fact, he *has* a decent life, *is* a decent person.

My life as an analyst teaches me most people are uncomfortable with themselves. There are all kinds of inner complaints, pains, difficulties that do not reach expression. People can be beset by chronic emotional colds without locating affected areas. It is odd, perhaps, to think of emotional lungs filled with psycho-spiritual mucous, that one is in danger of being depleted by, even dying from, undiagnosed emotional pneumonia, that emotional lungs or heart or liver may be damaged and unable to work well. What affects a life runs through a person. We chop experience into categories and forget their source.

Neither Hardy's physical nor his psychic dis-ease is life threatening. He will live. But how, in what condition? It is a quality-of-life issue, a personal matter. It has more to do with who he is, how he meets life, what life does to him, and what he does with it. What can he do with his chance at living? What does it mean to live a life?

I say that Hardy's dis-ease is not life threatening because it is unlikely he will die from it soon. But it is wrong to think his dis-ease is not threatening. He may not die from it, but his life quivers and shakes in its wake, his life is affected. *He* is threatened, lives under threat, and, in a way, *life is* threatening. It is not so unusual as one might think to feel persecuted by one's own life.

It has taken quite some time for Hardy to spontaneously begin a session with the words, "I'm broken. A piece is missing. Something is missing." He has bitched about his life, people in it, fate, history. But to come in and say that he is broken—I never heard it so openly, fully, immediately. For the moment I was taken aback, surprised at my good luck. It is good to have this feeling, to connect with it, express it. We wreak horror on ourselves, others, and the world at large by making believe we are whole. To be whole, we break others. No accident "total" is the root for "totalitarian." Humility is missing in pretensions of wholeness.

"Maybe I was right as a teen, when I felt something was wrong," Hardy continues. "I tried to talk myself out of it most of my adult life and gave myself to new experiencing. I feared I wouldn't live if I stayed with what was wrong. It's taken this long to get back to it, to be in a position where I can take looking at it."

For months Hardy has bemoaned his workaholic ways. He scarcely sees his kids during the week, and on weekends he gets involved with his own activities. Family activities often are disasters, complete with bickering, blowups. His wife and he are increasingly estranged, see eye to eye on nothing. This past week was different. There was a slowdown at work and he spent extra time at home. "It takes a while to get used to being there. They have to get used to me, and I have to get used to them. Our paces are different. We have to find a common rhythm, feel each other out, establish a way to be together. I gave it time and, for a change, it turned out nice. I didn't make them do this, make myself do that. No rush. We just hung out.

"I can't believe I'm saying this, but it was nice to be at home. Kids, doing small things. I liked it, really liked it. It makes a difference with the kids, wife—*and* myself. The kids were calmer, wife warmer. I made less money but got more satisfaction. I'm not very social. I'm self-protective. I'm apologizing for not going anywhere New Years. No one invited us. Without work, I don't have much. What surprised me was having a family. We had a good time together.

"It's hard to get used to having choices and the realization that my life is my own, up to me, at least in some sense. I'm so used to relying on external structures and doing things for outside reasons. Going to school, making money. Yet I have a feeling of *something* meaningful, activities I love, art, music, nature, being with the kids—things I do so rarely. There's a feeling of something more, something good, beautiful, in contrast with social and economic pressures." Hardy was surprised, too, at how good he felt for a spell, emotionally *and* physically.

The next week his energy ebbed a little, mood dipped. He looked at his life and was not happy with what he saw. "A good puppy dog is what I am. I did not know what I wanted for myself and got married young. When I went along with my wife, all was OK. I never really challenged my parents. My primary identification with them did not get broken up enough. I could not be oppositional. I had to be obedient, a good boy to fit my wife's and parents' frames.

"My wife resents me. Her mother was sick all the time. She was deprived and is angry with me for failing to make up for it. She stayed with the kids to make up for her mother's lack. She doesn't appreciate the support she got from me all these years. Now I resent her lack of support for me, her staying at home, my having to make all the economic decisions. She could have worked part time and I could have helped at home. Whether I go along with her or oppose her, she resents me. She might as well be angry with me for having my own mind than for doing what she wants.

"I have to move past this resentment. It's eating me up, damaging me. I feel it eating my body away inside my breathing, corroding my spirit. I don't know what will happen if she doesn't get past her anger, but I know I have to move past mine, for my sake, if not ours.

"I feel I see my life as it is for the first time. It's limitations, flaws. It's as if I'm breathing in a blameless moment, things as they are. I don't know how I got there, but I'd like to stay a while. I have to make a new relationship with my wife, move forward. I fantasize leaving her, but that would involve giving up our whole world, a world involving my relationship with our kids. I don't feel reconciled to our situation. I wouldn't go that far. People manage in their lives, maybe not so great, but they make their choice, make the best of it. I'm wondering how to go about making the best of it, what that would be? I feel a scary peace. I don't know what will happen. It may fall apart as soon as I leave this office, but for the moment I feel in contact with something worthwhile, although I'm not sure what it is. Maybe it's just me and a little more than me, a kind of deeper feeling for my life."

Amanda tells me about her migraines. She never knows when one will hit. They have plagued her throughout her adult life. She also gets irritable bowel symptoms, diarrhea without warning that lasts for months, then mysteriously goes away. Violence in her body.

When I was a young therapist, I learned a simplistic body scheme. Headache = daddyache, bellyache = mommyache. I don't believe such formulae uncritically. Yet Amanda's intestinal problems receded after finding a deeper peace with her mother near the end of her mother's life. It was not a reconciliation easily achieved. Most of her life, she felt underappreciated and criticized by her mother. When she did something she was proud of, her mother scarcely seemed to value it. Yet there were ways in which Amanda felt embraced and accepted. Growing into womanhood, being with men, finding her husband, sexuality, affection—her mother seemed at home with home and body and supported this part of Amanda's life. A woman achieving in the world did not make sense to Amanda's mother. Amanda's resentment and anger circulated between her mother, herself, her body.

Lately, her body ills are migraines rather than intestinal troubles. She takes medication. Real relief is hit or miss. Something is bothering her, something unknown expressed as pain. Emotional pain—physical pain: they are not always so different. Her father recognized her vocational efforts, her wish to be someone, when he was aware of them. He was off a lot doing his own business. But they had sweet times, joys, pleasures, good memories.

Eventually, Amanda spoke of not so good moments. When she was a child, she hated it when his penis showed through his underpants. He walked around in underwear a lot, too much for her. She felt shame, pain, anger, guilt all combined. Sweet memories, dancing together in the streets, treats, ice cream, fun things fused with a sense of something bad about to happen. His penis was about to come out. And often did come out. An ache was growing in her head.

She loved her father but for many years thought him an inadequate man, not a man among men. No one else she ever met felt that way about him. As far as people said, he held his own, congenial, dogged, reliable, not the worm she imagined at all. Where did her disgust and contempt come from? She was ashamed of him and herself. Were they conspiratorial in a way that left out her mother? Or were the conspirators she and her mother dancing around his penis like a maypole? One moment his penis is out, one moment hidden, now you see it, now you don't, here, gone. Father comes and goes, and she can't control him. The head of the family, too missing, too obtrusive. What better way to gain some ascendancy than rise above him by putting him down. She adored him and had wonderful moments with him. But she also was rendered helpless, vulnerable, at a loss. He exhibited, she felt shamed. Shame was contagious and spread, engulfing him in her mind. He did shameful things which made her fearful, and she protected herself with contempt and disgust. It was hard to put together his loving and life-loving side with the ways in which he was inadequate as a father. Her seeing him as an inadequate man transformed dread of ways he was an inadequate father. In a child's mind, inadequate man = inadequate father. In Amanda's case, the movement from father to man in general represents a kind of quasi-mastery attempt through displaced shame, the latter partly defended against by superior disgust. Faults in fathering tainted ways in which he was good. The snake in the garden has traumatic impact, whether or not the snake knows it's a snake.

When Amanda recounted her feelings about the many times she saw his penis (underpants a snake hole, a kind of *fort-da*), her head pain grew, and the words jumped from me: "When the father in your head gets an erection, you feel pain, penis rising, pushing into your brain."

Well, that opened a can of worms and a hornet's nest—creepy, buzzing thoughts galore. The pain subsided, and she spoke about the first migraine she remembers. She was walking down a street, thinking very hard about a philosopher and a flaw she saw in his thought. A light went on when she saw that he confused pleasure with happiness. A light followed by blinding pain. She wept from pain but welcomed it if that was what she had to pay for insight. Seeing and blinding went together, like castration and opening. It is not easy to give oneself permission to see, if one sees flaws. A child may not be able to bear seeing parental flaws if the parent cannot take it. A child not only battles to be seen but to see, a battle for one's mind.

"That was the first time I used my head, thought so hard. That can't be true, but it felt so. I never thought so hard before. I thought until I ached. It was worth it because I saw something important, a distinction between pleasure and happiness. I got a headache from using my head for thinking. My mother couldn't care less about this thinking, the thrill of *seeing* with one's mind. It's not important to her, but it's a source of happiness for me.

"I don't know if you could call my father a thinker, but he thought more about the world than my mother. He would be more likely to appreciate a thought I had, if I had one. That makes me more like him when I think, and that makes me dangerous. If I think, can I be trusted? Can I trust myself? What will my thinking do to others, to myself, when my penis starts to show?

"I got dizzy five years earlier, thinking about whether to get married, not sure whether I wanted to or not. I was very conflicted and got sick when I tried to decide. I was also very excited, and I think excitement turns into pain too. My head constricts and my body bursts. Sometimes in sex it's so exciting, it's painful. I've been experimenting by being a collaborator with my brain against the pain, breathing, meditating, feeling it, and sometimes I can stop it and it's gone. Like now, it's going away. It started getting worse in the session, and now it's getting better.

"I see myself in high school dancing with a boy I hardly knew, melting. To melt, who suspected this? Some form of melting is part of my personality, The melting self is different from fluff and icing. It's gutsy, not sentimental. It [the melting self] makes it easy to be with people. I'm adaptable, blend in. Not a conformist exactly. I took it for granted I was OK with people. People like me without my working at it, and I like that. But it's not the same as working hard at something important, getting *that* kind of satisfaction. I doubt if *that's* something my mother knew about.

"I had a sense of self when I was very young. Something happened to it when I tried to become something I'm not. It was a temptation to coast in college, to drift into something easy. It was easy to get along. I made choices I did not believe in and made believe I liked things I didn't. No one told me I was training for the wrong thing, that my studies didn't fit me. I took an easy way and people, like my mother, didn't ask for more. They thought the easy person they saw was the whole me. Either people don't have a clue or they pretend not to notice how stormy it is inside. Self-doubt grew and hasn't left. I had boyfriends, but they never made up for the insecurity and for not being at one with my work.

"Melting went along with my sense of self. Melting has a truth sense. When I melt into, around, or through things, the melting feeling tells me whether what I'm doing is right or wrong for me. It was telling me my studies and work were wrong. The only voice that kept telling me I could do something else or more was inside me. Most people do not associate melting with truth, the way you feel when you pour yourself into things and how you feel when they mold you. I knew I needed another mold, another arena to pour myself into and, in time, I tried. Melting can be gentle, sweet, thrilling, a relief to dissolve and take another form or no form at all. It can also be fierce or have fierce spots, an eye in the hurricane, a very windy emptiness. I poured myself into bodies, knowledge about physical processes, and cannot believe I ended up becoming a neurologist, Dr. Amanda Levy, but that is what felt right, a right mold for my strange liquid."

Amanda spoke more about her parents, her conflicts about doing better than they, doing things they couldn't, yet from an early age she knew she was not put on earth simply for their pleasure. They had lives, with each other, with other people, as well as with her. Her father's difference (and badness) gave her permission to be different, although it scared her, marred her. Her mother's acceptance was almost paid for by lower expectations. With her father, she paid for excitement with fear. Melting with father, with boys, blends of fear and fulfillment. She knew hard work was important to feel herself. It was good, but not enough, just to enjoy herself with people. Liquid yes, but water cuts paths. There were inner pressures, thought storms, body storms pushing for life.

The discussions above center on somatic storms that are not associated with fatal illness. Symptoms come and go, connected with a variety of factors, including mood, quality of interaction, the meaning of events, emotional flow. Nevertheless, the symptoms that come and go perdure. Headaches, intestinal aches, respiratory blocks are parts of lives. Life conditions repeatedly bring them out, yet how one meets such pains often influences the latter. Emotional pain and physical pain blur.

When a mother touches a body, she touches a person. Touching a baby's body is not a neutral event. *Someone* feels the touch, responds to it. It is pleasurable, painful, makes one feel better, worse, even divine or toxic. There is also room for touch that is more neutral, that simply involves a task, and babies get used to it and understand that what is happening is neither exciting nor threatening. But it is sometimes easy to lose sight of the facts that touch between a baby and its mother, even in the act of changing a diaper, mediates feeling tone and that when a mother touches a baby, she touches a soul.

To touch a body is to touch a psyche. Touch itself is psychically charged. Someone is touching someone. It is not just body touching body. Thus what affects body affects emotion, and what affects an emotional field affects the body. Basic permeability may be played down as one grows in awareness as a separate individual. The pride of self, the sense of becoming more and more a person, creates the illusion that permeability is something one can handle or ignore.

The fact of permeability and the subtle ways it works is demonstrated by the therapy sessions above. These illustrations were relatively benign, painful as they were to the individuals involved. If interweaving of emotional-somatic dimensions is so easily demonstrated, one wonders about interpermeability in severe and lethal illnesses. Loss and psychic injury can precipitate psychosis and somatic ills as well. There are many anecdotal happenings that give pause. The year a woman's father dies, she gets cancer. The year a woman's mother dies, she has a heart attack. A man gets prostate cancer following a series of guilt-ridden happenings. Immune-system disease gets worse or better for unknown reasons. A man dies of a heart attack after falling in love. One can only speculate on somatic and psychosocial factors that play a role. Often the physical origins of illness are obscure.

Synchronicity is not causality, and one is at a loss to draw conclusions. But one can't help suspecting the importance of psychic, atmospheric factors, matters of spirit. Of course, somatic conditions and tone affect the psychic atmosphere one moves and breathes in. It is usually not possible to pinpoint what does what or how the under- and oversides of our emotional and physical skins adhere in a reality encompassing both.

There are no formulas. It is not true that people doing body work are disease free, any more than people working with emotional states through words are. Therapy is no panacea, no escape from death and mishap. It does not solve the problem of pain and illness. But it is not without value. There is something to be said for growth in self-knowledge, awareness of one's personality makeup, one's patterns, and an ability to work with, if not control, those patterns, although this is not the main thing. More important than "knowing," is opening fields of experiencing, building a taste for life, for experiencing, problems of psychic taste buds. The head-mind and gut-mind that comes out in sessions with Stacey, Hardy, and Amanda connect with an ineffable psychic sense that runs through them, a feel of aliveness that has its own quality and tone. One is driven back to the feel of a life, to an elusive "something." An elusive something that is precious.

More resonant contact with this elusive, precious something does not make the bad stuff go away. "Probably the greatest suffering in the human world is the suffering of normal or healthy or mature persons," writes Winnicott. Why? Because they can take more? Because they feel more? Because they expose themselves to more of life? Freud's famous remark about psychoanalysis helping people tolerate the malaise of real life rather than be mired in neurotic suffering plays down Winnicott's reality. Perhaps Freud is protective about adult truth, like a parent shielding a child. It is not exactly a good "promo" for life to say, with Winnicott, "Get better and you'll expose yourself to suffering you never dreamt about." And deeper satisfactions as well.

No one is free from distortions that growth processes force on one, owing to environmental impacts, pressures, stresses, and the sheer intensity of life. Forces involved in growth are sometimes more than an organism can bear. People who are fully and deeply involved in life expose themselves to events and pressures that can prove too much. "Healthy" people are not immune to somatic breakdown when demands and injury take a toll. Sometimes the body pays a price for psychic strength (a caricature version in movies is when a fighter's will, heroism, or vanity makes him stand and suffer blows past a point his body can take; Shakespeare places the agony in human sensitivity and portrays psychic derangement, breakdown, folly).

Babies and parents go through daily terrors and joys at an intensity level most of life can't bear, but the relationship they are immersed in enables them to bear it. Much of life involves coming through disturbances and coming through again. If a relationship has decent enough elements, it helps us weather difficulties it gives rise to. Often we do not notice that a relationship absorbs feeling states a person alone can't handle. If things go well enough, we help each other just by being together, even if being together is part of the difficulty.

Being together as a human group *is* a major difficulty, but only working together as a human group can help. Emotional and physical suffering plagues us from our first to our final agonies, and part of making peace, if peace there be, involves growth in how we approach necessary pain. Prophetic, Blakean, or Tennysonian visions of peace implicitly rely on growth in which everyone (including psychic voices, all aspects of self) takes part, to which everyone contributes. That everyone is central to everyone else may be a lie or fiction. Yet in some way that involves growth of human feeling it is absolute truth.

Permeability and its emotional-somatic storms feed and challenge lives. Life does not stop impacting on itself. Our challenge is to partner ability capable of making these impacts worth the trouble. We are driven by a worthy sense that asks for worth. This chapter shows little moments in lives that tasted what it is like to connect impact (of life, of personality, of other, of self) with more nourishing processing and a fuller sense of being. In the general scheme of things, these little bits of work may not seem like much, and taken out of context they are almost caricatures. Nevertheless, they bear witness to a profound desire for growth of psychic taste buds and, with an impossible-to-pin-down psycho/spiritual/somatic body English, a need to steer a better course.

6 Dream Images

Dream: *An oldish woman who, to my surprise, appeared to be pregnant. A pregnant old lady. She seemed lively, moved around with a lot of energy. Maybe something funny about her. She seemed nice enough. Sincere, a slightly humorous tinge. Active, on the go.*

She reminds me of a chemistry teacher I had in high school who looked hillbillyish. I half expected her to start fiddling or burst into cheery song, even though she was serious, worked hard, presented the course straightforwardly. She had a gawky, homely strength and energy that, without my quite realizing it, felt life-affirming. Reminds me of a comedienne when I was young—I'm not exactly sure who, maybe Fanny Brice. Similar bone structure, homeliness. She got laughs making fun of her looks.

I could tear the dream to pieces with associations, trauma, wishes, life events—all the things that one can do with dreams —or connect it with creative urges, possibilities of growth. I'd like, for the moment, to pare away as many of these associative branches as I can, and stick with the surprising energy the dream evoked. The dream was alive, breathing, *this* old woman a surprise in every sense—her age, her pregnancy, her sprightliness. Now that I think of it, she seemed almost ready to move in all directions, as spirit moved her.

I feel a tinge of humor thinking of biblical angels on some kind of ball with proscribed possibilities of motion. If my pregnant old lady, at first glance an earth figure, were an angel, she'd be a more whimsical, less forbidding figure than awesome prophetic presences. Nevertheless, she is mysterious, startling, dumbfounding. She leaves me speechless, fascinated, not totally without foreboding, but generally feeling light and good. She is puzzling but not ominous.

I mention "foreboding" because I am sensitive to trauma waves in dreams. Dreams give form to a kind of formless annihilation dread that is part of the background radiation of the psychic universe. Dreams express myriad creative and destructive possibilities. On the latter side, dreamwork brings intolerable emotions into focus and tries to mediate digestion of troubling events and feelings. At times, dreamwork seems to spin its wheels, portraying overwhelming and damaging stuck points. My pregnant old lady melded creativity and trauma, a dense packing that pressed experiential nerves. Mostly, she jumps out at me, slips into openings of self I didn't know were there. Where does she come from? Who is she? What can she want, if anything? What is her destiny, if any? What does she say about life, my life, our life?

I feel a certain adolescent and child energy in her, as if her skin were tightly drawn around excitement that bubbles into anxiety like juice through the skin of a plum. Her skin doesn't exactly sag like an old person's and is not exactly tight. Maybe it feels tight because of the shower of electrical shivers that leak through it. Movement emits feelings, leaks feelings.

She is definitely not the image I would have thought up for "soul clap hands and sing." Just hand clapping, body moving, aliveness buzzing—one hand clapping. Energy too much for body, body too much for mind. Child energy, teen energy, old age energy. Raggy filaments too hot to touch one moment, feathering you the next. A sense of the whole universe, all of us crazily jumping up and down—all one hand clapping.

Old lady phallic energy jelly bean belly in your face going about her business propelled by forces that don't come from you, that you don't understand, autonomous, self-directed currents of her own. I've seen bugs dart around like that, especially when I tried to kill them. But there was no killing in the dream. This was, unbelievably, a nonviolent dream. A packed, darting energy, at once dense and mobile, unpredictable, a lot of potential energy with no one getting hurt.

The Bible tells us about old ladies getting pregnant. Moses didn't begin his birth-of-a-nation work before eighty, perhaps about the same age that wild, kindly, almost son-killer Abraham circumcised himself, cutting himself into newness. Freud tells us that circumcision was a way that ancient Egyptians demonstrated their superiority. For Abraham, it was part of a marriage contract between soul and God, a devotion, a promise to bring forth souls more populous than the stars. An association between cutting, purity, bonding, binding, offering, promise, recreation of self and peoples. A mixture of freedom, difference, newness, and service. One catches glimmers of all this in cutters and self-mutilators today, a kind of skin or organ anorexia that promises more for less.

Old ladies with special babies, God babies, blessed miracles, proof of God's commitment, presence, force. Goodness topping deprivation. God needs a lot of proofs of His existence and we need a lot of proofs of ours. A special moment should be enough but time moves too quickly, even for God. Down-to-earth old ladies baffling time. My dream lady was down-to-earth, practical like biblical old ladies, although, perhaps, more comical, a little haywire with bouncy energy. Are people who are mysteries to others mysteries to themselves? I suspect my pregnant old lady was as unknown to herself as she was to me.

My grandmother looked so old to me. I called her "Monkey." She died of cancer in her forties, but her face was lined like my dream lady's. To me she was one hundred and twenty. Maybe I was four. She lit candles on Friday nights, kept kosher. A few years before she died, she nearly died and came back, speaking of beautiful, radiant men with prayer shawls. She was so happy to have seen them. They told her it was not time yet, she had to stay with us a little longer. She came back to tell us about them. Now she is back again, mediated by my dream lady, a lightning bug in my heart, making me smile as I puzzle funny turns.

"You see, I did it," she might say. "Now I'm with them." She is with the holy ones. When I think of her, I'm surprised to see a baby in a tiny boat darting in the water. It must be me in her arms, feeling precious and loved.

There is more—always more. Birth is not limited by anything you can think of. If my grandmother is pregnant with death, it is death pregnant with life. She comes to show me that life goes on and I cannot understand it and neither can she. The dream figure is sheer presencing with a taste of incredible persistence and a taste of incredibly sweet joy. I am drifting away from the puzzle, the unknowable pregnant old lady, energic force, creative urge. Trying to tame the startling. Flying sparks bait me. I see a pregnant old lady rocking a boat, and I jump in and rock with her.

Old ladies can do anything. In the Bible and in Hollywood. Mary Poppins can do anything for a moment—almost. She comes to tell you anything is possible. My indestructible old lady is a bulwark against fragility, death, time. Almost a slide of pure strength. My grandmother, in contrast, was skinny, deteriorating, the disease eating her insides out. Not in dream life, not this dream. This old lady is a bit like a machine, an engine. She accelerates, not simply walks. She does not say anything. There is no speech in the dream. The dream is quiet but for the whir of energy and a mute insistence. Movement makes me hold my breath and watch. Am I listening for my parents' sounds in the night? The force of the old lady's compact pressure going nowhere, here, there, like up-and-down bodies in the night. Their movement stops me.

My dream lady draws power from many sources but is nothing but herself. The definitive density of being only herself is part of the fascination, the liberation. How can one be only oneself? Waves of strength pulse through my body when I think of her. I feel more together, able, ready, with anxious, steadfast energy that moves me I know not where. Able to come alive, fragile as a bird coming back year after year to the same site to nest.

An old bird grown kindlier with age. But no, I'm confusing something in my own heart with the woman staring at me from the dream, eyes open, staring—just seeing, not me, not anything in particular. The force that works in this woman is not human. But then, there is much that is not human in us. Life does not stop, the psyche does not stop, not when we are dying or when we die.

My dream lady is not sentimental. Is she indifferent? Part of an indifferent force that does not care about us, part of the pressure of a universe that keeps universing? Part of the force that is the work of mothering tasks, someone who takes care of the baby without knowing exactly who the baby is? Is she a look and an energy I do not grasp? Why call her indifferent if she appeared? She came to show herself to me. A new creation using some old materials, a figure creating herself out of dream substance. She could have remained hidden, unborn. Her coming into my dream, becoming a dream image, is something other than rude indifference. She turned herself into a dream gift to ponder, to take me places. If indifference, then an indifference that is part of who we are. The universe may explode, collapse, expand, thin, chill, but my pregnant old lady represents psychic force with no end.

My father called my grandmother a force of nature. She, for whom I was so precious, so loved, traumatized me horribly. When she thought the pet duck my father gave me was big enough to eat, she killed it and served it. "That's what she did in the old country," my father explained. "That's what she knows. A peasant. A force of nature." "Why didn't you stop her?" I wanted to know. "How can you stop a force of nature?" my father replied. He pleaded innocence, like all men and women since Adam and Eve. But pleading innocence does not stop pain.

My mother never liked having the duck in the apartment. It challenged her sense of cleanliness. One day she said, "Your duck is too big for the apartment. It's grown up. It needs a larger space. It will be happier in grandma's backyard." The hand of fate slices through all bones. Truth mixes alien desires. Grandma's backyard was big enough indeed. It looked like it would make a barnyard animal happier. You can't argue *that*. All I could say was, "Quackie is happy with me. Quackie will be happier with me in a small place than without me in a big place." Anywhere together was the happy place. This took no figuring at all, pure emotional arithmetic of a child not yet in kindergarten. Quackie was my best friend. He waddled up and down my body when I napped, wagged along behind me on the street.

One Shabbos I went to grandma's and Quackie was not in the yard. They told me he must have escaped. I went around the neighborhood calling, "Quackie, Quackie," but I knew. They called me in for dinner, and Quackie was on the table, our Shabbos meal. At first they said it was from the butcher, but my parents could not hold out. Even they knew there was truth that could not be hidden. After some attempts, they gave up trying to get me to eat it. I'd like to say I never ate duck again, but I tasted it in my twenties and ate it several times after my thirties, although it has been a couple of decades since I last tasted it. A hatred was born for parents, for adults, that never left, although becoming a parent and adult somewhat modified it. My father claimed he could not eat it either, that he was horrified, that he did not know beforehand. By the time he died, he achieved some sense of what good people can do to one another (it was obvious what bad people did). I know some of my faith in life— deep down in my being—comes from my grandmother. But she is also part of what shakes me to the core.

An inevitable insensitivity, indifference is part of child care. We are all seared by it. We try to personalize it, minimize it, think it doesn't have to be there. We can, through evolution of sensitivity, tone it down, take some of the edge off. But it will never be eliminated. We always will be partly monsters afraid of monsters. The inevitability of trauma is part of emotional storm.

We look at our hardness, indifference, insensitivity, feel it quiver, give way, and re-form again. We see hate attached to it, fed by wounds. But we cannot be sure that the energy of hate begins with wounds, or that all hardness is hatred. There is productive hardness needed to stand up to ourselves. We *can* work on ourselves, soften, become more compassionate and open. But we never stop being lethal. We want to help each other and do. We lift each other's spirits and lives. But there are moments when we forget to duck as the blade's edge swings our way.

There was no meanness in the face of the pregnant old lady in my dream. There was no predator-prey element that I could see, no drive to be on top, nor sense of being a victim. She was just being what she was, *is-ing*. Perhaps she was showing me something new in evolution. Or something old getting distilled out of top-dog–underdog paraphernalia, disengaged from above-below hierarchies. The pure momentum of life pressing into birth processes. Energy, endurance, persistence going on being, potentially omnidirectional, steadfast in density, inherently mobile. She was startling but not menacing, not a horror. She was attention getting, arresting, but did not stop you dead in your tracks, did not turn you into stone, did not slash your heart or pulverize your being. She just made you address her, experience her, wonder about her. This in itself would be a great step—to be able to get each other's attention without wounding, without having to hit or maim or bruise to feel we are there. She teaches by example.

Pregnancy does not stop with old age. Simply, pregnancy does not stop. The anxiety, excitement, patience, movement, endurance that never end are here attached to birth rather than murder. If we treated ourselves and each other as pregnant beings, murder might become a less addictive solution to problems. Imagine, pregnancy and birth a possibility of every encounter. The will to power might lose some of its appeal if its energy had better things to do. Emotional storms are here to stay, but we may have some input as to how we undergo them. Force without dominance—my old lady flashes on possibilities that are far from perfect, but something to think about.

Dream: *Kids on a roof throw another kid off, a little girl. It's time to flip her. "Flip-flop." She lies on the ground a bit, then gets up. You do this to "reset" yourself.*

At first I fear the danger of falling, of smashing to smithereens on the ground, then think people who jump to their deaths don't necessarily smash to smithereens but get all broken, a mess. You'd expect that if you got thrown off or jumped off a roof, the damage would be pretty bad. I think of someone I knew who jumped out a window; they didn't show his body at the funeral service because it was too messy. He was on LSD when he jumped, and maybe he thought he'd bounce back up or reset himself. Maybe he wished to jump through anxiety and pain toward the urge to start fresh, make the bad stuff go away. But renewal, like birth, and anxiety, and pain all go together. My dream moves through aggression, anxiety, surprising relief. What I fear is murder turns into play.

It has long been my belief that a kind of rhythm involving injury-recovery is part of a faith structure that is part of the foundation of experiencing. This may involve processes of renewal, rebirth, regeneration in many forms, always partial and tentative, although too often felt or conceived as totalistic and absolute. The above dream image is a semiwhimsical variant of this pattern. It begins in earnest, deadly serious (so it felt to the dreamer). A kid being thrown to her death. It was awful. All the terror, dread of dream, a sick storm increasing in force.

The compression of time in dreams is amazing. The anxiety attached to the girl being thrown to her death was palpable. It was acute and steady, on the rise, ready to accelerate, flood, paralyze the dreamer's consciousness. At the same time, it did not reach climax. It remained more of a steady state, like sound waves rapidly oscillating, background radiation ready to flare into something totally decimating. In fact, decimation was already happening: the little girl being thrown off the roof, on her way down, hitting the ground. Each part of the sequence simultaneously in slow and rapid motion, one after another, excruciating drama, yet in some way happening all at once. One can dip into each microinstant and find worlds of affect, infinite dread, limitless subcurrents of feeling, anticipatory and actual dread, dread of outcome, dread of happening. Parts of images could be slowed down and focused on as the dream sped along. The viewer-experiencer does not know the outcome moment within moment. Startle is part dream structure, moving from shock to shock.

The girl hits the ground, lies there. Death. The dreamer's affect drops downward, downward. Dread fuses with depression, shock with sorrow, nascent onset of mourning. A terrible happening, soul buckles, heads toward grief. The girl pops up. Surprise. Up, up. Soul smile in the startle. Relief. She is OK. She is alive. I mean, not just alive but *alive*. An active kid with kid energy, alive energy. Popping up, walking off. I can feel her body and now think of the pregnant old lady's energy. Except the little girl lacked the perpetual-motion machine feeling. She is not perpetual motion, irrepressible force. She *is* destructible yet wasn't destroyed. She *could* die, but didn't. The old lady's energy felt indestructible, whether it is or isn't. The little girl felt vulnerable, even if she wasn't.

It is said that Jesus truly died and was truly resurrected. If one gets into the infrastructure of my dream, it might be that the little girl truly died and came alive again. It certainly felt that way. She plunged to her death. Only death was not final. Perhaps she did not die but was lying unconscious or semi-unconscious, analogous to being in a state of shock, awaiting recovery. That's not what it seemed like. In the dream, she died and popped back up. Surprise was an important element in the dream feeling, part of the nucleus of the dream. The surprise of violence, finality, not-finality, renewal. A not-surprising sequence in retrospect, an ancient sequence, but real and consuming while in progress.

The dream entertained me with its prowess, its amazingness:

"Look what I can do." Life triumphs. Violence and death are part of renewal. Self pops up good as new. The dream caricatures my own faith structure, faith rhythm, my commitment to a rhythm of recovery. A basic feeling in the dreaming state is "Wow! Look at *that!*" And what is *that?* Something in me that keeps popping up, wanting more? Narcissism, élan, self-affirmation, love of living? Something irrepressible? Or more—the dream's *jouissance,* amazement at itself, at its own existence and its appreciation of itself as exemplar of the processes that make such worlds of experience possible. Amazement at itself as part of the thus-ness of things. The images themselves have the last word, although I keep writing.

The pregnant old lady and the young girl who dies and comes to life share a surprising energy. Neither one is business as usual. They evade space-time categories, not simply to shake things up, but to inject something new. They intervene in habitual routine and make one re-visualize events of the day. They stop the world for a moment, make you wonder. You have to appreciate the fact that there is more to life than you dream, as your dreams make you notice. They are part of the strange, the unanticipated. They make you stare dumbly at the scene as prelude to opening you up a little. Surprise, startle, shock is part of their method.

Whatever their differences, the old lady and the girl share a life energy that won't be put off, boxed in, easily packaged. Even though they fit traditional themes—pregnant old lady, dying and coming to life, birth and rebirth—they slip in between the cracks of personality, tickle a raw nerve, and won't let you get away with dozing off on your life forever. To some extent, they reverse the order of time, not simply to fulfill wishes (to evade death, live forever) but to keep you in tune with what you value most, freshness of being, the taste of experience, the shock of aliveness.

The girl and the old lady aren't involved in dramas about caring. They are forms of energy going on being, just themselves. It is not a matter of cruelty or indifference but of is-ness. They don't represent the whole, personal self, but give a sense of nervous endurance, momentum (pregnant old lady) and resilience (the dying–alive again girl, down and up—neither scared nor scary, just alive in herself). There is an X that keeps going, gets through things, never stops, carries one along. It is neither sentimental nor mean. While these images are surprising, they bring out something commonplace, basic—the nervous, vibrating propulsion and momentum of life moving you along.

Ordinary disruption in dreams takes many forms, sharing qualities of surprise, startle, shock, crackling at the edge of rigidities, inviting personality to stretch and be more inclusive. The remainder of this chapter presents a nearly random sampling from recent dreams drawn out of a hat.

Dream: *Not able to find my younger son. Train? Subway? Night? Raining?*

I wake up from this scary dream, which embodies parental fear. The dream fear shakes me and has power to shake me more. Waking puts the brakes on. Here the disruption is fear of a loved one dying or being lost, the most dreadful fear a parent has. There is no growing through a fear like this, no expansion of personality through death—just terror and living through fear of loss and the worst.

Even so, the literal portrayal of the dream fear acts as a channel for fear that runs through personality, rampant annihilation dread that is part of disaster terror attached to a trauma world. The worst trauma I can imagine now—the loss of a child —bespeaks terror and trauma in general through a specific possibility. It is loaded with all the fear of my life in a somewhat attenuated way, since there is no indication that my child is dead.

In the dream he is just not there. To be missing can be ominous but there are other possibilities.

The reality is that he has likely gone somewhere and is not back yet. Of course, the dream does not say that or stop there. To say my son is missing sets a tone that spirals. There are, too, subway, night, rain—place and atmosphere, partly filling out the mood, partly normalizing it. There is no reason to jump to conclusions, except dreams express affect through extremes. It is hard for me to give up control, to let him go, to tolerate autonomy. He has gone off on his own without me. I am left behind as he risks the world and the task and adventure of living his life. As it should be.

I had a very overprotective father, and it cost me much to break free. Is the dread that pursued my father embedded in me, part of an atmosphere of dread permeating generations?

Is the dream expressing the fact that there is something missing in life, in relationships, in encounters—as Lacan says, we are always repeating a "missed encounter"? Are we trying to discover something in life that isn't there, life that is nowhere?

I want to stick with the dream's incipient affect here, the impending dread, a dire feeling potentially mounting. Whatever its meanings, the fact of it is upsetting. It taps subseas of catastrophic anxiety that surround, subtend personality, sensed as premonitions of the worst or of something pretty bad. Semi-omnipresent disaster anxiety informs the background of experiencing that dreams grow out of, nibble at, try to digest or express. Hints of storm never far away.

Dream: *My parents called the cops, as I was missing. I'd been away from morning on and didn't call. I was at Betty's apartment. When I got around to calling at 10:00 p.m., the cops were on the way to find me.*

My parents jumped the gun. They could not tolerate my being away, out of their sight, out of their control. They could not take the anxiety of growth, aliveness, separation difference. The dream exaggerates to make the point: I must have been in my mid-thirties if I was at Betty's (my wife to be) apartment. Even my parents didn't track me down when I was in my thirties. But in spirit, the dream is right to hyperbolize.

I get anxious when my kid does not call. We live in a dangerous city, and he is supposed to let us know he is alive past a certain time. I went to extremes to break away from my parents. I had little urge to call when I left home. As a young man, I did not want much contact with them. I had as little to do with them as possible until I got married. I did not want to feel how afraid they were, as I feared that would break my life drive. I pushed past their fear, my fear.

I've thought of calling the cops when my kid is late in calling. Parents have to sit on a lot to be parents. Holding oneself back is part of love.

On the other hand, I may be missing something as a person, missing something in life—and no amount of police work will find it.

There is ebb and flow, balance between impulse and protection, life drive and police, although lives get weighted too much one way or the other. Here police function as tether to parents. A reining-in function, lest I get out of control, too far out, or just become myself.

I was living my own life with Betty, my wife. The dream flashes on her apartment before we were married. You'd think the superego lessens with experience. But the dream makes clear that it is a persistent force in personality, here a parental extension clustering around safety and loss vis-à-vis sexuality and freedom. It is delusional to think either pole absent. Conservative and adventurous tendencies work together, although tensions between them can mushroom. Freud cautioned that competing tendencies can be tyrannical, that one can be destroyed from the side of control or the side of impulse, while one needs both.

There is no getting away from the stormy situation of being a parent or of being a child. To grow or not to grow—what kind of choice is this? Often I meet someone who thinks growing solves problems. One does not leave personality structure behind by acquiring new territory. New territory, new problems. And inside new problems, old ones, with further meaning, significance, possibilities. Old and new are not reducible to one another, but are not simply outside each other either.

The child-missing dreams focus on parental anxiety rather than the child's growth anxiety. The two dreams cover an arc of experience, with me on either side of the fence, parent, child. However, the thrust seems to be on the difficulties of being a parent—containing parental dreads, letting go, separating, affirming the fact that we live our own lives, that attachment involves suffering. We grow through the challenges attachment presents, since there is no life outside these challenges.

In the second dream, the parental police proved unnecessary. My parents could not withstand compulsion. My inner parents need to grow more. It is unlikely *I'd* call the police when my son is late coming home, but I'm not above calling his companion's parents at three in the morning to see if there is any news (much as I'd hate myself for doing so). The anxiety-control nexus is gripping. But *that* is not the whole person. There is, also, a free and open feeling seeking development, a sense of treasuring one's chance at living. We are neither just clearing nor clot.

Focus placed on child development obscures a fuller realization of how much parents develop (or need to). Parental development is as important a fact as child development. We need university departments for the former as well as the latter. So much in life depends on how parental developmental challenges are met. I've gained enormously by staying with the internal upheavals, emotional storms, that family differences entail. Upheavals come from anywhere, often when least expected. My kids and wife are doing something that arouses anxiety. The urge to mold or shape the situation raises its ugly head, threatens to tyrannize. Helplessness, rage, control meld. A little thing, like who is going where when suddenly mushrooms into a threat against the self, challenging a constricting, one-sided conception of the day.

The wish to help and contribute skates thinly over the will to dominate. It is very easy for some aspect of family life, with all its potential intensity, to tip over one's individual balancing act, hit a nerve, rub an image wrong. Little twists and turns incessantly challenge imaginings of how things should be. How does one learn to wait when waiting is needed and let things sort themselves out? How does one let oneself become part of dialogical processes that open pleasures of responsiveness? There is a feeling of freedom and lightness and breathing easier that comes with learning that others know how to do things and that the spontaneity, resources, inventiveness of others is a pleasure. The gruesome fact is that many are intolerant of this kind of learning and substitute destruction for dialogue.

Over the years, I've accumulated a little catalogue of events that precipitate breakups. There are marriages that survive extramarital affairs but fail to survive a house renovation or family trip. The latter are but two triggers for exaggerating the clash of differences, stresses that distil or aggravate chronic, personal fault lines. Family life is made up of complex developmental processes or failures thereof. That enormous emotional pressures are involved is seen by flights from relationship occasioned by pregnancy or birth, which turn out to be more than one bargained for. Of course, flight can be better than murderous fights, although the two merge. For some, personality does meet the challenges that life together exacts, and one enters the mystery of profound development that connection entails.

As mentioned above, one of life's most freeing discoveries is a deeply felt sense that others can figure things out, that one does not have to think for everyone. As wisdom literature reflects, it is an odd property of self to think one knows what is good for others when one can't figure out what is good for oneself. Even more freeing is the realization that we don't know what we're doing (as Jesus noted, a basis for forgiveness). We grope along, and productive groping is what we hope for. Life finds its ways. There is such great fear in letting go of control—mental or spiritual or physical—whether control involves real or illusory power. Sometimes people fear growth or try to stop growth because some favorite method of control, one with a favored sense of self (even if hatred of self) is threatened with extinction. Such threats are apocalyptic and based on an all-or-nothing, totalistic style of thinking. Not to worry. Since the compulsion to control that is part of the anxiety of attachment does not vanish, one need not fear being deprived of the pleasure of letting it go some more.

The pregnant old lady and the girl dying and coming to life express the urge of life to go on being, keep moving, renew. As long as you are alive, life goes on, with or without your consent, sweeping you along, although you may try to channel it, use it your way (what you think or imagine is your way), slow things down, reflect on it. There is a division of labor of sorts: the dream images catch the dream gazer's attention, so that there are actors and observer. A mixture of movement, immediacy, and watching, two poles of aware being. If there were only action or only a watcher, the tension that makes the dream compelling could not exist.

The second set of dreams involve parental anxiety, with subtexts of annihilation fears, separation, control, and autonomy issues, as life pushes into life. Birth anxiety, attachment anxiety, growth anxiety fuse with parental fears. Parents need to grow. Pressures children exert can be overwhelming. The movement into full parenthood requires growth of capacities one scarcely suspects exist, as challenging a growth as a child's. What it means to be a child or a parent are boxes we are opening more fully now than ever before.

The going on being of aliveness in the first two dreams was carried by others—the old lady, the girl—not the dreamer. The parental anxiety dreams involved the dreamer as player, as anxious one or as "cause" of anxiety. It was as if life gave the dreamer a glimpse of itself and its processes in the first two dreams and touched on an enduring difficulty in the second two.

Some surprises in dreams are fulfilling for the dreamer or promise fulfillment. That a dream goes well for the dreamer both as actor and watcher can be more surprising than that things going badly. So many dreams nibble on the edge of disaster anxiety that it is a relief and something of a dramatic foil when dream life treats one truly well. But there *are* good dreams and dreams of promise, although fusion of good/bad elements and tendencies come closer to the rule.

Dream: *It is possible to have sex with different women who are delighted. Something sexually fulfilling is happening with me and several women, one of whom had been married. A lot of possible sexuality, affairs, nice feeling of girlfriends, of possibility.*

Here is almost an anomaly, a wish-fulfillment dream that doesn't get mutilated or blown apart by disaster dread. A pleasure, delight. Some anxiety in the background—there nearly always is, fulfillment being fragile, easily lost. Obviously, it will be lost—I wake up and the dream is gone, although there are pleasure waves I dip into through memory. But delight could have been lost in the dream itself, as often happens, potential fulfillment cut short. Then there would have been memory of aborted pleasure, pleasure lost as it was starting. Instead, I am vouchsafed a time of pleasurable fulfillment that did not get smashed or aborted—a good time. Could that really happen to me?

The women in the dream liked me and liked *it*. I got lucky. I didn't have to choose this one or that. Bountiful life. A sense of being liked, wanted, in my body, myself. There is reference to the oedipal mother, the once married woman, as pleasure slides across worlds. What is most important is that something good happens and is actually felt. The feeling is the reality. Good feelings exist and do not have to be spoiled. They claim reality as disaster does.

You might think this just a selfish wish-fulfilling dream, a harem dream. Narcissistic male repairing damage to narcissism. Sexual male repairing damage to sexuality. Wounded male imagining healing of wound—through fantasies of accepting women, good mother, desirous female. A power, conceit, entitlement dream. Yes, but more. It affirms life's generosity and delicious promise. There is the latent sense that women open to my desire through theirs because they experience something valuable in me. It is implicitly a dream of recognition—no one closes off. It is centered on me as an analysis might be! It is *my* life, my pleasure, but part of my pleasure involves their good feelings. Reciprocal delight hovers. I can't believe they like me this way, which implies something happening for them. But they are all in my dream, part of dream pleasure. Is fulfillment part of life? The dream says yes and proves it. The Other is part of dream pleasure. There can be no hallucination without another to support it.

Dream fulfillment does the self a world of good. That morning on the way to work my train got rerouted, and I had to travel by foot in a long underpass connecting train lines on Forty-Second Street. Suddenly—surprisingly as a dream figure—a gospel singer stood near me, playing a keyboard and singing fully, openly, "I'm satisfied . . ." Open-heartedly, heart to heart. A moment only, connecting with the pleasure of the night before. Heaven in the subway in a tough life.

Later that day I stop at a deli to get chopped liver as an extra for Thanksgiving. The girl behind the counter looks at me with heart joy and I feel peace, happiness. Instantaneous burst of affirmation—life is wonderful.

A few days later something popped in me. Someone on the internet responded to a note I sent to a mail list. She responded without resistance. I'm used to struggle in communication but this was different. She just got it, let it in, embraced it, without closing or pushing. I don't think this happens to me a lot. It surprised me and the pop inside surprised me more. Something gripping gave way. I breathed in a place I didn't know was not breathing. Once felt, I knew that before I was tight, never breathing in the place that opened.

How long before it closes again? Or something else closes? Or another tightness comes to the fore? After the pop, I felt more relaxed (sometimes) for the next few days (which is a lot). I feel it in my body now and am communicating it to you.

About a month later:

Dream: *Some sensation/image of not having to get away quickly from people, of enjoying being with people. A feeling of letting it develop, take its course, pleasure between people, between me and others.*

I feel this dream in my body too, a wonderful sense of opening, not rushing. So often I break off contact prematurely, thinking an interaction is over or wanting it to be done. This goes with a sense of trying to get through things, a fear of not being wanted, or of being wanted too much in a wrong way. What if we lingered together? Would we be uncomfortable, wish to break away? You think a moment is over, but another may be building or the same moment may be catching its breath, readying for more. It is possible to let time build, let more happen. The dream is antidote to the conviction that I can't take any more, it's already too much. Even pleasure is too much for me. Storms of pleasure. There are not only good but divine emotional storms. A good feeling growing between you and me—how much can I take before breaking off? Good feelings, once ignited, take work. The dream is a reminder to wait for more. More may be on the way. Little by little, over time, through practice, its message, its reality spreads through me, becomes almost second nature, but like any cultivated garden, needs work.

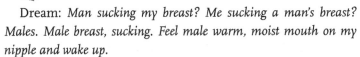

Dream: *Man sucking my breast? Me sucking a man's breast? Males. Male breast, sucking. Feel male warm, moist mouth on my nipple and wake up.*

Mixture of anxiety and warmth. Startle. I wake with a jolt. No question, I'm afraid. Homosexual? Freud wrote Fliess that the key to his creativity was sublimation of homoeroticism. Don't get away from it: I feel the ripple of male energy, male mouth. My father's open mouth warm, hollow, licking, taking me in, kissing, sucking my body. Someone else was in the dream at my nipple, I at his? Drawing on father's dark hollow, father's need. We are mother and babies for each other. Breast envy? Mother envy? Something deeper, more frightening, comforting. A hollow at the center of my being, where plenitude is. A dread. Sucking, filling, never getting enough. Always seeking, finding, frightening, taking. You are a thirsty, hungry baby. So am I. I am your nipple, you are mine. There is no end to sucking, seeking.

What milk can I give a baby? Why do I want a man to take my body? To be in a man, a man in me? It is part of the hollow of my being, my breathlessness. My heterosexuality is threatened and I'm scared. Scared by the immense depth of mystery, of longing that is boundless, with no regard for the normal. It is another kind of normal, another law. Law in darkness, where images howl and bowl one over, feeling from unknown places. Feelings from unknown spots support life as much or more than known ones do. Would I do this with a man? Could this happen? It scarcely matters. It is happening now in the depths of my being. My body feels it and awakes with trembling. Whole territories make mincemeat of who I think I am, who I am in daylight. Without them I'd be without a home. There would be no such thing as nakedness. There would be nothing to fear. No depth to wake me.

Dream: *Homosexual partner, guy with beard. Then it occurs to me that he really wants to be with me but that I really like women.*

Before the idea of sex came up, being with a man felt fine. Warm, calm. Moments like this with my father, just together with the feel of him. Sex intrudes, and I get scared. You mean, I'm really gay? Recoil. When push comes to shove and reality becomes reality, I am startled, pull back, and in the dream wake up to myself: I like women sexually. Sex with a man is too frightening, not that I'm not frightened by sex with a woman.

Typo: "I'm really like women" instead of "I really like women." I'm really like a woman. Like Schreber, who wanted to feel or be like or be a woman during sexual intercourse. Let that spread through me, through bodymind, the feel of me.

Sometimes homosexuality is about being a man, two men, males. Sometimes it contains aspects of being like a woman. Being like a man and being like a woman enfold each other, encode each other. Perhaps a man can only be like a man too, or a woman like a woman. Being *like*—because we are not *just.*

The dream brings up a possibility, a reality: my homosexual partner. Dreams are real. But homosexual sex scares me into realizing—no, when it comes to sex, it's a woman. I could do it with a man, cross the fear boundary, but respect arises for an inner structure that forms and guides me. Although things could be otherwise. And in the depths, so they are.

Asserting a normalized current does not end things. The feel of the warm male mouth on my body, in my insides, going through the underneath of me from the outside of me, the whiskery sensation (whiskey—whiskers), another set of insides emerging from someone's sucking, new ideas of warmth and wetness—they do not stop because I sleep with women. They add.

I think of part of Bion's fictitious dream of psychoanalysis, *A Memoir of the Future.* Rosemarie, the servant, turns the tables, grips her lady, falls on top of her. Surges of feelings unknown to either emerge. Alice, the mistress, feels sexual stirrings, complemented by Rosemarie's sense of power. Both sexuality and power feel new.

"For Rosemary, the vital force coursing through arteries, battering her heart and temples, brought thoughts from a reservoir unknown to her. As she gazed she knew triumph. When Alice at last brought herself to meet her maid's stare, the past had gone as if it had never been. Not only had her situation changed, she had herself become the home of feelings that might have belonged to someone else, they were so strange."

Sex and power, fused, reversible. An invasion was taking place. Bullets would penetrate the English countryside. Rosemary already knew rape, in contrast with Alice's stiffness, stuffiness, emotional monotone. Now dread, new kinds of menace, rage. Elements of emotional life spread throughout the landscape with no respect for who felt what, since soon enough everyone would feel everything. Menace everywhere, punctuated by streams of thought, passion, confusion, vacillation, calculation, and force. Vital force, unknown reservoir, home of feelings that might belong to someone else, that might belong to me, you, anyone. Storms gathering, one way or another, from storm to storm. Dullness, arrogance, stiff lips, even keels—indices of tumult to come, upheaval making its way toward the latest structural pretense. Phoniness and placidity attract dismantling. A sense of safety is important, but at what price, at the price of what reality?

We cannot hide from danger in our dreams. How many people never woke up screaming? Often the scream is stifled, nearly paralyzed. One tries to yell, but the voice fails. One cannot, dare not move. Effort is futile. If one is lucky, the scream comes out. If one is very, very lucky, help comes.

A scream in search of help. Amid endless dangers.

Men threatening to break through windows, doors. Hoodlums with knives. Man menaces me, going to kill me, fuck me.

A man with menacing power, and I cannot escape and wake up screaming. Nightmares or near nightmares resonate with day-mares, real menace in waking life. The real in dreams links with the real in waking life, storm to storm. A man is head of state— an almost cheery, mild-looking man who likes golf, family, fun —and talks war. The reverse is also true: the state of war talks through him, uses him. He becomes an instrument of war, an infectious spore colonizing lives. The only antidote comes from the same places in ourselves, from the same spore. Inner-outer storms intermingle, reverberate, create new storms. There is no way out of this dilemma. What we need to do is find ways in.

What life feels like to us, the raw impact. An impersonal, anonymous aspect. Pregnant old lady rolling on, aflutter like a bird, relentless as a pendulum, promising more, scarcely aware she is there, like an angel, part of a momentum that creates her, presses her to appear. Violent kids throw a girl to her death; she pops up, goes on popping up, alive in her bounce, proud of her moment. A buzz, whir—used to be angel wings, now part of medication. An electric buzz , fire, Walt Whitman, Upanishads, Chassidus. We try to put it out, regulate it, mentalize it, neutral-ize it, manipulate it. Exploit the fire, the buzz. Our life that we cherish bullies us, bowls us over. It takes us out to sea at the same time that it throws us into shore, bruised, choking. To con-trol it is our revenge, a resentful refuge. Yet to bob up with a great smile in the golden liquid light is something we live for.

Parental anxiety because grown-ups know how dangerous life is and how dangerous parents are. They've tasted the apple and dare not, cannot stop their children from tasting, no matter what the apple is like in the latters' times. We wish the air, water, and earth were better, but children breathe, drink, move, and take their turn no matter how we leave things.

Children's anxiety because they feel pressure to grow, to be-come part of something, to shape something. To live and give life to others, heat of spirit, necessary cries, the long birth life is. Everything one is and is not assails one, the apple's juices, the tongue's sweat, fields one works and that work one night to day, beginning to beginning. Another meaning of hide and seek. Where do all the endings go, where are they hiding?

When I was five or six, I told my parents I saw grandma walking on the street. They looked at each other, as if doubting reality for a moment. Could I be right? Then the look settled into a what-can-a-child-know kind of peace, a gentle, sour peace. I swear I saw her. Was I dreaming, imagining, hallucinating? After all, dead people talk to us in dreams.

Killers in Dreams

Some killers in dreams attack truth, others goodness. Many attack lies, phoniness, falsehood. Some just attack. A tendency to attack anything, true or false, good or bad. To shred and keep on shredding until nothing is left. Then go on annihilating nothing.

Flannery O'Connor's destroyers aim at self-presumption, smugness, pride, self-satisfaction in belief about self or life or religion. They take particular aim at the smallness involved in feeling "saved." O'Connor gets to a point where there is nothing to hold onto. Faith is this something in which there is nothing to hold onto. Faith is a mystery, and anything that infringes on this mystery, anything that diminishes, explains, understands it—is taken away, over and over.

A relentless ethic, a nakedness, everything stripped so that faith shines more brightly. Brightness is stripped too, especially brightness. There can be no consolation exterior to raw presence of——. Already too many words, too many dashes. Raw presence of Unknown Unknowable disappears too, superfluous, misleading.

O'Connor's killers, spoilers, cleanse the psyche. An uncompromising element of the psyche in which the devil, father of lies, is a conduit of truth. The devil as lie surgeon, scientist, artist. Who but the devil can scour the psychospiritual landscape and ferret out every lie speck, big, little. Who has vision as acute? A lie detector in every speck of being.

Job's Satan, prosecuting attorney, channeling God energy to strip Job, like a shark cleans water. Away all goods of life. Not just pretenses, lies. Satisfactions, the good, full life, riches of living. Flocks, wives, children, respect. A God-fearing man, afflicted in soul, body, mind, attachments, loses all except maybe God. He is left with nothing but his God-connection. Friends try to uplift him, explain God's ways. But Job has reached a point beyond explanation, a point ordinary justice cannot do justice to. He has fallen into a realm of excess. Normal discriminations, normal brakes on the shredding instinct fail. Job goes from being normal to being abnormal. To the point where, as songs say, there is nothing but God.

Isn't this where O'Connor takes us? All her characters are unconscious Jobs stripped of consolation, without even the consolation of thinking of oneself as Job. Zero point of soul, a clearing where any lie that scampers by can be seen for miles, for all eternity. Merciless. But what does one really know of the mysteries of mercy and grace? Those who stay with O'Connor can scarcely believe what opens at the annihilation point, what begins as the stories leave off.

A patient, Leila, dreams of a bulldozer. It wipes out everything in its path. A mindless force. Just bulldozing. She thinks of parents bulldozing children, children bulldozing parents. People bulldozing each other. A bulldozer self that can't be stopped. It rips through nations, across social structures, flattening, clearing. It happens anywhere, anytime.

Her father was a more obvious bulldozer than her mother. He yelled, barked orders, gave sensuous bear hugs that made her want to scream, that repelled but interested her. His presumptuous body made her claustrophobic. When she burst out, she had nowhere to go. Her mother was dying. Incurable disease another bulldozer, implacable, ripping body away. Life itself a bulldozer, breaking down walls, pushing toward exuberance or despair.

Bulldozer killer, wiping out everything in its path. Not the same precision as O'Connor's destroyers or Job's Satan. Aim is missing. No specific appeal to God or mystery. The alchemy of transmutation, growth through suffering, is stillborn, dead in outrage. No God is worthy of this kind of life, not even a bull-dozer God. No mystical experience of God's power is jaw-dropping enough to make Leila cry uncle. God has explaining to do. He can't bulldoze evil away, His evil. He can bulldoze us and twist us out of shape but can't stop our minds from demanding something better. No bulldozer can stop our questioning self.

Bulldozer self—questioning self. Double imperatives. If we are in God's image and God is rock-bottom, we are in big trouble. And we *are* in big trouble.

There are bulldozers of mind and body, and Leila scourges herself with them. A tyrannical bent of mind sifts others and self through needles no camel can pass through, pinning mortals with ineffable, spiritual failures. Bulldozer eyes of needles. She is even more heartless with herself, taking any sort of failure as a sign of moral, spiritual, and personal defect. A basic defect no amount of work or good feeling undoes, but any failure exacerbates. She has an inner layer or fabric made of barbed wire trying to scrape defect away, keeping wounds fresh, itching for pain. When pain comes, it is evidence that she is bad: something is wrong with her, something basic, incurable, which she keeps trying to cure.

She, like her mother, became ill in adulthood, incurably, mortally. Unlike her mother, she lived through it, only to be overtaken by another lethal illness. So far she survives, grows stronger, meeting the bulldozer head-on with medical, psychological, and personal help. With help from her own depths. It is a dreadful thing to say that illness forced her to dig deeper, to care more deeply, to struggle with despair more fully, to struggle with her bulldozer self more carefully. Even without such illness, there is no way to avoid how evil life is, an extravagance of evils. But the more horrifying, fervent truth that there is no cure for evil—evil is incurable—*this* dreadful truth Leila might have avoided if she had remained healthy. She might not have confronted this particular gruesome needle eye, whether to pass through or refuse to enter. She could have gotten by with truth less deadly. There are plenty of truths for everyone, even bad enough ones, not all so horrible.

She might have been able to pretend she was doing *it* to herself or parents or society did *it* to her. A lot of talk in psychoanalysis rotates around freeing oneself from toxic objects, inner or outer. Years ago emphasis was more on modifying the hold of indomitable drives. Now emphasis is more on relational patterns: modifying, through present interactions, accumulated negative patterns that afflict one. Whether the emphasis is cognitive, behavioral, interactive, or on unconscious patterns, the person as agent is central. There is therapeutic belief in persons able to participate in change and influence life for the better. Some combination of will, insight, new possibilities of relationship, and practice can modify destructive patterns and create better ones.

Some try to sidestep work on relational patterns, internalized objects, drives, attitudes, whatever—in one blow, with medication, if the latter makes one feel better, gives energy, opens paths of living. More often, hopefully, medication enables individuals to work on themselves and ways of relating, so that physical and psychological therapies enhance each other.

I'd like to sidestep warring factions of psychoanalysis and other schools, even though I know that not stepping on toes is impossible. I share therapeutic faith with many workers in my own way, although I hesitate to downplay our killer element. My pursuit is less theoretical, more like a hound following a scent, tracing a killer with many aliases, whom many claim to have sighted but none has slain. My vision is not exhaustive, just some indices of what we are grappling with, what we cannot wish away. Call it damage, defect, evil, sin, madness, folly, organizational patterns, systems, constructions, representations. Pick up the scent anywhere, we will be sniffing under our own tails. We need to confront, in whatever way we can, with whatever lights and sensibilities, our killer psyche.

The curve in Freud's thought from sexuality to death provides an array of windows to open. A lot of Freud's early thinking clusters around vicissitudes of sexual vitality, eros, love. In his seventies, death increases momentum. In *Beyond the Pleasure Principle*, sexual power wanes, the power of death waxes. However, things in Freud are never so simple. Every psychic act, he emphasizes, combines life and death drives. Death does not take sexuality's place, but adds shade, counterpart, drama, a horizon of doom for life's fragile light.

Even near the beginning of his thought, sexual vitality varies. Some people have less, some more. A form of neurosis, psychasthenia (he fears he describes himself), is characterized by depression, anxiety, lack of energy, malaise, or weakness and is attributed to deficient sexual energy, which is genetic in origin. Psychasthenia has subtle ties with environmental conditions. Use of condoms or anything that dampens sexual pleasure might bring it on. But then, you probably possess a psychasthenic disposition to be so affected or to consent to using condoms in the first place. A more vital man would never tolerate such an imposition.

The above little sketch of psychasthenia is only partly tongue and cheek. It hints at Freud's obsession with sexual vitality and the latter's link with potency generally. Freud's great formal gambit was to tie a poetic, informal sense of vitality to the concept of a fixed quantity of energy capable of taking many forms (doing many kinds of work)—transferring an idea from physics to psychology. A kind of libidinal monad or clock, an individual's energy innately fixed, its patterning partly up for grabs. More informally, Freud sexualized the will to power, saw the latter powered by sexual currents. Individuals had inferior or superior endowments of vital power. Power storms erupt in particular lives and history (tantrums, Holocaust, Hiroshima, explosions mixed with manipulation).

Rising energy vis-à-vis a lower energy threshold can be translated into killers in dreams, and, vice versa, a fall of energy after adaptation to a higher energy level can be represented as a threat to life. On the other hand, too much control, toning down, cutting off energy flow can find expression as a killer in dreams. Dream killers spontaneously give expression to changes in energy (from high to low, low to high) or control (too much, too little, along a severity-diffusion continuum). It is tempting to view dream killers as being "constructed" out of the dialectics of energy and control (the background rise and fall of energy and stimulation, the pressure of control), but I feel "construction" is too formal a term. Translation of state to image is more immediate, expressionistic.

The notion of eruption and control or channeling of vital energy has been a staple signifier of the human condition. It is not the only way to image what the self, personality and society are about, but it is important—taming the wild, sublimating or inhibiting the vital. Plato's white and black steeds drawing the chariot raise the issue of what to do with Dionysian, unruly, aggressive, sexual, power-driven, rage-driven currents. What sort of education does the black steed need; what sort is possible, is valuable? Where does the bad fit in with the Vision of the Good? What sort of transformation processes must the bad eternally power? What will be lost or gained if the anti- or negative-pole equus dissolves in a sea of goodness? Is it only a matter of reining in? And who is the charioteer who can be trusted with such a task?

Henri Bergson's image of ripening differs from the eruption-control model. An action or decision falls like an apple from a tree when an energy form reaches its time (akin to vital unfolding, Aristotle's entelechy, the acorn's potential to become an oak, given adequate nutrients). A vision more Taoist than Heraclitian or Empedoclean: interweaving of complements more than war between antagonistic principles or elements.

Freud asks, what about the weak ones? If I'm deficient in energy or vital flow, should I be left outside the city walls to languish and die? Am I destined for an inferior life? How inferior is inferior? Is there any overlap between Freud's preoccupation with weakness of energy and biblical concern with the weak, the helpless, the casualties—those in danger of being run over, left out by the energically favored?

Too much or too little—the criminal or the neurotic? The corporate criminal of abundant energy wedded to a fatigued society. Is widespread fatigue because of sleep deprivation or something deeper, more pernicious, a dehumanizing treadmill run by power mania? The fatigue of helpless rage. A new hypersex in which it is difficult to say who feels less, those on top or bottom, a simultaneous hyper/hypo, intensity/anesthesia, black hole orgasm/antiorgasm. Who can keep it up?

We are told those on top have more testosterone, drive, will to power. Once again, a vision of maximum vitality. Very Freudian, Nietzschean, despite our society's hullabaloo about religion. Thou shalt know them by their economic gonads. We are told, too, that tall people make more money. I have not heard whether thin or fat make more or less but can guess. A rich society of giants on the way. Freud was very short and not very rich, except in a wealth that can't be measured.

In a Thomas Mann story, a writer with little energy creates a world of fiction teeming with energy. He must sleep between short writing bouts, but these efforts add up. If only people knew how little the author resembles the world he creates. Mann's writer is on the psychasthenic side, but the words he forms are powerful. Where does such imaginative power come from? Mann contrasts it with the physical power of the athlete, the man of action, the political, economic, military man who wins the real world and the real woman. Real vs. imaginary energy.

Freud says that thought takes less energy than action. The poet Elizabeth Sewell might disagree. I once heard her say that she knows when she's thinking because she has to sleep afterward. Einstein claims to have thought once in his life. What about the rest of us? Not too many people have the strength, will, autonomy or bravery to think, as Socrates pointed out. Yet we know what Freud means. One can try out courses of action mentally, entertain diverse possibilities and trace imagined consequences. One can perform thought experiments, mental trial and error, without lifting a finger, in a way, like dreaming.

One can easily see the importance of thinking in terms of practical planning. To construct a bridge or building requires the kind of forethinking engineers can do. Clearly, proper forethought is economical if one wants a bridge to stay up or a building to last. But what about planning a life, thinking through a life? Freud himself wrote expressively about the intense effort it cost Moses to control his rage, how in Michelangelo's sculpture of Moses, mental and moral intensity pervades Moses' entire body. To think a feeling through, to wonder about rage, its basis, its consequences, its makeup? A thought few are up to.

Such problems are built into the fabric of social life. Nations lie, cheat, kill, and injure to uphold power. It is amazing that moral feeling survives the corruption that kills all over the globe. But it does survive, and people speak for it, often without realizing what will be unleashed, unable to stand the consequences of being silent. It is amazing that moral feeling, caring for others as well as self, for self everywhere, survives massive abuse of morality. Moral hypnotism keeps people in check and gets them to act against their interests for the interests of a few. We have neither will nor ability to correct evils that spew from systems we create. Nevertheless, we accomplish much to balance and keep brakes on the worst that is in us, in spite of destructive hemorrhages. Perhaps we can play for time while we learn what to do with ourselves.

To translate Freud's note on the economy of thinking, given what we know now, not to think would be more costly in human terms than the nearly impossible effort thinking requires. Especially when it comes to thinking about living, preserving life, getting along with each other. It is very easy to create a thought that can destroy. It is, after all, thinking that develops weapons of mass destruction, making it easy to wipe out and maim each other. Physicists have not invented a thought that can do *for* people, with similar visible magnitude, what it can do *against* them. It is easier to destroy than to build. Thinking about caring is something else, more difficult it appears. What would technologies of caring look like? Caring requires a different kind of effort than destruction.

It is this ease of destruction that Freud's Michelangelo's Moses pits himself against, that we must pit ourselves against. What to do with destructive urges? Holding back is not enough and often adds to the explosion later. Freud's work opens a path. He begins meditating on sexual energy and ends meditating on destruction. He spent the greater part of his life thinking about what drives us. Whatever lapses and failures, that is not a half-bad place to take off from. To spend more time thinking about destruction, less time doing it.

Add to this the further consideration that long-term planning and calculation is now a staple part of rage. This may sound odd, since rage is spontaneous, instantaneous. Still, revenge, traditionally, required planning, waiting, timing. Rage and hate are part of getting back at someone, even if only as a matter of honor. Rage fed blood revenge, tribal revenge, personal revenge. But today rage becomes part of a killing machine, drawn out killing that goes on and on, less for honor than for self-interest (individual or group). Self-interest is used to justify the most outrageous proposals and actions. To stop destroying would risk destroying society. To stop destroying would stop the world. The fact that so much rage is impulsive (road rage, desk rage, erotic rage, holy rage) masks the long-range aim of the most lethal rage today. Today's tantrums or emotional explosions can be spread out slowly, tantalizingly, over long periods of time, with the aid of scientific thinking and technology harnessed to political/economic/personal ambition and control. Destructive intentions transcend individual eruptions and cannot be satisfied by any particular outcome.

There is a terrible kinship between waking life and dreams. The trauma list of daytime corresponds with dreads at night and the terrors of dream life are, too often, unleashed in waking hours. The safety of sleep for thinking dangerous things (Freud noted we cannot act out disasters while disarmed in bed) no longer acts as a natural division between what we imagine and what we do (if ever it did). The barrier between waking and dreaming has been eroded. They spill over, inform each other, so that it is difficult to tell whether we are dreaming or awake. Dream killers and waking killers enhance each other. Waking killers can be worse because use of science and technology (planes, guns, chemistry, physics, cosmology) multiply dreads with concrete possibilities more nearly approaching boundlessness. Concrete images of death (total obliteration, immense mutilation, turning bodies inside out in an instant that can be duplicated any time or extended over time), paradoxically, approach infinities of destructive power.

The raw energy Freud imagined finds its realization in thermonuclear power—in the horrors of war that seem to satisfy or tease orgasmic need. The orgasm of destructive release, at this point in history, seems more satisfying or entrancing than ordinary sexuality. Have weapons, need to use them. Have hate, need objects. We do not know whether there was less rage in the past or whether there now are more ways and means to give it massive expression—more opportunity to amplify rage through prosthetic devices, to raise terror to greater powers. Once upon a time we invented the idea of hell as a terror device, but now we possess more immediate and tangible ways to push limitless fear buttons.

There are still many dreams in which sexuality is dominant and upsetting, and many in which erotic moments are uplifting, life-affirming, sometimes bringing satisfactions lacking in daily life. But there are more involving loss, mishap, mayhem, helplessness, attempts to escape capture, torture, annihilation. Attackers, invaders, death or disappearance of loved ones, street gangs, thugs, mysterious killers, figures from the movies, national figures, FBI, CIA, faceless figures, monsters.

There are, perhaps, more dreams about addiction and abuse than there used to be, although I have no hard data, just an impression. Addiction is emerging as a crucial image for so much of what we do and are obsessed with today. One of the most important addictions is an addiction to violence, unconscious rage addiction. It is too easy today to blow the other off or up when we blow up. We are addicted to violence not only as a means of solving problems or avoiding them, but gratuitously, for its own sake, as an experience. The high of violence, destructive highs. Our worry about drugs, partly, masks our fear of unconscious attachment to destructive processes extending far beyond mere literal addiction. Drugs become a symbol of the way we drug ourselves with power, the mania of being on top, no. 1, the biggest and best. A fantasy of grandiosity all too real in what it does to how life feels throughout the world. Our economic, military intimidation is one arm of it, but it merely writes large the addiction to power and intimidation all humanity faces.

CONFLICT

Conflict is embedded in Freud's thought. Nothing escapes it. In the Freud that is well known, conflict involves forbidden impulses toward incest and familial murder. We are in conflict with desires and drives, and they are in conflict with each other. Nevertheless, the informal Freud portrays all sorts of conflicts. Many thoughts conflict with self-esteem, and self-esteem itself is drawn from many conflictual sources. Being proud of self in one way entails being ashamed of self in another. Freud's women in early studies on hysteria tended to be in conflict with sexuality, and Freud in his dream book had problems with ambition. A romantic stereotype lurks behind these portrayals: woman injured by anxious guilt over love, man the warrior with guilty anxiety over aggression. Put the two together and you have a psyche in conflict with itself, its wishes, its urges and what it does with them (since desire leads not simply to fulfillment, but also to injury). One is not only afraid of success or love, but afraid of the harm success or love brings in its wake.

Another Freudian binary is conflict between self and species preservation. Species evolution may or may not be kind to individuals. Bion pulled this thread when he wrote of a woman who fought her urge to exist because the latter threatened to destroy her. A woman cut herself off from life because the thrust of aliveness exerted pressure toward coupling and childbearing that she might not survive. Her contraction and isolation protected her from forces she felt had no regard for her, ran of their own momentum without caring whether she lived or died. One might call her schizoid or borderline and show how she sacrifices chances at living fully, to protect an island of self. Yet her predicament brings out how anonymous and impersonal many forces (social, physical) that pressure us are, including the very aliveness of our bodies and its demands. To what extent one can and should and must personalize the body, to what extent the latter remains foreign and threatening constitutes a perennial challenge in every life.

Whichever way one turns in Freud's work, binary conundrums multiply. For Freud, the ego is a hallucinatory organ that develops antihallucinatory properties. It grows out of the id and is allied with it. It is stimulated to grow by the impact of the outside world on sensitivity and functions to regulate multiple tendencies of personality, including itself. Its hallucinatory dimension continues all through life, a kind of psychic magnifier, idealizing authorities, loved ones, self, activities (becoming critical or disillusioned as the smoke begins to clear). Thus the ego transfers dream activity to waking life or, rather, is a vehicle in both waking and sleeping for dreaming to do its work.

Freud values the civilizing work of the ego—ego as scientist, business executive, psychic engineer, knowledge and adaptation machine. And he values its role in art and literature, exploring, shaping and cultivating sensibility, form, and feelings. Nevertheless, he remains keenly aware that ego is prone to glorify and denigrate itself and others, misreading and misappropriating experience, and that it can run amok on the side of ethics or instinct (e.g., becoming overly judgmental and/or impulsive). Nowadays, too, it runs amok as a work machine, caught on an economic treadmill, reducing experience to fit an age of technological and economic intimidation (we keep stressing benefits of our way of life to play down the injury of being caught in money and power machines).

The superego, by far, gets the worst press. The overly moralistic, critical superego has been depicted as devouring ego functions, so that ego capacities (thinking, feeling, will, ambition, directed movement) become extensions of a self-destroying force. You would think the explosive id is the culprit, and often it is. But emphasis tends to be on how the id is used, forms it takes, how it is organized and channeled. Ego and superego are committed to securing instinctual gratification one way or another—through work, through morality, feeling good about oneself for doing the right thing, or through practical and cultural achievements. Organizing processes can run amok, and a warped superego breeds and feeds off deathwork, increasing severity to self and others. It turns the ego against itself, against life. There is a gruesome pleasure in addiction to antipleasure, destructive gratification. The death drive gets its own kinds of orgasmic satisfaction, and appropriation of the moral faculty to destroy life is a premier method. Destruction milks the juice out of the life drive to produce a store of ecstasies that exert a mad, mesmerizing fascination on humankind. Add to the brew that destruction vitalizes *and* saps life and one is dizzy to distraction.

Sandor Ferenczi spoke of psychoanalysis dissolving the superego. Barriers to instinctual gratification would diminish. Life could be more satisfying if superego condemnation and strictures were loosened or undone. Seeing through tyrannical aspects of superego intimidation will free people to live more openly. A utopian vision, to think that sex could ever be free of trouble.

Ferenczi's own practice zigzagged between a more utopian picture of what things could be like and what in fact we must work with. He opened the door to a deeper sense of mother-infant relations, threading common sense through the eye of psychoanalytic needles. Freud (with common sense) noted that part of mothering involves offsetting an infant's distress, making a baby feel better when assailed by painful states and conditions. Mother transforms pain to bliss, well-being, feeling OK again. Ferenczi dramatized this by noting how mothering helps offset the death drive, maintaining the baby in life. The latter includes supporting the infant's trust or faith in the face of agonies, stresses, and pulls downward. Infants go through immense depressive and persecutory pains and the mold the ego gets set in depends, partly, on the quality of help received. Parental help initiates modeling how we help each other in the face of distress, a capacity that grows (or fails to grow) with us all life long.

Ferenczi's semi-utopian clinical vision (a person's caring for another can offset rigid prohibitions and destructive pulls: love sets you free) was balanced or ruptured by his dramatic vision of a death drive working in nature and personality. While his work spoke to the punitive superego, it gravitated toward a deeper destructive force that made a punishing tendency possible. Ferenczi has been criticized for trying to cure with love, holding patients as a mother might hold a baby, transgressing boundaries sacrosanct to many analysts. In his personal life, his open attitude sometimes created havoc. Nevertheless, he paved the way for greater sensitivity to moment-to-moment emotional transactions, how two people vibrate to each other and affect each other in nuanced ways. He drew attention to the importance of emotional fluctuations in personal encounter—what they mean, what they add to life—at a time when clinical work was on the brink of facing problems having to do with lack of feeling and meaning. Basic elements of his discourse—mothering responses in the face of threatened dying out of self—would soon take on importance that neither he nor Freud might have predicted.

This is not to underplay the importance of the id, which Freud came to see in terms of two major instincts, life and death drives. The life drive is envisioned as creating greater complexity, forming energy into greater unities. The death drive unwinds, unbinds, tending toward entropy, homogeneity, simplicity, chaos. A double movement, one toward animate, vital being and heightened consciousness, the other toward inanimate being, collapse of psychic organization.

In some passages, Freud feels life wears itself out, grows weary of itself. Character is eroded by its conflicts. In others, there is an active destructive force that life cannot handle. Perhaps the difference is illusory, or perhaps each tendency is part of the brew. Life is too much for itself, arising against the force of gravity, giving birth to consciousness and psychic complexity that is hard to sustain, falling back into vast inanimate forces through which the universe began. The pull of or drop into the inanimate is felt as anxiety, a background persecutory sensation, part of the fluctuations of fragile awareness vis-à-vis lifelessness. Nevertheless, there is more to destructiveness than passive collapse as a result of inability to sustain life's tensions and complexities. One also feels an active force working to undo the building of good things.

Before Freud formally developed the idea of the death drive, destruction was built into the life drive. Aggression is part of eros. Desire for life and more life has an aggressive thrust and often carries destruction in its wake. Frustrated desire increases rage, hardens into hate, molds self and personality, works in secret ways to get its own back and make the other pay (If I can't have you, I'll hurt you). Love and rage and hate often belong together. It is said that power is an aphrodisiac, and intimate links between eros, power, and sadism are endemic. Eros involves possessiveness, territoriality, problems with boundaries, control, surrender, power—isn't that enough to account for what we do to each other? Recall, too, that Freud saw the id as a cauldron of seething excitations, raw energy both awaiting and subverting form. Isn't an additional destructive drive a redundant luxury?

When destruction is on the side of life, perhaps. But what we have witnessed—brutality of cultures, economies, massive abuse of individuals—seems more on the side of death. For Freud, as time went on, the extravagance of destruction between nations, cultures, and individuals called for a category of its own. A destruction that co-opts life, exploits orgasmic properties, turns juicy excitement into hell. Orgasmic destructiveness— life's properties pre-empted by a destructive force for its own use, turning life against itself.

If we play the song of life in the key of destruction, all psychic structures and functions can be killers, co-opted and deployed by a seek-and-destroy command. What does destruction seek? Any sign of life. How does it work? By turning life functions into death functions.

The commandment not to kill can add to blood lust, since prohibition, punishment, and desire fuse. A man feels divinely commanded to kill his child or brother. He is told by a whisper or voice or shout that he will go to hell forever if he fails to kill as ordered. He may have some hold on everyday life and find himself in conflict with the destructive command and not know what to do. In such an instance, indecision can be a life-saver. The force of indecision attached to unconscious murderous urges plays a larger role in decision making than ordinarily acknowledged. We ally sanity or goodness with creating the least murderous decisions possible, although practicality occasionally tells us killing X now may save Y later. Sanity, sanitize, clean—a kind of sorcerer's apprentice situation, trying to clean up psychic bad stuff that keeps coming

Command, then, is a tricky business. Id or superego or ego

may command us to kill. Command is subject to reversals (kill, don't kill; kill X, don't kill X—kill Y) and endless amalgams of psychotic commands, ethical commands, realistic commands, impulsive commands. Commands frequently fuse delirium and calculation, rage, love, hope, suppression, tensions between pulls to preserve and enrich life and pulls to wipe life out. It is unlikely any command is as simple as it seems, since multiple pulls plague it. Indecision as a general policy might save the human race a lot of surplus misery.

Abraham's psychotic command to kill his son highlights tensions between multiple tendencies. Crazy God tests Abraham's faith, akin to a psychotic, possessive partner or parent who says, "If you love me you would . . ." A tyrannical litany in mad intimacy, exacting absolute obedience, where desire and command are one: "You don't love me if you don't do what I ask." God goes for the jugular. He aims at what is most precious for Abraham. Do you love me more than life, more than yourself, more than your own son? The son of your old age, Sarah's son, son of our covenant? Isaac—carrier of God's promise, link with the future.

Intrafamilial murder: a familiar theme. Play of cross-currents, to kill, to cherish. God (like Cronus, or Laius) melds with a host of real and imaginary characters who murder children, partly portraying Abraham's (or Sarah's) infanticide wishes. The urge to kill children, to hurt children, to hurt each other all life long. Kill your child—what better authority than a command from God for a dire tendency that is part of life. When the urge to murder hits, it often feels like a command from God. Whether a quick jolt or simmering over time, the need to kill acts like a categorical imperative. The command not to competes with a commanding imperative to kill.

In the Bible story, Abraham does not kill his son. Precious life wins out over the obliterating urge. The biblical tide goes back and forth. God's wrath portrays a smidgen of what we face in ourselves. Human evil is bad enough, but the surplus of fury God adds tells us we are not simple creatures, that the magnified anger expressed through God must be solved or tempered or somehow engaged, if we wish to minimize mutual injury.

What Abraham goes through is, one way or another, repeated by parents all over the globe (in my view, millions of times a moment). To kill, not to kill, to kill *and* not kill, a kind of unconscious pulse gives rise to the feeling that life is threatened, precarious, saved in the nick of time. We escape the knife—once more, but not always, not forever. Relief after fright creates a powerful rhythm in emotional life. Shock, fear, threat, danger—coming through, survival, renewal. A basic rebirth sensation partly involving living through dangers, especially our own dangerous natures. When this works decently enough, the destructive urge adds spice to life, makes for drama and suspense.

Not all people survive themselves. Killers in dreams portray aspects of pressure that personality exerts against itself, that life exerts against itself. The Abraham-Isaac story is a special expression of such pressures. It straddles madness and sanity, often fused. It shows the command nature of murder, its imperative aspect. Unconsciously, it feels as if it comes from God. Murder promises to make one feel like God Almighty. One reverses weakness and helplessness in a burst of might and glory. The ego fuses with God, giving an uplifting, if momentary, sense of authority, a sense of rightness, at times a sense of purity.

One good thing about uncertainty is that it tempers the conviction that one is right or has the right to kill. The image of placing the child outside the door, the city gates, the garden, expresses how exposed and weak we feel, beholden to the elements, to chance, to the kindness of strangers because intimates are so virulent. Abandonment protects the child from ourselves, a sense that baby's better off without us. "It must be better elsewhere 'cause it sure ain't better here." When elsewhere approaches, difficulties obtrude.

Ousted from the garden, Adam and Eve make terrible discoveries but go on with their lives. How, we wonder, after Cain murders Abel? How? Certainly, as broken people. Broken people do not stop living but go on with the cycle of joys and fears, the care of days.

God, the parentless one, exiles his children. To save them from becoming as the gods, to save them from becoming like Him (we know the pain of personhood, how much more the pain of Godhood)? To save them from incest? To save them from deathlessness? A patient asked, "What's wrong with God? Is he angry because he didn't have parents? Is God a feral child?"

A parental unconscious might think getting rid of children gets rid of disturbance. A wish to be disturbance-free attaches to the child: free of children, free of pain. Mad logic jumps to the conclusion that murder will set one free. There is no question Freud was on to something when he traced the path of this logic to zero: zero stimulation, zero sensitivity, zero life = zero disturbance = zero pain. The Bible associates pain with children, not only suffering in labor (a name for birthing), but pain of upbringing and what children do to each other when grown up (endless growing pains, like pleasures, endless birth pains, endless death pains). Childbirth and death belong together in many ways, not least of which is murder.

In ancient Greek literature, fathers exile or murder sons to protect themselves. Mothers kill children, jealous of the latter's lives or to get back at husbands. There are enough images to show that mothers don't need men to hide behind. They devour in their own right, though having a partner to bounce off of can thicken the stew. Children do their share of murdering. In the Bible brothers trouble brothers. One solution to disturbance, conflict, complexity, pain is for everyone to murder everyone. Another solution is modulating frustration, respecting differences, building relationships inclusive of difficulties. However, there is only so much tension one can bear, and getting rid of it equates with murder unconsciously.

We are caught between double murder. Annihilation dread increases with increasing tensions. The more intensity, the more energy, the more tension, the greater the danger of feeling flooded, overwhelmed, sinking, dispersing. It is also true that heightened tension and energy can increase pleasure. But even the rise of pleasure can feel like too much, more than one can bear. One swoons, goes under, blisses out, dissolves in a sea of pleasure. For some, wonderful. For others, death. So much literature, music, and cinema associate maximum intensity of love and pleasure with death. As noted above, killers in dreams can depict a feared, overwhelming rise in energy, aliveness as destructive (life too much for one). On the other hand, loss of tension, energy, intensity threatens loss of meaning and feeling, death from too little rather than too much. Zero points are reached from either end, maximum or minimum tension, intensity, emotion. Loss of self with loss of tension, loss of self with too much tension. Either end may not only feel like death but mediate dread of murder, expressed in dream killers and dire threats.

Some people manage to kill off the capacity to feel anxiety, or the latter dies out. Usually, anxiety, like difficulty, survives the murderer within. Everyone blames everyone for difficulty, but difficulty has a life of its own. Wherever difficulty is located, anxiety about it remains. We survive as partially murdered beings.

The obverse of getting rid of children is getting rid of parents. If the parent thinks the child causes disturbance, the child may feel the parent does. There are brutal and whimsical stories and fairy tales of parentless children (by choice or force) that echo the sentiment that life would be better off without parents. Get rid of parent, get rid of child = no disturbance. Stories of children without parents. There is always hope that fulfillment of wishes will do the trick. No parent, no pain. No child, no pain. No rival, no sibling, no pain. No people, no pain. No self, no pain. Fantasies of being without children and doing away with them may mask fury at parents for family pain carried since childhood. A child who harbors the delusion that children might be better off without parents may abandon a child later to prove the point.

But no, the baby needs parenting to survive. This means loving, murderous, indulging, depriving beings. We think someone else can do it better. Someone not so close, swamped, overwhelmed, rageful. Abraham shows that parental life has traumatizing elements we must learn to work with. As the rabbis say, at least he didn't kill Isaac. He sided with life—but what a struggle!

What rescues a baby feels angelic, allied with saving aspects of love. But baby is not always rescued, not in time. In Benjamin Britten's "War Requiem," Abraham kills Isaac, unable to stop the dynamic set in motion. Michelangelo's Moses (Freud's version) does the opposite: Moses, like the biblical Abraham at a crucial moment, holds back his anger rather than smash God's commandments. For Freud, murder was a founding ingredient of religion, murder of the father by the sons, rather than the reverse (a nexus of murder, repression, guilt, return of the repressed, prohibition, punishment, reparation). Religion, whatever else, struggles with the aggressive nature of humankind.

I stayed within one part of Abraham's story, the command (temptation) to kill his son, Isaac. Add any other parts and you compound the dialectic of cruelty and compassion. Having to exile Hagar and Ishmael, his first-born son. Sarah's bitter laughter at turns of fortune. Complicated stays in Egypt. His split with Lot and saving Lot. A rich and difficult life on the edge of disaster. Abraham tried to temper the wrath of the God he loved. To temper God's temper. To temper destructiveness. To temper the murderous tempter, inflated rage, vindictive mind.

Sometimes God acts as a good parent who helps the child go into the world, taste experience, grow through knowledge of suffering. Adam and Eve bring suffering on themselves, but they had help—the serpent, curiosity, wonder, wishing for more or something else. To be like the gods is to strive for infinitude, which takes Adam and Eve deeper into finitude. You can't stop the world from being dangerous for children. Far from God stopping Adam and Eve from finding out for themselves, He set up conditions that led them to do just that. If Adam named animals, God named suffering. In this He was a bit ahead of His children, but they caught up soon enough.

Bion writes that it is important to be murdered and survive. Not simply survive in a dead way—too often one survives by turning off and deadening feelings. There is only so much sensitivity we can bear, and we partly murder ourselves to make it through life. We do this in benign and lethal ways, toning sensitivity down, insulating it, suffering partial anesthetization, numbing, shutting off. Deadness is suffocating, makes us claustrophobic, and we sometimes become violent to break out of self-deadening processes. We try to murder the self-murdering tendency. A manic high may be achieved, but deadness regathers and vicious circles mount. We murder to breathe easier but poison the air more.

A question Bion raises is how to be murdered *into* life? How can being murdered help us come alive, wake from lifelong asphyxiation? Bion suggests it is possible to survive being murdered and feel all right, a variation of the ancient death-rebirth theme, in which surrender opens larger possibilities. In Bion's account, endurance and persistence lace surrender.

His special twist involves enduring, tasting, meeting the murderous superego, an object that stops dreaming and freezes and fragments experience. The murderous superego is a code word for infinite destructive force that destroys personality, time, existence, aliveness, and keeps on destroying in subzero worlds, after everything imaginable is destroyed. In psychic structure it manifests as murderous superego aimed at other psychic structures.

Of special concern for Bion is a life-and-death drama between murderous superego and dreamwork. He believes dreamwork plays an important role in digesting feelings, especially traumatic impacts. Catastrophic impacts, however, can be so over-whelming that dreamwork gets damaged. In such a situation psyche is in the position of needing to process damaging impacts with damaged processing ability. It gets caught on a viral treadmill of trying to process damage that stops processing. The murderous superego represents and condenses damaging forces, but to constitute it in dreams is to constitute obliteration.

How can one dream the object that destroys dreaming? This is a developmental task the human race faces. Human beings need to evolve an ability to digest destructive feelings rather than be pulverized by them. Such growth will take time. In therapy, individuals chew on a little catastrophe at a time, initiating what digestion is possible. Even a little assimilation and reworking of what is injuring one's capacity to process injury can make a big difference as life unfolds.

One consequence of immobilizing affect processing is a sense of unreality. Life and self become unreal. Bion and Winnicott believe that in order for life to feel real, it has to be dreamt. Dreamwork helps make life feel real. Dreams are steeped in emotional subsoil, and the figures appearing are dipped in streams of feelings. To say that dreams help store and process feelings means that life is taken in, becomes part of one's insides, becomes significant, becomes real. Many individuals do not feel real and feel life is unreal. Bion, partly, links this with effects of trauma on dreamwork, injuring ability to dream life. Sessions become a place where therapist and patient dream each other into life. A place where dreamwork can thaw out.

Murderous superego kills off a capacity to feel life is alive, that one is an alive and real part of life. Selective use of murderous superego gives one the right to feel alive at someone else's expense. The other is treated as somewhat unreal. Real enough to attract attention, not real enough to be respected. The dream of the other has somehow failed, injured by a mixture of self-interest and trauma. An incapacity to dream the other into reality reflects a failure of feeling on the part of the dreamer.

Murderous superego is sprinkled in dreams as various killers, invaders, kidnappers, rapists, shadow figures, predators that threaten annihilation and damage. The annihilating force is never vanquished once and for all—there are no final victories. Murder, mayhem, annihilation anxiety continue into old age, when the specter of death picks up momentum, egging one on to the edge of personality, as far as one can go. To the extent it is able, dream life regulates doses of destruction it can work with. The dreamer tolerates smaller doses of destructive energy without having to wake up. Waking up is not necessarily bad. It can be a call from one state of mind to another. Destruction reaches a point the dreamer cannot handle, and the dreamer passes it along (e.g., through the jolt of nightmare) to its waking partner. Waking and sleeping, together, divide attention to destruction, nibbling at it from both directions.

Individuals can use waking (or sleeping) as an excuse to ignore destruction, to make believe it does not exist or is unimportant, even though it just scared them out of their wits or skin. Defenses work either way. One may get tired and sleep to escape difficult feelings. Destruction wears one out. Once again, when awake, one may downplay the jolt of nightmare by saying, "It was only a dream," or some such gambit of disregard. One tries to talk oneself or sleep oneself out of fear. But fear is an index of something real, emotion needing attention, destructive energy requiring work. We can do this work only, if at all, a little at a time.

Emotion is a double threat. Insofar as emotion represents life, it threatens the murderous superego, which is set in an antilife mode. At the same time, emotion is an important part of what murderous superego feeds on, converting life to death, mowing down, devastating, eliminating anything in its path (path being a misleading image, since the destructive force, like emotional life, is not, strictly speaking, localizable). One pins down local representatives of destruction, small- or big-town bad guys, but such triumphs, significant as they are, open other

Pandora's boxes. One does not end destructive energy by working with some of its images. Nevertheless, what work one does increases a sense of familiarity with destructiveness, develops one's sense that there is something there that is important to learn about. Such awareness may make one less tinny and abrasive, as one searches for ways to care.

A devastating reversal occurs when murderous superego turns emotion into dread of emotion. One dreads one's own life insofar as it will be devastated by a murderous function—one dreads one's own life insofar as it is subject to psychic murder. Murderous superego carries a negative imperative: thou shalt not be alive. The threat is annihilation of aliveness insofar as the latter dares birth. The murderous superego aims destructive energy at aliveness, turns the latter against itself, absorbs or channels its power, adding life to destructive force. On a relatively superficial level, an individual may say, "Why bother living if you're going to die." The capture of aliveness by destructive energy is more than this statement implies. Negative momentum reaches a point where life is part of destruction (rather than the reverse) and infusions of aliveness automatically empower destructive action. Dreading aliveness (it will be destroyed or used for destruction), individuals jump on or give in to destructive bandwagons for the giddy, tragic, somewhat mad and perverse assurance of momentary destructive victories.

Not so fast, says emotional life. Destructiveness feeds aliveness, as well as the reverse. Emotions threaten the murderous superego, not only fuel it. A feeling comes and goes, but its traces, its effects go on working. Feelings resonate to feelings across their fading and dying out—not only within individual lives but between individuals and generations ("A thing of beauty is a joy forever"). Generative emotional work continues through feelings and images and actions mediated by all of human history: concerns of Sophocles are reworked by Shakespeare, are reworked by Freud. We hunger for each other's images and adventures and listen to voices of those who find ways to mediate feelings and thoughts that matter. We tell each other our dreams and sometimes listen to what they try to communicate.

Nonetheless, in spite of all the claims of life and the aliveness of emotions, emotions can and do appear as killers in dreams. It is hard to overestimate the importance of this realization or the importance of neglecting it. A crucial part of what makes us feel alive threatens to murder us in our dreams. Our sense of aliveness transforms into fear of annihilation, expressed in murderous images. Dreams embody and condense a diffuse apprehension that pervades us, a fear that aliveness is destructive.

To some extent we can dissect and parse out aspects of this apprehension:

1. Emotions threaten the anti-emotion aim of murderous superego. The latter expresses a force that destroys everything. But no aspect of psychic reality is an absolute winner over all others. A destructive force may convert emotion into anti-emotion or no emotion. But more emotion may arise to threaten as well as fuel it. To some extent, emotion and anti-emotion offset, even balance, each other. No matter how much aliveness feeds destruction, the work of the latter is not total. Not in our world, not so far.

2. Murderous superego incessantly threatens personality with annihilation. For personality to be, it must withstand, to some degree, the weight and pressure of annihilation anxiety. It must be in the face of and in spite of dread of being. Love of being offsets dread of living as well as teases this dread. It adds to dread of living by increasing vulnerability and openness on the one hand, inflaming envy and hatred of aliveness on the other. Destruction envies life, seeks to drink it dry, suck the life out of life, a deranged feed, sometimes imaged as monster babies wholly bent on destruction. Shakespeare catalogues variations on the ways emotion attracts destruction and, more generally, characterizes emotions as multiedged, multivalenced, multifunctional.

3. Id, ego, superego, introjects. From a simplified id perspective, killers in dreams might represent passions or drives, often

fused with superego elements. Since sex is regulated by taboos, certain objects (mother, father) forbidden, libido must be redirected. Guilt and anxiety spread from primary prohibitions to libidinous activity elsewhere, and since libido is part of all activity, nothing is immune from sexual guilt and anxiety. A dream killer may be sex in disguise, sex as threat to ego/superego, as subversive to business as usual (although, to some, sex as transgressive *is* business as usual).

However, sex as killer (dire threat to structural organization) is not only tied to guilt or anxiety and "moral" regulation (often puritanical or practical rather than really ethical). It also has pure energic significance related to intensity. Individuals vary in their ability to bear feeling or stimulation of any sort. Freud spoke of early trauma as flooding—personality flooded by stimulation, excitation, emotion.

Nervous system flooding itself. In accord with nineteenth-century neurology, Freud depicted the brain as a field with diversity of functions, involving neural excitation and its regulation. The "old" subcortical brain exerts drive pressures, allied with emotions and passions, while the "new brain" exercises cortical control, including functions like attention, inhibition, and selection. Regulation is variable and at times faulty, so that cortical functioning is overwhelmed or threatened. Anxiety may signal variable states of drive control or, more generally, reflect in the psychic domain the ongoing, delicate, mutual adjustments of neurological structures and functions to one another, a kind of neural hum, which can get stormy.

Phenomenological translations, extensions, revisions. Our ability to take stimulation is variable. There is only so much of ourselves or the world we can bear. To what extent can we take rise of emotion, follow its rhythmic arc as it builds and dies down again, fading into the background of being? Insofar as attention and processing ability fails, the raw fact of emotion can be threatening. We may fear being thrown by feeling, its sheer presence and intensity. The opposite is also the case. Persistent lack of feeling can be tormenting and frightening (a cruel conundrum, feeling pain over lack of feeling). How much of ourselves—aliveness or deadness—can we bear?

Surges of feeling can be imaged as killers in dreams insofar as they threaten to flood or paralyze the ability to tolerate and process them. Too little feeling can be imaged as killers in dreams because of the threat of depletion, emptiness, nothingness. Too much feeling can equate with psychic blood bursting and splattering: too little equates with psychic blood gone. We are dangers to ourselves by *being* feeling beings, although without feelings we may be even more dangerous.

Ego. In Freud's depiction, the ego's first cognitions are hallucinatory, and through life's impacts, antihallucinatory perceptions develop. The ego remains a double agent, hovering between delirium and the mundane. Analysts vary in their respect for ego's ability to discriminate between fact and fancy and their skepticism about its self-aggrandizing ways: ego as scientist and businessman vs. ego as god. One way of stating our doubleness is that we are never completely psychosis free, nor are we totally without curiosity about our psychosis.

Freud hits the nub of a bad rub by attributing to the mad, calculating, power-driven ego the function of balancing psychic forces, regulating psychic tendencies, creating homeostatic, adaptive blends out of conflicting ingredients. A mad killer in charge of the psyche. But not only a killer. The superego originates as a self-regulating part of the ego, self-observing, mediator of moral considerations, a system of checks and balances. As noted above, superego can take on a life of its own, become a moral monster, a destructive power. The ego, thrown back on itself, may rise to the occasion, appeal to common sense and practical considerations, and thread its way through destructive tendencies. The ego may become more ethical—try to find the least harmful, most productive path—than the "moral" superego. Quite a balancing act, an executive function modulating passion, morality, and the need to survive. Add to that a taste for truth and deception (yes, a double taste), and we are never far from stormy weather.

In clinical work, ego mediates transference dialectics between idealization-disillusionment, over- and-underestimation, deification-demonization of self and others. Our sense of self and others mixes hallucination and delusion with perception of real impacts. I like to think of ego as the guardian of hallucination and of fact, performing a double protective function, since we need and value contributions of imaginative extravagance and everyday perception. Freud often pits one against the other, emphasizing antagonistic competitiveness, for example, the ego's bossiness, tending toward grandiosity and megalomania, competing with reflective consideration, seeing things in perspective, a mediating, conciliatory function. Freud's vision was of growth through dialectical conflict, which left room for competing tendencies to offset each other and contribute to overall development. Often, however, his rhetoric was one of war, struggle between forces with the outcome of the great battle in doubt, latent intimations of Armageddon pulsing through desire for compromise.

Freud wrote of the ego dividing itself in dreams, distributing various of its functions among dream characters. He insistently hammers home the intriguing point that one aspect of personality is experienced as threatening by another. There is hallucinatory extravagance in dream processes, and in psychic tendencies generally, which measures things through extremes. Magnification-minification, hyperpole, exaggeration is part of the way our psyche works (easily veering into lying). Threat magnifies into murder, infinitizes into absolute annihilation, a dread that spreads through body and psychic being. Actual murder concretizes and momentarily stops a murderous feeling that has no fixed beginning or end. A sense of destruction permeates dreams. To some degree, we take possession of destructiveness by building images of killers who frighten us, but have, for the moment, particular forms. Specific forms seem almost handleable, although if we try to touch them, they turn into pure, formless menace. Inner democracy is difficult when we have to make room for murdering, being murdered, and wordless, imageless menace.

A common way to organize and distribute areas of conflict is thinking vs. feeling, either threatening to enhance or kill off the other. Freud described cases in terms of conflicts between thinking and feeling, for example, obsessive killing off of feeling, hysterical killing off of thinking. Thought or feeling can appear as menace in dreams, depending on defensive predilections and fears. The ego's bureaucratic thinking appears to murder aliveness, while its idealizing tendency creates gods to worship and destroy.

Bion suggests exercising our ability to see life, world, body, personality from many vertices or "viewpoints": how life looks from the "viewpoints" of eyes, ears, breathing, skin, digestion, etc. Marion Milner suggests contracting (expanding) into one's big toe to get a different sense of being. To imaginatively sense the world in many keys of experience requires growth in respect for diverse experiential domains. In life across the globe, few things are needed more. Attitudes in dreams and toward dream figures carry over into waking life. Waking and dreaming consciousness structure each other. Killers and menace in dreams reflect and constitute dangers in relationships, whether dramas of injury and repair or cycles of spiraling injuries. The kind of psyche that is involved with murder while asleep is involved with murderous tendencies when awake. It is the same psyche in two states, and it is up to us to work with it.

Superego (again). Caricatures of psychoanalysis focus on ameliorating a virulent superego, so that one feels less guilty about living. Often, an emphasis on diminishing guilt is used as an excuse for getting away with selfish behavior and escaping self-criticism. One sides with impulse or desire over silly or lethal prohibitions. Sometimes this makes for superficiality of development, inasmuch as guilt is an important part of sensitivity to injury and requires serious attention. Nevertheless, there are many for whom a too severe superego attacks aliveness, using guilt to batter life-affirming aspects of personality. Bion depicts a position in which devastation spreads. The life-destroying superego uses what personality functions it commandeers to further its work of destruction. It then becomes less a picture of a hapless neurotic trying to get permission to be more sexual or assertive, than a horrifying sense of personality being hollowed out from the inside, left to collapse into a dense hole or nothingness.

Destructive superego can masquerade as ego or id elements as it commandeers their functions. The personality can appear to be thinking and feeling and trying to live decently, yet subtly leaves destruction in its wake, destruction that gathers momentum. Thinking and feeling get deployed to think and feel about how to kill thinking and feeling and how to use thinking and feeling to destroy. The dreamer may get the message before the waking self and picture attacks, expressing attacks on thought and feeling, their attacks on each other and on personality. The dreamer flashes the catastrophe that personality is undergoing long before the latter catches on in waking life.

One of the extraordinary achievements of destructive logic is to turn morality into a moral hole, a caricature of itself, a kind of psychopathic ethics. A destructive sense turns conscience, in Bion's phrase, into "immoral conscience," a negative of itself. The sense of "right" becomes an adaptive or political strategy, aimed at getting one's (individual, group) way. One of the mesmerizing ploys in current politics is the indignant ease and complacent assurance with which "self-interest" is elevated to an ethical imperative. Exploitation is fused with moral posture or, worse, moral conviction. Dreams are part of our sensitive underbelly in which falsehood registers. In dream images, lies transform into killers attacking self-aggrandizing complacency, the latter itself a killer. The killing ways we cheat our way through life show up in dreams, even if we are the victim. A lot of what goes on in sleep may be amoral, but there is, also, an ethical dimension in dreaming, in which trespasses against others transform into aggression against self, as well as the reverse. In dreams the "kill or be killed" notion is shown to be the sham it is. A kill *and* be killed psyche is closer to the truth, for killing spreads and becomes uncontainable (many kinds of killing, literal, moral, economic, psychic, aesthetic—including the most widespread abortion practice of them all, murder of *embryonic personal being*).

Introject. Introjection refers to taking something from the outside in, so that a quality, function, set of traits, image of a person, or action pattern pressures and molds experience. At times, it is a shorthand way to mean a person or influence impacting personality in significant ways. It is an elastic notion, which has suffered wide uses in psychoanalysis but which contains endless puzzles when examined closely. One thing that is fun about it is that it suggests something elastic, permeable, open about personality. Things go in, come out (introjection-projection), like eating, breathing, only here we are in a mental realm, even a spirit realm.

A toxic introject ordinarily refers to a bad object, or bad parent or aspect of parenting, a set of injurious traits or patterns. The traumatic agent or situation is taken in and becomes part of a person's feel for life, part of the way he behaves, and part of what he fights against. All this is a kind of metaphorical thinking—poisoning personality, poison milk, taking in hate, fear, indifference. The unconscious becomes peopled by bad spirits, fantasies, graves hiding unborn goodness, or monster births with second thoughts about being born. An introject can be a picture of another person, competing pictures of a person, aspects of conscious or unconscious functioning, parts of a person fused with fantasy, fabrication and germs of truth. The idea of taking in objects or presences is ancient and has many historical twists and turns. In psychoanalysis, it is grounds for drama, the struggle between good and bad introjects or objects, good and bad feelings about self and other.

Ironically, a notion that seems to express the psyche's permeability tends to be used to express its rigidity. For bad introjects are conceived as rigid structures or fantasies or objects or representations that keep the individual mired in destructive, self-persecutory patterns. The bad introject, installed in the patient's ego or ego-ideal or superego, attacks a person's being, his very wish to live.

One of Lacan's ways of tuning into this is to depict a tragic element built into desire. Desire is a play of desires, including desire to capture the other's desire, the other's *jouissance*. One keeps an eye on the other's desire and molds oneself to lure it. Mutual molding is the rule. The watcher is everywhere seeing who's desiring who and how personality twists itself to make the interface of desires work. The story of desire is the story of influences: since the desire of the other infiltrates personality, tones it, shapes it, indeed, one unconsciously reconfigures one's own desire to better attune oneself to the other's.

Desire is allied with the torture and deforming of desire, even the death of desire, depending on the structure and force of influence. Desire, which one imagines should enhance the vitality of living, too often culminates in the seizure of one's being by the desire of the other, a kind of death. Yet even this death can be enlivening in a certain key. When we awake in this death we feed on the other's *jouissance* that our deformation secretly accesses. Desire survives in twisted forms that suck on other desires. Desire is always multiple, desires nested in each other, serpents with many bellies, many heads. Look closely at one, others come running.

Can aliveness survive the desire that quickens it? We try to free ourselves from, as well as enjoy, each other's desires. We need each other's desires to grow, but feel stifled by their impositions. The other's desire, as one's own, may appear as a murderer in a dream, one reason dream love often ends in frustration. The very fact we bungle things in dreams acts as a kind of protection against desire co-opted by the other. In the movie *The Loneliness of the Long Distance Runner*, a man in prison loses a race his hated warden wants him to win, even if winning means being set free. The warden is a dream killer the runner wants to kill, so much so that he "wins" by losing, one kind of murder substituting for another.

And what about the good core, offsetting the killer within, giving it food? Doesn't the killer rely on it? A comforting thought, that even the killer, especially the killer, is looking for something good. But once killing reaches a certain point, can goodness satisfy? There are those who say goodness is a fantasy and those who claim it as ultimate reality. Bion reaches for a grim truth by positing a destructive force that goes on working after goodness is destroyed, that does not stop destroying after time, existence, and personality are destroyed. It goes on destroying because that is what destruction does. It goes on destroying when there is nothing left to destroy. Apparently one need not posit goodness for destruction to work. A bull, whose horns we barely see or grasp, gores our lives.

It is at this point that we have to take the measure of our faith. Is it possible for a therapist to face the therapy killer, the killer element of psyche manifesting in individuals and groups, sometimes rampaging, sometimes seeping through lives, without hope of good wind to fill our sails?

8 Training Wheels

Eva reminded me of a distancing remark I made about a dream she had about a bicycle with training wheels. A few days earlier I said something about never having thought of therapy as training wheels, but now that she dreamt it, I saw it and it made sense. Why was that distancing? It sounds OK enough from the outside. But I knew immediately it was a wrong thing to say or a wrong way to say it.

The truth is I felt touched inside, a heart feeling, when she told me the dream, because of the delicate and deep connection in therapy, the emotional threads that knit us together. I betrayed my true feeling by making a sort of pleasant, affirming, objectifying remark. A remark *about* an image, not an expression *from* the feeling, perhaps an expressive gesture once or twice removed. Is that the best I can do? Often it is. It is hard for some people to link up with themselves—it is hard for me. I am sort of linked up in a wordless kind of way. Getting affect to words is another matter. A lot gets lost along the way.

A heart feeling. How much heart? One can't exactly measure, but there definitely are variations in intensity, fullness, range, depth, totality. In the heart region there are relative totalities, now more, now less. No sense in ordinary logic but real enough for heart logic. Of course, there are no regions when it comes to heart life. The physical heart has a specific place, but the emotional heart can't exactly be located. But let's talk a bit as if the heart is findable just to make communication a little easier.

What is it to say one's heart is moved in therapy, *my* heart, with *this* person? The hour ends, we go our ways—but the emotional moment is real. It has effects, irradiates in our lives and beings. It can be affirmed and betrayed and our—*my*—relative openness *and* defensiveness is not confined to one moment, one person. Even a little heart opening has consequences, especially when compared to a little closing. One develops sensitivity to the relative opening-closing that characterizes micromoments and to an overall sense of fluidity-rigidity that tones personality.

I felt relief when Eva fingered the distancing place. She felt set aside by me just at the spot where she touched me. Calling my evasion enabled me to link up with what she knew I felt. She felt a subtle jolt when my real feeling hid away. Why did I hide? Perhaps out of embarrassment, fear, shame, feelings she well understood. I think, too, a quiet sense of being on top feared being toppled. Hiding is a baseline habit.

These things are complicated. I didn't feel totally distancing. There was a drawing closer together along with a pushing away. Even as the objectifying words came out, I was feeling her and me, our work together, being together. This connection came through the distancing words, making them stand out as distancing. Therapy as training wheels: when I said therapy, I substituted therapy for *me*. There is a distancing *twinge* I sometimes feel when the wrong words or the right words with the wrong feeling leave my mouth. Eva and I felt that twinge immediately, although we said nothing until Eva brought it up next time. It's not only a matter of evasion. It takes time to link up with oneself through the layers of fuzz and walls and semishapeless stuff.

Eva said it simply and clearly: "Having strong feeling for you makes me feel like a human being. When you distance it and talk about 'therapy,' it's like cutting off a respirator. *You're* my training wheels. When you say 'therapy,' your breathing sound goes away." My breathing sound means life to her.

It's the difference between talking about and being. Her words opened being. Eva's words were feelings. The warmth I felt and meant came alive and was close. She did not force me to feel anything, but showed, through what she went through, how my fear or disability affected us. The aftermath of self-betrayal led back to the original feeling, how we touch each other inside.

Such moments go a long way. What we do is not just practice or modeling. It's real exchange of feeling, repeatedly, in different ways. We cut off air by choice of words or how we speak when words are walls rather than feelings. In just the few years we've been together, Eva and her husband fight less, love more. Not that they care more, but they feel each other's caring more. Fearful, controlling rages with her children diminish. Feeling feelings extends. Faith in subtle touching grows. She dreads losing her children because of too much rage and closeness. She fears they will turn against her. More and more, she finds them in new places.

Sometimes I feel an inner vagina in my heart or chest opening and enfolding, opening and enfolding. But it is better than that.

Eva already had twenty-five years of analysis. The last ten were just marking time or worse. She felt intimidated by her analyst, who berated her for self-defeating acts. Whatever went wrong, she caused it. Internal bad objects persecuted and blackmailed her, and *she* failed to stand up to them in order to chart another course. With all her work, she *should* have power to abandon addiction to negative patterns. She sees through them. She and her analyst have gone over and over them. Why can't she let them go? Guilt, shame, suffocation. Analysis, once helpful, stuffed and choked her.

She screwed up her courage and left amid threats that if she didn't stay and work out her relationship with him, she was doomed to self-destruct. She felt the most self-destructive thing she could do was stay with him. Breaking away from persecutory blackmail was what she had to do.

When she began with me, she felt battered. And was battering. Fights and rages between husband, children, and herself were incessant. Flare-up after flare-up. The only peace involved getting out of the house, long walks, movies, working. Rage and wounds—a way of life. It was what she had known since childhood.

What did all those years of therapy do? Well, she had a husband, children, work. And if she had a raging, wounded self— it was self! Therapy was not a loss—far from it. It not only saved her life; it gave her a life. Before therapy she had been a scattered, fragmented mess. Now she was a more put together mess. Life before therapy was a chaotic succession of jobs and men leading nowhere. With therapy, she built a real, if awful, life that meant something, a life not without riches. There is no doubt in her (or my) mind that her therapy bond had been enabling before it became bondage. Bondage, too, discloses truth, forces truth on her, presents paths to enter, explore, escape, succumb to.

Eva breathed easier with me. I was less likely to stuff or hijack her with interpretations. More room to stretch, more room for error. A different touch. Criticism is what she was raised on. Her mother was ready to jump on her—she ate too much, too little, she was too fat, too skinny, too brilliant, too dumb. Whatever she was was too much this, too little that. Distance was upheld by negativity, closeness by vampirization. Her mother sank fangs into Eva's psychic blood, living off her talents and accomplishments. A cement mixing criticism with adoration. Eva became bewildered by her own blissful intoxication with a creativity she was increasingly unable to use.

Therapy bondage differed somewhat from maternal bondage, although they shared a lot. Eva's therapist did not idolize her, so the blend of idolization/persecution was not identical. He stuffed her with responsibility for self-destructive states, insisting she could do better. She stayed stuck in shame, self-hatred, disability. She *should* be able to stop acting out, she *could* do better and felt badly that she didn't. Bad feelings about herself mounted and became a chronic underpinning. Somatic symptoms blossomed together with fury, despair, helplessness, frustrated omnipotence. She felt amazing powers she could scarcely use, like a centipede that felt it should fly, but could use only one foot to drag itself along.

Eva's therapist tried pulling and pushing her past this over/under self-estimation. One reason he fell short was that he wished to be idolized in place of herself. The onus for failure fell on the patient. *He* could do no wrong. *She* did not try hard enough, was too regressive, too attached to bad things, guilty for wanting good things. Her desire to get better was split, tainted. Guilt held her back, pervaded her, but he was guilt free. If she criticized him, he turned it back on her. If someone was going to be the idolized, it wasn't going to be her.

Eva felt strongly that her analyst's failings got worse over the years, and not only was he blind to them, he could not bear others seeing them. "I wasn't allowed to notice he was self-indulgent, that he'd given up his self-appraisal as an analyst. When I criticized him, he turned on me, told me I was grandiose for seeing what I saw. Puny and grandiose—I felt both. But I saw what I saw. To get along with him I'd have to blind myself. I acted blind and my outside eyes became more hating and my inside eyes more self-loathing."

Such compacted guilt, hatred, fury. I thought and thought about it. Visions of so many kinds of guilt, survival guilt, guilt over being or not being, guilt over individuation or stagnation, guilt for doing or not doing. It is dangerous to think one can do better than another analyst, especially a past one. One does not know what impassable core lies ahead. It is too easy to get flattered and flattened by comparison with one who failed, and only partly failed at that. Years have taught me that awful things go on in almost any kind of contact between human beings, with help relationships no exception. Hope of intimacy drowns many dreams.

A guilt wall. There is a place where we are surrounded by guilt, a dense and impenetrable area. We follow the guilt so far, then the trail disappears. Reasons fade, guilt remains. Guilt out-lasts reasons. We stay with the guilt as far as it lets us, in hope that this time something will give way, something more will happen. One does not do justice to guilt by putting it in neat packages ready for disposal. One must face the fact that it out-lasts the ways we try to get rid of it.

Meanwhile, Eva was thinking of two ways of feeling sorry, one that bears fruit, one that makes things worse. "Sorry when you're in contact with real hurt leads to change. Sorry when superego makes self the victim doesn't." Eva thinks of her children. When she feels sorry for injury she inflicts, she thinks about damaging consequences and works on herself. She feels the hurt of others. Injury she causes gnaws on her, works its way into her, reworks her. This kind of sorry inflicts inner pain that is useful, related to her actions. Feeling this pain is motivating. It digs into her, breaks barriers, drills soft spots. Pain drills through self-hardening and reaches deeper sensitivity.

Superego self-victimization spins and goes nowhere. Useless pain mounts. Eva can be sorry from now to kingdom come but the only thing that happens is feeling worse. Painful oblivion scratches her insides, persists like a toothache. But when she looks for the source, there is nothing to be found. An ache of self-hate without end, more and more bitter frustration. Endless itching, endless scratching, nothing to show for it but blood. But the pain of guilt is not solvent. Blood does not dissolve it.

Feeling sorry while in contact with the other's hurt is some-thing else. It spurs Eva to do better. She tries. Scratching wounds and falling deeper into holes is unsatisfactory in com-parison with the real thing. She longs to get the job done, to have a good effect on others and herself. How to go about it? It is a sorry that asks to learn more about contact.

It is difficult to know what to do about sexual feelings with Eva. Things get intensely erotic. She talks about erotic hate, what she wants to do together, things she wants to do to me. Her sexual escapades are arousing, sometimes frightening. The room heats up. Brain heat, genital heat. My body pump works overtime. She tells me about things she does in sex now that she never did before. Anything is possible.

My job involves keeping ears open. In literal fact, ears do not close. In psychospiritual fact, they rarely open, not enough, not fully. Listening, hearing, feeling. What is it that goes inside ears? Ears go directly to the heart.

Bion compares the analyst to a soldier needing to keep a clear head in danger. He also writes that the gut brain works faster than the head brain and that the former is necessary for survival in battle. Head brain, gut brain, heart brain—in therapy they all come into play.

It was harder near the beginning when I was trying to get used to the level of arousal Eva brought. What made it a little easier was her reliance on sex as a way of holding self together. The picture of early desperation, overreliance on sex with many men, acted like brakes for me. It might be terrific for a few moments but would not help. It would ruin therapy. I did not want to go through it. She was clear about it sometimes. She wanted to express everything and wanted everything. But what she most wanted was a healing experience. We could drive each other crazy but were after something more. It would have been awful had I given in before we started. Before she had a chance to see what was at stake.

I can have sex with lots of women in my mind. It is not as good as the real thing, but sometimes it is better. I picture all sorts of things with Eva. She pictures all sorts of things with me. Incite, excite. In-sight can be hot indeed.

The hard rock of sex. Eva knew immediately that she was freer with hate in sex than I. She feared she would be too hating for me. Would our disjunction be bearable? Any less bearable than our conjunction? A lot of deprivation went into Eva's hate. A lot of deprivation goes into therapy. But we are not deprived of sexual imagining. Often what we imagine is tantalizing. But there are times touch opens worlds we could not have imagined.

We taste each other psychically, a special apple on the tree in and out of the garden. Emotional taste takes the edge off deprivation. It heightens the latter, brings it to fulfillment. To fill with feeling, even the feeling of deprivation. Many speak of being filled with emptiness, filled with pregnant void. The opening of psychic taste buds is what therapy offers.

Something got fulfilled in Eva's promiscuity and in her marriage. But no matter how much aliveness there was, how great an embrace of life, nothing slaked a deeper deprivation. Excitement added, but lack could not be taken away. Deprivation bored into her, the more she tried to appease it. An inexhaustible measure of emptiness acts as a kind of protective coating, resisting self-exploitation. An unappeasable measure of emptiness— which means an unseducible core in so seducible us.

Eva's former therapist thought she should oppose emptiness with a gratifying life. Cycles of gratification and self-destruction intensified. More room for pleasure, more costly sabotage. As her physical problems mounted, Eva recoiled. Something was harming her and she became more frightened. Her body complained with symptoms, her psyche with rage. Her fear for herself, partly, precipitated changing therapists.

Pain and fury in Eva's sexual fire, distress in heat. Distress speaks to distress. No amount of sex could change this fact. On the contrary, use of sex turns heat into a medium of distress.

When I published *Coming Through the Whirlwind*, a criticism I received was that I should have been more expressive of my erotic feelings with Cynthia. I described what I felt to the reader, but held back with Cynthia, my patient. A couple of experienced analysts felt she left after two years because I sat on my feelings. I'm unable to decide if the criticism is altogether fair, since my feelings played a role in transformation processes. One scenario I heard went something like this. A little girl needs the father's desire on many counts, intellectually, emotionally, physically.

Such recognition is enlivening and releasing. Maybe Cynthia would have benefited more from more expressiveness.

I suppose there were reasons for my caution. Cynthia had lots of sex with lots of men, including authority figures she came in contact with. Sometimes to her disadvantage. She was used to affirming herself through masculine desire and elicited this desire in me. I hoped to offer an experience in which other aspects of herself found recognition, including wounded aspects and strengths she might dare to use more. Sex may be used to soothe wounds but rarely solves them. It affirms, adds life to life, but if one imagines it will solve basic difficulties, the wrong thing is being asked of it and disappointment must follow.

Nevertheless, it is possible to be more affirming throughout the spectrum of experiencing. The erotic charge in sessions could have been put to better use. Hopefully, I can do a little better with Eva than I did with Cynthia, on this as well as other scores. Perhaps freer flow of energy and feeling will emerge. I hate to think I am just as stuck now as I was over ten or fifteen years ago, although in certain ways this may be so. Even logjams that do not seem to budge are subject to processes over time and cannot stay the same. My work with Cynthia had bright spots, and she and I benefited overall. Our work and my written expression of it make a valid contribution, whatever their limitations. Further suffering, enjoying, living, learning of the past fifteen years will be to Eva's benefit, again with whatever necessary restrictions.

Eva raises the possibility that starting menopause is giving sexual intensity an added edge. It is more important than ever to feel desired and desirous. Not as important as in her teens, in her twenties, but important in its own way, with increased hunger, fervor, expectation. There are times life rises sharply, efflorescence before decline. Eva cannot bear that she may not pack the same erotic intensity some day soon and takes hormones to forestall that.

Even so, orgasms are not the high she habitually counted on. Not as acute, they slip into tenderness, melting. Sometimes they run off on a lower ledge, as if not happening, as if she could not find them. "Tenderness is new," she said. "I know it's from you."

It is not that the hard edge of hate is not there. It *is* there. "It will be there. It is part of me, part of who I am. I know that much. But the tenderness is something that hasn't been there. I've had it for my children. I've wanted it with my husband, but he has rejected it. He likes hard stuff. These past few months he has been softening. We've been tender sexually. It's something new, and I like it, even if I'm afraid it is growing because the way I've experienced sex is fading. We still enjoy hard hate. But something different is beginning."

She feels vulnerable quivers, and I feel them through her. "Sweetness," she says. "Sweetness we pushed away or tore to shreds. It's come."

I think of drawn-out sunsets, brightening as dark quickens, sweet orgasms without end or place, threading hearts.

"It was a nice weekend," she begins a session. Nice weekends are rare. Nice things happen but spoiling spoils them. Weekends are a hothouse for destruction. I have a penchant for destruction, a taste for wounds. I'm pulled to hurt spots. What hurts is hot for me. There is a gravitational pull toward injury. The black hole suits me well, density from which no light escapes. And in this most desolate landscape, illimitable joy. Not everyone shares this double nucleus of experience, indomitable joy kernel, indomitable death. But Eva and I do. We have this in common, which may be a reason we are together. Her past therapy made her feel bad for going down. Maybe this was meant to be encouragement, you can do it, a you-should-do-it-better pat or kick. For me, dropping down is limitless as rising.

What almost spoiled the weekend was her starting to nag and rage at her children. She held herself back to a large extent, but negativity escaped her, piggybacking on the need for control. "Fantasies of my kids on drugs, getting AIDS, going down the tubes—I was like a nuclear-powered sub getting hit by underwater missiles. Pow, direct hit, psyche explodes, takes on water, explodes and drowns. Was the goodness of the weekend suffocating? Did I have to add a touch of disaster?"

Maybe, but not so simple. The weekend involved some very hard components, the difficulty of which Eva underestimated. For one thing, she visited her mother, which meant being criticized, put down, dropped. There were few greater challenges to self-sustenance that a visit to her mother. She imagined she felt good enough to take it—always a mistake.

Eva's mother could not tell the difference between love and control and suffocating closeness. A kind of mad love that made promises it could not keep. Eva's mother was not there, mindless, the more she poured into Eva. As gone as she was infusing. She drove Eva crazy. As Eva veered toward explosion, she kept herself together by an acute rise of her own need to control her children, the latter fantasized as disorderly and self-destructive. All loose ends dangling in life's abyss. Nagging was a kind of rage at helplessness, dread of internal disorder and loss of control. In fact she did quite well.

"I kept breathing when volcanoes threatened to erupt. My nose was icy burning inside. A genie threatened to erupt from my nose. I pulled him back inside. The ghost that comes out my nose is fat, white, disgusting. I dissociate around my mother's madness, the sick love oozing into my pores, my cells, my organs. I tighten harder not to be a formless blob. Not to be eaten by the spreading ooze. A cancerous ooze."

A moment with her mother. It does not take long to break down. Volcano, icy burning, holding in, cancerous blob, ooze, a genie, a spirit. Her own stormy, dying, gruesome, warped, thrilling insides. Eva works hard to get past the emotional self-indulgence she sees in her mother. She tries to work with herself. She tries to keep breathing, finding ways out and in. Two spirits fight for her, one sickly cancerous, another fiery, determined. She joins the struggle.

There is good reason she is happy with her weekend overall, even if she complains about giving in. She admits her collapse was not so bad, slivers squeezing through cracks, not a total caving. Not a total wild woman. Her kids didn't mind her, flicked her off. She could take being flicked off, glad.

She is of two minds. Her judgment against herself magnifies. Nagging rage is a hemorrhage that never stops. She speaks of losing her sex and sees herself as an old lady pushed out to sea. She becomes an iceberg, good for nothing but destroying boats. She is drying, freezing up, except for rage. She sees a monstrous image of herself. She sees an ugly magnifier, a mind that magnifies the worst. At the same time, she feels a budding gentleness toward her hurting insides, insides that are growing outside the magnifier. Real growing pains, not just twists of trauma. Not just an ability to keep things in perspective, but an ability to be.

Two minds become two eyes in a dream. I don't remember Eva's dream exactly, but it has two eyes different in color, lighter, darker. In the dream her husband has eyes of different colors.

She thinks of the Bible story involving Jacob and two wives who were sisters, Rachel (lighter) and Leah (darker). Maybe Leah had eyes of different color. Eva recounts a "drosh" in which Jacob loved Rachel but sex was cool between them. Sex was hot with Leah, but he was not romantically in love with her (as she was with him). Two attitudes Eva and her husband knew well. They had lots of hot sex, a lot of hot rage, a lot of coldness and emotional frigidity as well. Rachel was thought to be cool physically, relieved when Jacob went to Leah. Leah loved Jacob with body and heart (a word "accidentally" containing art and heat). Eva speaks of splits of self, icy-hot with the same partner, the same self, taking different forms in messy, complicated marriage.

Hot eye, icy eye. Another patient thinks of masturbating while studying. Thinking turns her on. Or, perhaps, not being able to take too much thinking diverts to sexual excitation. Stimulation in one sector radiates through others.

Eva connects the dream of her husband with me. Is Rachel an imaginary elsewhere I stand in for a while precisely because we don't have sex? An ideal beauty that can't give itself? If I drop her emotionally, the fall is not mitigated by touch. But she has her husband to go to, her Leah, real life. Their love-hate sex, their friends, their chores, partners in daily miseries and pleasures that body and soul squeeze out of living. Lately, things have been better and she is appreciative. Hope reappears with its heartening fright. She is at life's mercy once more.

Two eyes, two minds, two hearts. There is always more to Leah and Rachel, life tendencies, ways of organizing life. Through them Eva conveys the sense that she is not one thing. Whatever grabs her, there is more, another take. Something else is possible. She is not trapped in single-eye hardness. Her dreams mark the difference. Soon after dreaming her husband had eyes of different colors—two ways of being with her, of being together—she dreams of telling him to go, while wanting him to stay. He reluctantly agrees, but divines the truth and finds ways to keep in contact with Eva in case something changes. Her dream leaves a door open for mixed tendencies, reversals, unknown movement. She is linking up with the dangers and opportunities double tendencies provide.

"It's too easy for me to turn people into things," Eva says, feeling her way into another contrast, a variation on doubleness. "It's easy for *you* to turn yourself into a thing. I watch you do it. I feel you becoming human, becoming stony. You turn therapy into a thing. Calling my training wheels therapy, something out there, not you, not you and me. I know what it's like to turn therapy into stone.

"You turn therapy into a thing because you are afraid, and I think you don't like me and can't take me and need to get away and shut down. I send you away in a dream to make believe I control this. I want you to want me. I turned my mother into a thing to get away from her turning me into one. If I didn't, there would be no me left. You're like me this way. I fear you see me as I see my mother and you turn therapy into a thing or no you will be left. We turn into things, turn each other into things to protect our persons. What would person to person be like? Sometimes I feel that happening. I feel that more and more.

"For years I turned myself into a need-gratifying thing for my therapist, for my mother. It didn't work. They tossed me into the garbage. I tossed them into the garbage. It's not a matter of not feeling guilty and being free of sin and crime. It's a matter of getting out of the bubble. In the bubble there's carbon monoxide. It's sickly sweet. A toxic bubble, a garbage bubble."

When Eva says I am her training wheels I know what she means. That inner sense is enough at times. Why pretend it isn't happening or is something out there? A you and me tremolo. We struggle for a feeling language so that what happens is not iced. So that what happens can keep on happening. Of course, training and wheels have a mechanical edge. We resonate rapidly to each other's tones, our inside "chooser" trying to find the most fruitful wave of moment. Sometimes we select well and wave adds to wave. Often, we work with missed chances, wrongly read emotional cues, misperception of experience. This means that the possibility of emotional disaster is never far away. But it is precisely our challenge to be sensitive to disaster intimations and keep discovering how to respond.

9 The Binding

Crazy God tests crazy Abraham's faith, akin to a possessive partner or parent who says, "If you love me you would . . . " A tyrannical litany in mad intimacy exacting absolute obedience. A case in which desire and command are one, crazy desire, crazy command: "You don't love me if you don't do what I want . . . " God goes for the jugular. He aims at what is most precious. Do you love me more than life, more than yourself, more than your son, the son of your old age, Sarah's only son, son of the covenant? Isaac—carrier of God's promise, link with the future. Is your son more precious than your link with me? The son who is an earthly-godly link, born past the time Sarah could bear children, a miracle.

God said he would not destroy the world after the flood. He did not say man would not destroy it. Now he puts Abraham in the position of destroying a rainbow to prove faith. Isaac, outcome of faith, signifier of faith: to destroy faith to prove faith. Love of God vs. love of children vs. love of self. This against that never stops.

There are many hot points in the Bible, and this has got to be one of the hottest. The story of Abraham binding Isaac is part of the daily Jewish prayer service and is read as a special part of the High Holiday service as well. It is seared into the Jewish heart, psychic circumcision, indelible vision, for better and worse.

The fate of a psychotic command is mesmerizing. Mad commands grip us today, in our personal lives, in the body politic, throughout culture. Psychotic commands play a role in cementing groups together (couples, families, socioeconomic, political, military, cultural groups). Groups are called upon to contain and process the destructive tendencies that help bind them together.

Psychotic commands tend to gravitate around destructive nuclei. An individual is commanded by God to kill his child or partner or brother. The command often involves a close bond, someone who is part of him. One is supported and threatened by those who are closest. Bonds are packages of intense feelings fusing excitement, hate, caring, warp, frustration, injury, striving, longing. Bonds suffocate and nourish. An aim of murder is freedom, to break away, to clear out, but, Freud points out, guilt intensifies bonds.

Guilt is somewhat lessened by killing enemies, those a little farther away, strangers, "others." Other groups, other lands, other interests. Psychotic command invisibly works through stubborn, if imaginary, self-interest, urging destructive scenarios as solutions to grievance. Lack of guilt, however, boomerangs, has its own destructive consequences, involving growth of arrogance, self-righteousness, and ghastly misjudgments concerning what is happening in those one attacks. Loss of ethical sensitivity and feeling for others goes along with poisonous lies about one's own state of mind.

There is plenty of biblical destruction of enemies. My emphasis is on intimate destruction, destruction of what is close. We are made of so many emotional cross-currents and conflicting tendencies—intimate bonds bear the stress of everything in us, everything that makes us up. Most murders by individuals are of lovers and family members and, also, of oneself (suicide accounts for nearly half of individual murders worldwide, more than half in the United States). Proximity plays a role in murder between national groups as well. There is often some kind of bond with the other that one tries to kill.

The closest bonds sometimes bring out the most madness. The Abraham-Isaac story is packed, a veritable repository of insanity, a fossil of strands of madness left by ancient human beings, a psychic fossil still alive today. Packed, impacted, impacting. Fascinating, chilling, repulsive, challenging. In the madness of life today, it is important to be sensitive to insanity. Without such sensitivity, one is endangered by becoming one with, or deflecting, dementia that needs attention.

The Abraham-Isaac story, called the *akedah*, "binding," in Judaism, relates to other stories from antiquity. Cronus kills his children; Oedipus and his father try to kill each other and one succeeds. It almost does not matter who wins. The murderous impulse works both ways, parents killing children, children killing parents. Murder goes in either direction within and across generations. The impulse is a constant, while subject and object reverse, oscillate, shift roles. Infanticide, matricide, patricide, fratricide—among the great themes of literature. Literature turns the flashlight on destructive desires, part of a vast, ongoing attempt to see and feel who we are. One would like to think that awareness of our makeup plays a role in the evolution of sensibility, but that remains to be seen. We do not appear to tire of murder.

Fantasies involving death and murder are part of parent-child relationships, often melded with dread of loss. Unfortunately, they are not confined to fantasy and feelings. But even feelings have powerful and long-lasting consequences. Parental death wishes toward a child may precipitate a lifelong tendency toward depression. Psychoanalysis suggests that such feelings are mutual, part of being an alive human being. Karl Abraham depicts infants as having cannibalistic fantasies, eating mother's insides, taking feelings in with milk. One makes mother part of oneself, a process involving making another oneself and oneself another. Hans Loewald suggests that the fight for life between parents and children is intensely real, with health costs to each. He depicts a struggle in which a parent may have to choose which life to support or even save, his or her own or the child's. Influence and fear of influence have early roots and are double edged. We take in others or aspects of others in order to grow, yet what we take in distorts as well as releases us. Influence can seem a kind of death, a possession, infiltration or taking over of self by another. Fusions of death and enrichment haunt and spur the self and partly account for the state of permanent bewilderment of human personality.

Why did Abraham listen to God, if not because from the place of permanent bewilderment, nothing sounds too crazy (it all is crazy). This mixture of madness and bewilderment is what everyone tries to rationalize. The *akedah* is nothing if not bewildering and mad. One rationale involves a sense of being better. Others may kill their children, but *we* do not. Child sacrifice is out. Human sacrifice is out. When I was a child in Hebrew school, it almost sounded as if human sacrifice was the norm and only Jews had moral sense enough not to kill their children. How proud to be a son of Abraham, of a people who respected life. The point was not simply that Abraham listened to God, but that God and man managed to swerve from intrafamilial murder in the nick of time, establishing a higher ethics (just the opposite of blood libel).

God and Abraham's "solution" to the death impulse was not permanent. Human destruction of humans continues. There is always some portion of humanity that conceives an irresistible urge to take control of death by perpetrating it. Even in Abraham's family, deathwork, once started, had consequences. The story does not end happily. It is said that Sarah died of a heart attack upon hearing that Abraham was going to kill Isaac or upon thinking, afterward, that he might have.

There are many rationalizations of the *akedah*, including mystical ones. In Kabbalah, Abraham represents divine lovingkindness, which unites with and tempers severity (so that caring can be effective in a world where severity rules). Abraham's knife on Isaac's throat mediates transfer or infusion of love into a cutthroat world. The swerve from murder at the crucial moment is a victory of love over cruelty. May it always be so. Ambivalence binds, and which side wins at any time is part of our drama. The *akedah* unfolds as a narrative but suggests a psychic field in which multiple tendencies densely fuse and incessantly redistribute themselves.

Some say Abraham did murder Isaac, but Isaac was resurrected. The hand that holds the knife cannot stop once it swings into motion. Death has a momentum of its own. Benjamin Britten's "War Requiem" explores the knife that does not stop.

For Kierkegaard, as for many Jewish interpreters, what is most important in the story is precisely what can't be rationalized: Abraham's faith in God and God's in Abraham, a faith subtending or transcending usual, naturalistic ethics, a mystery to be entered with fear and trembling and, one might add, deepest joy. The heart of mystery is awe—trembling, boundless wonder, curiosity, dread, and miraculous joy.

Add a dash of psychoanalysis and one sees in the *akedah* dense compression of a most troubling parental tension, struggle with one's impulse to injure a child one loves. A tension more widespread than many imagine. I have seen many parents bravely struggle with urges to injure, even kill, their children, and I have heard of many who failed in this struggle. Stories, myths, fairy tales, dramas of harm befalling children, especially at the hands of intimates, express realities on many levels.

From this vantage point, God's order to kill Isaac represents a displaced and disowned destructive movement in Abraham himself, a destructive element that typifies God's reactivity throughout the Bible. God is like a parent who breaks down and rages when faced with a bad child, lashing out destructively. It's as if God can't take people as they are, not too much of them, very like a parent who can't bear the mounting tensions of child-rearing. Humans push God to the brink and over to fatal tantrums. Something of a nuclear rage in family life, at the navel of the unbearable, hemorrhages through the pages of the Bible.

We hear of Spartans killing weak infants in hopes of strengthening their city-state. In almost opposite fashion, there are variations on the theme of killing babies one fears will grow up to displace existing authority. Freud's fantasy in *Totem and Taboo* of sons killing fathers was not pulled out of an empty hat. Important as they are in their own right, such threads of destruction mask deeper questions the *akedah* hints at: can people bear themselves? to what extent are they up to their makeup? how much of themselves and each other can people take? Anxiety festers and thrives at the root of the human capacity to nurture and raise children. The issue of destruction in the family, the fusion of destructive and generative aspects of bonds, complements issues of destruction in the state.

Destruction is the more awful because of the intensity of love. Destruction alone is easy to grasp, if not bear. But mixtures of love and destruction at the core of family feeling stymie the soul. How can you hurt me if you love me? How can you love me if you hurt me? Questions every person lives with. Sometimes hurt is beyond bearable bounds, piercing the heart beyond repair. Sometimes so much destructive energy melds with love that love becomes damaging.

Some manifestations of destructive energy seem relatively innocent. A mother voices fear for her baby. She is afraid of dropping or otherwise harming the baby by motherly ministrations. Natural enough, perhaps. One empathizes with this mother's fearful care, lack of trust in herself, fear of her own energy. But probe a bit and reach dread of destruction. Her own parents knew pogroms and fled Eastern Europe in hope and anxiety. Catastrophe anxiety spread through generations. Once-real dangers translate into parental apprehension, so that mother's touch mixes boundless worry with boundless tenderness. Even while the baby is affirmed and prospers, it starves for the other energy held back out of fear. Here the mother is too cautious, her grip on the knife too tight, her grip on her strength too tight. Self-suffocation is buried in love. The balance between thrust and holding is jeopardized, and the baby grows in nearly constant inner crises. In this case, the father was given to outbursts of rage. As in the Bible, rage and gentleness suffer dramatic distribution. I'm not sure there is real tenderness or personal intimacy in the Bible, but the play of anger and mercy or lovingkindness, try to make up for it. It is perhaps the rule, rather than the exception, that in human history, generic emotions run off without real intimacy.

Some analysts might see in the mother's fear a hidden desire, a repressed wish for infant destruction, mixed with a history of repressed/dissociated destructive tendencies and strangulated trauma. One seeks what one dreads. A formula like this, true as it can be, must be used cautiously. A deeper law is compassion in the face of possible truth: do not pin a person to her psyche. There is always more to warrant care, creases in the soul as yet invisible.

There is gain in comparing the *akedah* with Freud's version of Michelangelo's Moses. For Freud, Moses burned with an intensity of rage restrained with even greater intensity. He imagines Moses holding back his urge to destroy the tablets, absorbing or, at least, for the moment, binding a destructive surge. There are many obvious differences between the *akedah* and Freud's depiction of Moses binding his rage. Moses is coming down the mountain, Abraham and Isaac are going up. God told Abraham to destroy his son and Moses to give laws binding destruction. These and other details have significance, but they are variations around core affect constellations that persist through changing emphases.

Freud's feeling that Moses was holding back rage so as not to destroy the commandments differs from the usual view that Moses was about to trash the stones, the actual Bible story. Such an innovative interpretation, characteristic of Freud, has enormous significance. As usual, Freud fingers an Achilles heel of the psyche, putting the searchlight on struggle with rage, a privileged destructive nerve. To smash the tablets, to kill a child, not exactly strong literal parallels, but compelling lineaments of a destructive pulse are there. The intensity of struggle in the face of destructive energy in Freud's depiction of Moses illuminates the possibility of Abraham's struggle as well. A turn of the

Freudian kaleidoscope and one sees intrapsychic tensions as well as tensions between individuals and groups. One of Freud's layerings on an ancient theme, humanity's struggles with its passions, sears the *akedah*: a father binds death wishes toward his son, barely averting disaster.

As ragers know, the temptation to unleash disaster is always there. It sneaks up on you, takes you from behind, exploding the moment your guard is down. You never know when you'll be at its mercy. Destruction comes, and the price is paid in injury and grief. What we have with Abraham and Freud's Moses is momentary victory through struggle with oneself. Both point to a crucial dimension of experience that needs cultivation, a sore spot in human nature that needs every ounce of strength we can muster: the perennial challenge to oppose oneself. A kind of self-strengthening and growth through self-opposition.

Conflict is an important tool for intensifying subjectivity. Without intensity of conflict, personality remains jejune. In my version of Abraham and of Freud's version of Michelangelo's Moses, emphasis is on intensity of struggle, holding back but not simply holding back. One develops a holding environment for one's own being, a frame for waiting. Waiting on a feeling is not simply waiting a feeling out or putting oneself on hold, important as these are. To wait on a feeling allows reverie, imaginative reflection, a "feel" for oneself and one's situation, to grow. At the height of impossible struggle, one holds the self like a mother holds a baby. Holding as a prayer for development.

It is unlikely Abraham and Moses consciously thought of developing a holding environment for themselves. They hold themselves to bind destruction, to swerve from a destructive outcome, to hold the other safe from themselves. The "other" in each instance is one close to themselves. The child, too, is Israel, the Jewish people, and the particular seeds of God-awareness they mediate.

It is fitting that the Moses story begins with the saving of a child. Tensions radiate through a diversity of pairings, within and between families, peoples, territories, genders, generations. Moses, found in a basket as a baby, is over seventy when his true life's work begins. Abraham's most profound challenges occur in old age in relation to a child. Tensions between old-young reverberate within a single life, as well as between generations. A constant theme is the saving and protection of life from death dealing forces within self, God, nature, communities—vicissitudes of strife. It is not clear from these stories that difficulties can be solved, but it is clear that they must be worked with. Struggle begets new capacities. Abraham's and Moses' God-connection evolves into new possibilities of faith and law. The promise of further growth and struggle is passed on to us.

Abraham and Freud's Moses refuse to give in to themselves. They signal a grueling victory of love and faith over the destructive urge, a faith requiring fierce effort. One holds and grips and presses oneself with all one's might. The child self held by the mother undergoes enormous development. Faith babies born in fierce struggle inevitably are problem children, a fact humanity needs to absorb. It is a dangerous illusion to think that anyone is outside pressures of basic growth difficulties.

Freud described incessant struggle between love and destruction (e.g., life and death drives). In mystical Judaism, the conflict is between good and evil inclinations. In Freud's earlier writings, destructive tendencies are built into love as well (e.g., aggression is a part of desire; libido manifests itself in sadomasochistic ways). A hope is that love-faith-knowledge hold and work with destruction, turning the latter to good use. A fragile balance, often reversing, all the worse since love, faith, and knowledge often take destructive turns.

The sheer force of wrestling with oneself is important not only for growth and ethical behavior but for filling out one's sense of how life feels, what is possible and, perhaps, a little beyond possible. We push edges of experience in many directions, including poles of indulgence and severity. Some people favor physical exercises that pit muscle against muscle, muscle against barriers. Exertion reaches a maximum at which muscle gives way, leading to strengthening. There are times one needs to exert this kind of pressure on oneself psychically, with the paradoxical result that experience gives way, opening previously unavailable dimensions of experiencing. The capacity to pay attention does amazing things. Whatever it burns into opens. We use this gift to make money, weapons, art, medicine. Is it possible to become the kind of persons that can use entrancing physical, mental, emotional, and political gifts in less deforming ways?

Destruction—and the turn away from destruction—has been a nearly ubiquitous theme in myth and literature. A subspecialty of Abraham and Moses is talking God out of destruction. To talk God out of rage, to talk through feelings rather than evacuate them—an informal model for a bit of psychoanalysis. Psychoanalysis plays on this corner of human nature, mutual influence through affective verbal exchange. We see from the Bible that bargaining was an ancient art. With Abraham and God we have an intimate form of bargaining, like a mother trying to lift a baby's mood or realign attitudes when they go off kilter.

A key bargaining chip for Abraham was any bit of human goodness. Recall the story of Sodom and Gomorrah. Abraham reasons with God. What would be the minimum goodness required to avert destruction? Fifty, forty, thirty—ten good men? As it turned out, there were not ten good men in Sodom, and God destroyed the city, although Abraham's kinsman, Lot, was saved. As happens throughout the Bible, God's destruction is not total. Germs of goodness survive.

A key bargaining chip for Moses was faith, manifested as fidelity to contract, God's covenant. God repeatedly threatens to destroy His people and Moses talks Him down. He appeals to God's shame, pride, and loyalty. Does He want people to think ill of Him? Does He want others to think Him a lesser god, powerless in the face of wayward man? How will it look if He destroys those He chose to serve Him? Who would His people be then? Is God helpless in the face of human evil? Is He fickle? Can God be guilty of infidelity? Fidelity filtered through ego, ego filtered through fidelity. Annihilation waves are unleashed time and again, but circumscribed. God sends plagues, fire, and righteous people to kill the unrighteous; but his wrath is appeased with less than total destruction, and life goes on. By the time the Hebrews begin their campaign to occupy Canaan and Moses is going to die, their head count is about the same as when they entered the wilderness. Moses succeeded in protecting the Israelites from themselves and from the God he mediated. Replenishment continues.

The Bible oscillates between dialogue and destruction. If the former cannot stop destruction, it may at least lessen it. Had Noah tried to talk God out of the flood, the disaster might not have been as great. It is hard to learn that talking feelings through matters. In so much worldly life, the power of destruction might appear the greater argument. Still, one hopes that talking gains some ground. Psychoanalysis, the talking cure, the listening cure, the writing cure, the relating cure—one way that dialogical reality grips the soul.

To struggle with oneself with all one's might and come down on the side of caring for the life of others is how I read the *akedah*, a binding that is transforming. One cannot take for granted that this kind of caring will occur. Too often the Bible cares more about principles or ideals than people. To protect the sanctity of the other, the right of others to live, to live fully—a necessary, if difficult or even impossible, striving, let alone achievement. To grapple with destructive tendencies, one's own and others, is an ever necessary beginning. Part of the horror of the *akedah* is the horror of recognition of severe and deeply lodged ambivalence toward children, as experienced with our parents, they with theirs. It is hard to see and bear so much destruction in love, love in destruction. This omnipresent mixture is part of what makes us recoil in recognition when Abraham takes the knife to Isaac and does not use it. A scenario we know too well, central in our makeup. Impulse and counterimpulse, an identity-defining pattern. If we are alive, we survived, many times, parental threat of destruction. We pray we destroy our children less. Yes, we hope for their economic well being, their oedipal triumphs. But deep down we pray they survive us, their familial beginnings, with less damage to self.

I have parents in therapy who fear injuring, even killing, their children. They mean something literal and final, not just psychological: throwing a baby against a wall, drowning, smashing, stabbing, burning it. Many times a day they are tempted and draw back, a repetitious *akedah* of sorts, love clawing its way through destruction, the two *nearly* indistinguishable.

What Abraham goes through is, one or another way, repeated by parents, sometimes myriad times a moment. The feeling of life threatened, precarious, saved in the nick of time. We escape the knife once more, not always, not forever. Relief after fright creates a powerful rhythm in emotional life. Shock, fear, threat, danger—coming through, survival, renewal. A profound sense of living through dangers, especially our own dangerous natures, becomes part of the background of our beings, part of an unconscious rhythm that molds and grips us throughout life.

Freud analogized life-death currents to anabolic-catabolic rhythms of metabolism: building up, breaking down. He saw every psychic act as made up of the two tendencies, at times functioning more creatively or more destructively. My emphasis has been on affective attitudes that penetrate our being, a nuclear sense of threat and survival, danger and relief. How, moment to moment and over time, we move through destruction to a little more life—or fail to.

The movement through destruction plays out in many ways. It includes a double sense of destroying other and self, then finding both alive. We re-form after destruction. For example, destruction by the flood (emotional storm) followed by regeneration and renewal. After massive destruction of humankind by the flood, the Bible emphasizes repeated destruction of Israel and survival of a (good!?) remnant. Of course, many other peoples are killed in the process, for "good" or "bad" reasons. Twists of ethics and survival is a mean and lethal business. The identification of self-interest with the good is a widespread malady today, masking as health, and extremely dangerous.

The children of Israel. The use of children as an image of godly relationship—Israel, God's children—is alarming, not just comforting. We know what happens to children in the Bible. God's blade on Israel's neck, a blade that binds. A binding blade? And Israel survives—barely.

As the Bible darkly hints, familial pressures are exerted every which way, children on parents, parents on children, sibling on sibling, within and between couples. Children are idealized, cast off, killed, almost killed. Parents are heartbroken. The Bible is littered with broken bodies and hearts. God, the parent, is ever grieved, destined for disappointment, righteous rage. The Bible alerts us, if we can take it in, to the rage that parents and children share, that courses through humanity. God is the aggrieved and injured parent par excellence, writing large with cosmic lettering the story of wounded parental narcissism. Fury and forgiveness are two of God's horns that gore us, as we try to dive through space between them.

God's children forever provoke threats, although we are not told how Isaac provoked Abraham, not only to lift his hand, but a knife. The fact that we hold Isaac blameless brings out more intensely conflicts and tensions that parents are heir to. The very fact of a child and pressures of child-rearing are enough to bring out monstrous tendencies in human beings. One can imagine Abraham trying to control feelings that the pressures of parenting provoke. Even good children, precious and loved, wreak havoc in parental souls. The image of Abraham lifting his hand and battling with the knife bears witness to deformations parents go through, if only by trying to keep up with a child's states and crises, as parents and children succeed or fail at growing. A reality the biblical God and His people express is how difficult it is to be a parent or a child. The challenge exerted on each by the fact of being themselves requires growth in ability to suffer being human. To suffer being human includes wrestling with oneself.

Meditation on what it means to suffer human personality is part of lifelong stretching processes. Hopefully, better balances of flexibility, resilience, and persistence will lessen the horrors we perpetuate. But if the Bible teaches anything, it is that we ought not minimize the difficulties of living together. If we cannot solve them, if we are not up to grappling with them, we still can grow by living through them.

Whatever else the *akedah* means, it expresses a drama between destruction and care that plagues the psyche, constitutes the psyche, in some sense *is* the psyche. One ought not discount the emotive dilemmas because power is given to the male parent (God, Abraham). Nor should one dismiss emotional struggles by viewing male power as a way of downplaying or controlling the defining impacts children and women have. Gender politics, important as it is, does not have the last word when it comes to suffering our beings. Even when the roles and rights of women and children have their new day, the struggle between destruction and caring will continue. Subjects and scenes vary, but core agonistic tensions go on begging for creative, compassionate work. The Abraham-Isaac story teaches that murder need not have the last word. Something else or something more can happen. We can hold back, but not only hold back. Our relationship with God and self and others can take a different turn. *Must* take different turns.

10 Guilt

Guilt tends to act as a barrier against emotional storms but creates its own storms. It binds, suppresses, holds back—a kind of brakes associated with bad deeds, thoughts, inclinations. We try to stop ourselves from doing what we might be guilty for. Stopping refers to inner as well as outer acts, as we avoid or stamp out thoughts and feelings that arouse too much guilt.

More recently, guilt is associated with transgressions against self, as well as against others. Not simply bad we do, but good we fail to do, especially with regard to living the fullest, best life possible. We speak of existential guilt, failure to actualize potential, guilt over unlived life. A strange but powerful bird, this newish guilt, life not lived, a person one failed to become. More broadly, guilt is suffered over failure to do others or self justice, to do life justice. It connects with the ability to enrich, deplete, or damage the life of others or oneself.

Guilt is one of the great themes of literature. Before our time, it tended to be associated with bad things done. Oedipus blinds himself when he sees his guilt. Lady Macbeth washes fathomless bloodstains off her hands. The connection of guilt with blindness cuts deep. It is not simply that we are guilty for things we know we do. We are, also, guilty for actions that escape attention, that we fail to relate to or understand. It is not simply that Oedipus killed his father and married his mother or that he did this without knowing it. It is more that rage and eros are parts of our makeup, and we cannot escape their destructive aspect no matter what we do.

This may sound like cause for despair, but it is also goad to repair, to make reparation, at-onement. A vicious circle for some, destruction and repair ad infinitum and ad nauseam without change and without benefit. But guilt and reparation, deeply felt, *can* open unsuspected dimensions of personality, lead the way to uncharted areas of experience. Guilt as discipline, spur, penetrating agent into something unknown.

Lady Macbeth is something else. Unlike in Greek tragedy, where guilt catches us no matter what we do, even when we try to do good, Lady Macbeth tries to rise above the evil she intends, hardens herself, hopes to be immune. The power of ambition, the power of power, should be enough to blot out guilt. Throughout history, guilt is associated with violence and, with Lady Macbeth, not just murder but mental violence, a violence toward her self. She aims to amputate the breast of guilt, as if her feelings were a cancer. To shut out guilt is to shut out weakness. The insight of Greek tragedy prevails in this psychological experiment, as guilt returns at night, in dreams, in sleepwalking—the stain of the blood of feelings. That the blood of guilt cannot be rinsed off indicates something bottomless about guilt.

Lady Macbeth and Oedipus are different psychological creatures. He seeks to right things, to expiate, to reconcile. Of course, things cannot be righted, but he can take his sin and leave the land, shoulder his life, seek another way. She is unrepentant. For her, guilt signifies failure. It is not that she feels bad about murdering. She feels bad about not murdering successfully enough. Like Hitler's, her suicide is not penitential, but a result of power-driven hopes unraveling. She chose to murder her way to the heights, murder in service to lust for power. She is never humbled from within. She goes as far as she can before reality thrusts her back. To kill herself as she wished to kill others expresses the arc of her drive returning to its source. Passion and malice destroy her as surely as an overpowering storm or the sword of betters. Will strikes against limits and discloses madness.

One could argue suicide as failed expiation, repentance gone wrong, aborted rebirth, and sometimes this is the case. Had Lady Macbeth been able to be repentant, she might not have had to kill herself. Again, Lady Macbeth's murderous hand, murderous mind, turning against itself, can embody the judgment of the world. My larger sense is that her suicide was the culmination of a process that led to hell when gold at the end of the rainbow was envisioned (although her rainbow was largely black and red to start with). She could not believe her plans went wrong. She tried to snare and encompass the world with a contracting self the world would not shrink to fit, and she followed her contraction to its gory end. The weakness she refused came back to swallow her. If repentance fails in its developmental function, weakness collapses in on itself and takes us with it. She could not undergo the deeper psychospiritual suicide Oedipus tasted, which makes living possible.

Bloody and blind. Realization that humankind does not know what it is doing, which Jesus linked with forgiveness, is a start.

Do not worship false gods. Do not kill or steal or envy and take what is your neighbor's. Respect your parents, love God, love your neighbor as yourself. Don't do to others what you wouldn't want done to you or what you find hateful.

When I was young and hated my father, I used to joke about the commandment to respect your parents: if you can respect your parents, you can respect anyone. It was a joke that went along with a variation of the love-your-neighbor theme. *Ahavas Yisroel*—love Israel—love your fellow Jew. My joke: if you can love your fellow Jew, you can love anyone.

When I was older I came to feel that these commandments gave exterior form to an inner principle, a particular inner experience, an ethical revelation. The ethical sensation may or may not be associated with guilt. What seemed to me more primordial than guilt was the felt realization that we were alive, precious, amazing, thrilling—capable of injury, joy, caring. This was not a matter of guilt but an immediate, positive apprehension of reality.

Similarly, the injunction to love God with all your heart and soul and might. An experience of loving God that permeates one's whole being is translated into an objectified, exteriorized commandment. Moses saw God, spoke with God. If only he could have kept expressing *that*. But he channeled personal encounter through commandments, laws, rewards/punishments. Immediate vision and ethical realization became dos and don'ts, a handbook. What a handbook! It may have short-circuited the God-experience, but also preserved it, bound it, embalmed it, whet appetite for excavation, for renewal.

When I was young, I never understood aspects of the Jewish service that emphasized returning to the way things were at the time of the ancient temple in Jerusalem. The wish to return, to go back. One of the most beautiful moments of the service, *chadesh yomanu kekedem*, a melody of heartfelt, soulful beauty, translates something like "renew our days as of old." I don't think most Jews want to go back to the way things were, sacrificing animals in Solomon's temple. The thought of doing so constricted my heart, shortened my breath. At last it dawned on me that a few lines before, the song cries, "Let us return to You, Hashem." To You, God Himself, not an angel, not a messenger, not a temple. Turn to God, return through God. A life of renewal as such, the thing itself, an affair of quality. Not turning back the clock. Turning to the breather of life, transformational tuning in. A challenge to remake life, to make life better. A moment that opens everything. Going through God opens a heart smile that never ends.

A heart smile is not enough when it comes to daily living. The Bible documents aggression, seduction, vanities, jealousies, power lusts, you name it. Laws work up to a point but proliferate in the face of breakdowns. As Jewish codification mushrooms, nearly every part of life is regulated by law. Still, transgressions continue: infidelity to God, murder, robbery, destructive rivalry, together with a good thread, remnant, seed.

No law can take the place of immediate experiencing: O my God. We are precious. Life is precious, not cheap. How can we murder, steal, envy? How can we live without a primacy of love?

Guilt signals something less than love. As a signal, it keeps us growing, aiming for better.

As a signal, it can spread, go haywire, rush to keep up with proliferating laws. Even then, it can help inculcate respect, drive a wedge between impulse and action. But guilt, like law, can become cancerous, lose touch with basic vision, basic goodness. Lose touch with the fact that it mediates something more, something beyond itself. Guilt, like law, can take on a life of its own, turn into an idol. Guilt becomes a kind of god one worships, trapped in guilt.

An instinctive reaction to traps is to break free.

Would freedom from guilt entail freedom from social organization or freedom from law? In the collective, laws and punishment seem necessary. This is likely for individuals too, insofar as fear and guilt modulate behavior and thought. Guilt piggybacks, parasites on law as well as supports it. At their best, law and guilt sustain and renew each other in positive ways, even if they are easily degraded.

Yet a moment's loving God—loving anyone—is its own reward. Love is intrinsic, the thing itself. Nothing exterior to it is necessary. In reality, we need to incarnate love, make it daily bread, live it with real others. Law from the outside and guilt from the inside act as signals, as guides, help us steer. Still, the moment in which the heart sees God or feels the heart of another person is a privileged reference point. No stick or carrot can take its place.

An originary dimension before or deeper than guilt seems to be implied by the Garden of Eden story. Paradise first, then guilt and punishment. An age of innocence followed by suffering. Are things so clear? The serpent was in the garden too, right there in the age of innocence, already afoot (belly came later). Freud cracked a taboo relating to childhood innocence-sexuality. A greater taboo is recognition of the ubiquity of infantile suffering.

Serpent awaiting his cue might be translated as potential awaiting unfolding. The right time, the right circumstances and, poof, up comes the devil in a Punch and Judy show. As in William Blake's prophesies, evil appears.

Before and after in the narrative represent concentric states, or states condensed and enfolded into each other, or coincident. A simultaneous layering of moments that feel better or worse, more heavenly, more hellish. An ordinary before-after manifestation of this sequence represents change of states—now I feel great, now I feel horrible. Better and worse moments get blown up, infinitized, absolutized, abstracted from their counterparts.

While I affirm a joyous moment unsullied by guilt—heart's ineffable smile—guilt lies waiting. While unbeknown, with unconscious serpent wile, we sail, like the Titanic, to meet it.

In my translation of Bion, guilt has no head or tail or legs. It is an emotion or state or intention or disposition awaiting subjects and objects to form it. It is part of an emotional field we are born into, an emotion awaiting experience, awaiting an experiencer. Like thoughts in search of a thinker or characters in search of an author, feelings are sometimes in search of a feeler. Guilt awaits us as we grow into it. We are inserted into guilt as we are into language or a social field. It is part of a field of experience we cannot step out of, anymore than we can breathe without air.

The oedipalization of guilt gives some toehold, some method of organization, a way to try to grab it. Here is sin, crime, murder, incest. An explanation. We are guilty because we are unconsciously incestuous murderers. Not always unconsciously. Eros and destruction are psychic movements that guilt feeds and piggybacks on. One tries to break free of guilt by means of transgressions that give one a high for a while but increase guilt in the long run. Violence and sex compound problems they try to solve, problems they partly give rise to, leaving us mired in an emotive morass with no solution. At some point, it is important to realize that we live in an emotional morass with no solution. If only it were so easy as incest and murder, baby, mother and father—if only we could pin tails on psyches. But baby, mother and father are born into seas of guilt they form into patterns. They spontaneously distribute guilt between themselves in a variety of typical ways.

Bion writes, "The idea of cause belongs to criminal investigation." Feelings of guilt attach to causality as a mode of organizing the latter. "I am guilty of, you are, or someone is, guilty of. Someone must have done something." From the criminal, causal viewpoint, person precedes guilt, does something to bring it about. Someone must have caused it because here it is. For a time, guilt resolves into searching for a culprit, a criminal thing. Guilt contracts into causal notions that try to control or contain it, mastery attempts that often make the infection worse. Overestimation of control where emotions are concerned is partly delusional.

Where does guilt come from? People create stories with their lives to track it down. Stories are like lenses that bring guilt into focus. We pin guilt down with our stories, even if we have to kill, subjugate, and seduce to create explanatory handles. Even if guilt and injury go together and someone is always doing something to someone, it can be difficult to discriminate who is doing what to whom. Formless guilt spreads through scenarios involving subjects and objects claiming credit and clarity. To explain guilt is to explain injury.

Sometimes it is possible to say, "That parent is beating her child." It *is her* fault, and indeed it is. She *must* be held accountable for this beating. One looks into the parent and sees mangled insides, scars, wounds, madness, hurt, deformity, no beginning or end to injury. To start with this parent is real but also artificial. There is a sea of injury we share, and handles we grab slip away. Surely, a parent that beats her child can be helped?! That is a question and exclamation because sometimes she can and sometimes she can't, and we may not know how things will turn out. Can a social structure that starves (emotionally or physically) its citizens be fixed? Do we have to know where guilt comes from in order to feed and comfort? To think or pretend or feel we have to know delays caring, reaching out, trying to find a healing way.

To be inserted into an emotional field—here a guilt field—or to claim possession of it is an important crossroads. There is a tendency to suppose that if guilt appears, then a person or thing must have "caused it and be antecedent to it." This forecloses the possibility of an emotional field without ownership, a field we share.

Bion goes a step farther and notes there is "denial that the guilt caused it." The guilt caused what? For one thing, guilt in search of an explanation, a home, causes the oedipal situation. Life lives itself in ways that create plausible reasons for the guilt that one inhabits and that inhabits one. There certainly can't be reasonless guilt, can there? Guilt as an open set, part of our equipment, awaiting use?

Guilt in search of a home, a reason, acts as a force or pressure that people accommodate with all kinds of dramas, comic and tragic. One molds oneself to one's picture of guilt, as one attempts to give the latter form. In pride of self, egocentricity, we think we, or someone like us, must be the cause of what we are going through. Little by little, it is dawning on some of us that we are in this together. Solutions do not exist for the emotions we feel. This is less a cause for alarm than an occasion for freedom, if we think twice, and twice again, about how we justify the way we are.

What can it mean to say guilt is bigger than we are, that guilt precedes us, rather than the reverse? Is it a lie to humor us into better existence, to tease us out of delusional mastery? Or an attempt to broaden our sense of feelings we live together, that we partly co-create as we go along, an interactive, permeable field subtending one-sided ownership? "Cause" masks a dance of possibilities.

Bion muses, "In 'space,' does the infant have a left or right, before or after, or what? If it sees its foot and then its hand, does it feel its foot caused its hand?"

For the moment, space over time, if time is reduced to before and after. In space, at least, an appearance of simultaneity is easier to grasp. All the parts of a field are present at once in space, for a time, although we perceive them in unfolding profiles.

Can movement of eyes from foot to hand give rise to a causal intuition? Foot causes hand? Eyes cause both? The infant does not see its eyes when "it" is seeing. Yet a seer sees. Is the seer cause of all it sees? In time, seer will ponder who or what causes seeing as branches of thought and experience akin to religion and science grow.

Bion conveys the sense that hand and foot and eyes are parts of a larger field that "cause" does not quite cover. Guilt, like joy, sorrow, dread, fury, pity, caring, is part of a larger emotional field that "cause" precociously organizes and obscures.

John Heaton characterizes Wittgenstein's thought as rhizomatic rather than arboreal. "A rhizome (bulbs and tubers) . . . has diverse forms ramifying in all directions. Any point can be connected with any other. There is no ideal point closed on itself that serves as a foundation. It changes its nature as it increases in connections, but follows lines. It can be cracked and broken, but it starts off again following another of its lines. It is not answerable to any structural or generative model."

This sounds a little like what I have been trying to say about guilt. No beginning or end. We get inserted into it. It awaits use. It grows in all sorts of ways.

I doubt that Heaton's characterization (or mine) is adequate. One might suppose generative processes at work in bulbs and tubers. There are implicit generative processes at work in guilt. But *this* leads to *that* is hard to locate in any precise way. Generative principles or models fall short. Experience is quite a tangle. We can be cracked or broken but "start off again" following another line. It is not even clear that starting off is a clear starting off so much as a picking up of previously unnoticed threads. When does something start growing? By the time we discover a thread of consciousness a good deal of work has gone into it.

Freud speaks of a dream-wish growing "like a mushroom out of its mycelium." He speaks of the "dream's navel," "a tangle of dream-thoughts which cannot be unraveled," and which does not "have any definite endings," branching "out in every direction into the intricate network of our world of thought." One is tempted to bring Freud and Wittgenstein together, but how? Through Deleuze and Guatarri's image of the rhizome?

"A rhizome has no beginning or end; it is always in the middle, between things, interbeing, *intermezzo*." A middle that picks up speed, transports one between, between, between. Transitional.

No precise start or finish. "And . . . and . . . and . . ." In contrast with the tree and the verb "to be." Freud's mushroom and mycelium point to a theoretical beginning that reality loses, a foundation that can never be found. For Deleuze and Guatarri, Freud's mushroom may not be rhizomatic enough.

I think there is truth to Heaton's characterization of Wittgenstein's thought as rhizomatic. Nevertheless, Wittgenstein's writings on religion lead somewhere, which I might wrongly call a region of experience or being. Wittgenstein does not like to localize experience. As Wittgenstein points out, it is not a matter of a religious dimension, but of a religious life.

Over the years people have asked if Wittgenstein really was a believer and what that might mean. Was he *really* religious? This reminds me of high school in the 1950s when one asked, "Does she *really* do it?"

Wittgenstein mentions three kinds of experience that might be termed religious or that religious life draws on. He speaks from *his* experience, expressing how life is for him. One is wonder that the world exists, an experience of the miracle of existence. Another is a deep sense of safety, "the calm bottom of the sea at its deepest point, which remains calm however high the waves on the surface may be." A third is "absolute guilt." This last is associated with God's judgment, a judgment that runs through us with regard to how we feel and act toward others, a shudder of disgust we have at things we and others do. Feeling absolutely guilty is a ganglia with many filaments, one of the latter being a sense that "only religion would have the power to destroy vanity and penetrate all the nooks and crannies." Given absolute guilt, there is need for all the nooks and crannies to be subject to God's work, to transformation, to be part of the great change of life that religious experience portends, seeks, asks:

"Sound doctrines are all useless. . . . You have to change your *life*, or the *direction* of your life" (italics Wittgenstein's). Religious struggle, transformative struggle is necessary in this process, but it is not a boring, drab process. Everything is at stake. "'Wisdom is gray.' Life on the other hand and religion are full of colour."

Intense guilt can lead to God. In Wittgenstein's notes, God is associated with judgment and redemption, with suffering. Intense suffering connects with God. Of course, suffering can make us loathe God, deny God, render God irrelevant. But it also links us, some of us, to each other and to God.

"Life can educate one to a belief in God. And *experiences* too are what bring this about; but I don't mean visions and other forms of sense experience which show us the 'existence of this being,' but, e.g., sufferings of various sorts. These neither show us God in the way a sense impression shows us an object, nor do they give rise to *conjectures* about him. Experiences, thoughts, life—can force this concept on us."

Experiences, sufferings of various sorts force God on us. In this context, we are not debating whether or not God exists, or about particular details about his nature or our relationship with him. We are not asking what is possible. We are expressing what is.

We express God a little like we express pain. We might have less doubt about pain. But when suffering brings us to God, doubt is not what we are about. Nor are we about bludgeoning others with God, forcing our God on others. We are with God with our suffering. Not teaching a class, fighting a war, or making conversions.

A result of reaching God through suffering is renewed struggle with self. Suffering shows us something wrong with ourselves, a way of being, a propensity we are guilty about. We are suffering, in part, because we are guilty about our way of life.

We live from a place where there is a connection between suffering and ethics.

This, we know, is dangerous business, linking ethics and suffering. We are aware of guilt as cancerous, proliferating, stifling. Guilt infuses pseudo-morality, moral tyranny, murderous superego. It is, as so much is, Janus-like, depressing life, opening possibility. Guilt is cruel, persecutory, inhumane, pitiless, demoralizing. Yet it is humanizing, allied with caring. How can guilt be pitiless and caring? It contracts us, narrows us, pierces through our heart, brings us to deeper places.

At this point, I do not want to speak about useless suffering, suffering that is a by-product of illness or exploitation of power. There is a lot of meaningless suffering that is part and parcel of what life does to us and what we do to each other. My wish is to paint a picture of an amazing fact of suffering—at least for some people, some of the time. My aim is not to celebrate suffering but to bear witness to a possibility.

Suffering opens worlds. Not always, not with all people. But frequently enough to warrant appreciative regard. There have been times when suffering compelled my attention, sucked my mind into it so totally that I almost blanked out, perhaps did blank out, and what a moment earlier had been acute emotional pain turned into: (1) beatific, radiant light; (2) more variegated emotional fields with bright and light spots of shifting density-diffusion; (3) appreciative apprehension of the miracle of feelings and the magical transformations they undergo; (4) an ethical commitment to bettering life, living better, or, at least, sharing appreciation for our amazing experiential reality.

The above four elements scarcely touch the surface. The moment-to-moment nuances of feeling to feeling waves and reverberations permeate over and underneath skin, trickle through insides, dissolve downward, tingle with fingers of delight, invisible brushes turning unknown insides into canvases. Heart opens, love grows.

Such moments subside, and the work of love requires real living, setbacks, fresh tries, scraping shells, more suffering, more struggle.

As time goes on, struggle becomes a constant. The fight with one's nature is never-ending. Yet struggle interacts with grace, with good feeling, beatific feeling, with faith. So that neither feeling good nor struggle has the last word.

Guilt does not necessarily stop one from doing other things. But it adds to each moment a dire import, as if the future hangs on what is happening now, every moment a generative womb. I will still go swimming, hear the waves, stare blankly out the window, watch TV, waste time. I like to feel my body doing nothing. But I will also fight personal battles, struggle with addiction to vanity and abusiveness, modulate capacity to injure self and others, fight against settling for less than what I can give. Life is precious, a miracle. We are parts of this amazingness. We are this amazingness. Guilt is part of this miracle too. It signals, goads, guides. If anxiety is a signal of danger, guilt is a signal of caring.

Two people moving a filled-to-tipping wheelbarrow across a bumpy terrain rely on mutual sensing to get from here to there. It is not something one thinks out. An implicit intelligence gets the feel of the load, terrain, and partner, modulates subtle movements to shifting factors as one goes along. Guilt plays a modulating role in getting along together as a relationship moves from here to there. It is part of a larger field of social sensing, self-to-self sensing, spontaneously adjusting volume, intensity, affect coloring as we move along. At times, guilt helps us sense who we are and how much we can take before the wheelbarrow tips. Of course, tipping can be fun, like tipping a canoe over in a refreshing stream. One does not want to pull back in time or wants to only a little. There are less benign situations in which one prays to be able to stop or prays that, at least, destruction leads to learning.

Concentration on anything opens worlds. Not just guilt, joy. Is it harder to concentrate on joy than on suffering? Suffering compels, galvanizes. When we suffer, we know something needs attention. The gift of joy comes and goes freely. We enjoy it as we can. It lifts us, and we sway with it, light branches in wind. We know it does not last and take pleasure in its passing. We welcome it as it comes, express gratitude as it leaves. Why focus on joy as we do on pain? Yet a certain kind of attentiveness coupled with immersion in experience opens worlds of joy, as Dante's reflective persistence discovers infinite gradations of heaven.

Few writers other than saints express links between guilt, self-opening, responsibility, and caring for others more intensely than Wittgenstein and Levinas. The latter two share a sense that guilt engenders open-heartedness, open-handedness. Living engenders guilt as a caring about the life one lives and the lives of others. Both find God in the life of man.

For Wittgenstein, at times, radical statements express radical living. He read the gospels in the army during World War I and gave away his wealth when he returned. He wrote tortured confessions of weakness, his sinful nature, which he showed to superiors and friends. Did he imagine he could rid himself of sin by exposing it? Life regroups, and the worst of life regroups too. He could not get rid of himself by giving away his wealth or through painful confession. His honesty was lacerating, but self persists. Even late in life he turned down talks and positions, not wanting to represent himself as better than he was.

There is a suffering, a torment in his life that reminds me of

Hazel Motes in Flannery O'Connor's *Wise Blood*, the erstwhile "saint" who wore barbed wire under his coat, a barbed wire inside us. A torment more part of the human than many like to believe.

One can point to Wittgenstein's trauma pool, a history leading to suicide for his three brothers. One can correlate torment with trauma. One can, also, do the reverse and say, "Look where trauma and torment can lead, what suffering can distil." Not just what one does with what one is given. There is a watering down of experience by saying, "Many are traumatized, what will *you* do with it?" Wittgenstein opens this box and lets the real shine out. Look where suffering *can* lead, what torment *opens*.

Experiences, thoughts, sufferings, living, force the concept of God on us. God as an idea that is not speculative, not maybe—not if, and, or but. A concept of God that is part of the grip of life. There is nothing trifling in this thought of Wittgenstein's. It is a life-and-death matter. For Wittgenstein, Christianity is not a doctrine, not a theory about the human soul, "but a description of an actual occurrence in human life. For 'consciousness of sin' is a real event, and so are despair and salvation through faith. Those who speak of such things . . . are simply describing what has happened to them."

In a similar vein, Wittgenstein is less interested in the gospels as literal or historical narrative than as a force that changes living. To take it as a question of history waters it down. As food for living, spiritual necessity, as attitude-altering experience—life is raised, galvanized, taken somewhere else. In the gospels, life reveals itself more fully.

"*Here you have a narrative, don't take the same attitude to it as to another historical narrative!* Make *a quite different* place in your life for it.—There is nothing *paradoxical* about that!"

"And faith is faith in what is needed by my *heart*, my *soul*, not my speculative intelligence. For it is my soul with its passions, as it were with its flesh and blood, that must be saved, not my abstract mind."

"Historical proof . . . is irrelevant to belief. This message (the Gospels) is seized on by men believingly (i.e., lovingly). *That* is the certainty characterizing this particular acceptance-as-true, not something *else*." (Wittgenstein's italics)

That certainty is faith because truth pierces the heart. It is not "paradoxical" because it really is, or ought to be, life changing. At least, life awakening, awakening life to the response its torment calls for. Wittgenstein reverberates to Kierkegaard's tormented faith, or link between torment and faith. Faith holds fast to a redemptive response to torment, redemption torment plays a role in opening. "Wisdom is passionless. But faith by contrast is what Kierkegaard calls a *passion*."

A passage that begins with Kierkegaardian echoes:

> The Christian religion is only for the man who needs infinite help, solely, that is, for the man who experiences infinite torment.
>
> The whole planet can suffer no greater torment than a *single* soul.
>
> The Christian faith—as I see it—is a man's refuge in this *ultimate* torment. Anyone in such torment has the gift of opening his heart, rather than contracting it, accepts the means of salvation in his heart.
>
> Someone who in this way penitently opens his heart to God in confession lays it open for other men too. In doing this he loses the dignity that goes with his personal prestige and becomes like a child. That means without official position, dignity or disparity from others. A man can bare himself before others only out of a particular kind of love. A love which acknowledges, as it were, that we are all wicked children.
>
> We could also say: Hate between men comes from cutting ourselves off from each other. Because we don't want anyone else to look inside us, since it's not a pretty sight in there.

This is a thread not everyone experiences or wants to: torment gives rise to faith, gives rise to an open heart. In Bion's work, this means letting others in, letting others become part of one, letting others seep into the deep unconscious and become part of one's creative life. Bion and Wittgenstein share the sense of faith as opening, an important part of which involves the realness of others as central to *lived* life. So much of life is unlived: one can only live so much life. At least, some life is lived and lived fully. We are touching an Archimedean point where the good of others is in our heart. At this point torment is about injuring others, closing off, finding oneself unable to do the good that calls. We are tormented because we are not saints.

An unbent soul rings hollow to the deeply needy. Wittgenstein suggests that only one whose soul is sick "has the right to pity someone else." Someone outside illness pities without cost. The condescension of the "healthy" misses the mark. Compassion is for equals. A fraternity of sinners is ground for empathy. We are equals in guilt toward one another. The heart of the other calls for a caring gesture, and we share much experience looking the other way.

Absolute guilt never tires of calling for a response. It is a guilt we share, that obligates us to one another, a challenge requiring the use of all we are and have. It brings us to places we could not have imagined had we asked less of ourselves. Guilt sticks to us, pressures us toward loving belief. Holding fast to belief opens a special heart. Guilt acts like training wheels until the ride takes over. Love, guilt, faith, belief intensify one another, opening possibilities. Belief is believing redemption, holding fast to the latter. Wittgenstein goes so far as to imagine us suspended from heaven, not simply grounded on earth, his own version of super or supraman. Holding fast to redemptive belief "can come about only if you no longer rest your weight on the earth but suspend yourself from heaven. Then *everything* will be different and it will be 'no wonder' if you can do things you cannot do now. (A man who is suspended looks the same as one who is standing, but the interplay of forces within him is nevertheless quite different, so that he can act quite differently than can a standing man.)" A holding fast that is a suspension. A dramatic portrayal of life changed by belief and practicing what belief brings.

Wittgenstein confessed failure. He professed a talent for philosophy, rather than a vocation for sainthood. He pointed to his vanities, contempt, disgust, his wish for admiration rather than love (he wished he wished for love more than admiration), his failure to do more good. He prayed his thinking did more good than harm and that, at least, some of it came from God, yet worried about others stealing his thought and put himself down for this vanity. He acutely felt his failures and deficiencies, real and imagined. He was haunted by the specter, the principle of sainthood, the latter's commanding realness. Perhaps nothing was more real, except for realizing how far from it one was. Yet even this distance brings one close to God.

Few writings, if any, on Wittgenstein are more touching than Malcolm's wrenching tribute on Wittgenstein's last reported words:

> Before losing consciousness he said to Mrs. Bevan (who was with him throughout the night) "Tell them I've had a wonderful life!" By "them" he undoubtedly meant his close friends. When I think of his profound pessimism, the intensity of his mental and moral suffering, the relentless way in which he drove his intellect, his need for love together with the harshness that repelled love, I am inclined to believe that his life was fiercely unhappy. Yet at the end he himself exclaimed that it had been "wonderful"! To me this seems a mysterious and strangely moving utterance.

I suspect the coupling of wonder and torment is not so strange after all, but part of what it feels like to be alive. Guilty torment takes us to a deeply human place.

The saint as image of the soul or model of aspiration is an explicit part of Levinas's portrayal of a fully human being. He touches a place where guilt is associated with failure to put the other first or "to put oneself in the place of the other." As Bion and Wittgenstein suggested, this call, this guilt, is in place awaiting us. We grow into it, meet it, but it is already there inviting, urging, demanding us to grow into more caring, responsive beings. Responsibility is here associated with responsiveness, particularly response to the vulnerability of the other.

For Levinas, the face of the other evokes an ethical dimension, calls for an ethical response. Not a conceptual ethics, not a representation or idea, but a propensity to do good, to do the other justice. The other's face precipitates a call from one knows not where to do one's best to help. Levinas emphasizes vulnerability, a nakedness, a destitution of the other that evokes response. The other's face awakens us. It does not merely enliven our being but awakens responsibility for the well-being of him who faces us. It is an infinitely inexhaustible, transcendent call, since the work of responsive goodness has no end.

Levinas writes of this call, this order, as being older than thought, older than words. An infinite beckoning or demand that we are born into, that we inhabit, a face-to-face awakening that puts us at our neighbor's disposal. This is not the life of being, of will, of desire, the élan of vital power. It is an awakening into a life beyond chronic self-interest, triumph, survival, and pleasure to something Levinas believes more fundamental for who we are or can be. We are awakened by the neighbor's approach. Indeed, an approaching stranger is neighbor par excellence. We wake up to other people.

His formulations are extreme and take us off guard. Our awakening toward sainthood requires us to take the other's place in the face of death and to make us responsible for his evil. Our responsibility for the other is radical, insistent, relentless.

The call to help is boundless, an all-giving. An all where new-ness resides. Not the newness of novelty, fashion, or even self-creation, but the fresh response, new ways we find to help. News we bring that help is possible: we are there to help, even if we don't know how. "It is not because the Other is a novelty that it "gives rise" [*donne lieu*] to a relationship of transcendence—it is because responsibility for the Other is transcendence that there can be something new under the sun."

The quotation above is difficult, even mind-boggling. The cap-ital "O" is used because it is not a specific other, not a particu-lar you or me with our individual personalities. It is not quite a generic other either, not quite otherness of other, although that comes close. The emphasis is on "absolute *difference*," absolutely other. The assertion, the principle, the experience, the reality at stake is not just your particularity (your golden hair, dark skin, talents, skills, ambitions, postures) but your infinitely, ab-solutely, precious humanity. It is the prophetic insight par ex-cellence, to help the needy and *all* are needy. How can we be responsible for the whole world, for everyone, for anyone who comes our way? How can all strangers who approach become a neighbor? Is this fantasy? Does it fit reality as we know it? It does not sound realistic.

Responsibility for human beings is transcendent for Levinas because nothing in being can cancel it. It is—and here you have to suspend your normal, representational, cognitive thinking—before being, older, other than being. Levinas advances an idea that dislocates much of our usual thinking about being. Being, in which people kill and find pleasure, discovers an ethical pres-sure that places it in question. Beings question being from a sense of something better, other; for one thing, life without mur-der. Levinas asks, "By being, by persisting in being, do I not kill? . . . Do I not kill by being?" Natural perseverance in being, naive self-affirmation, is placed into question by "the explosion of the human." The idea of the humane permanently questions the violence of life.

One can say that Levinas is taking a part of life, the caring tendency, and reifying it into a transcendent reality or principle. That may be so but misses, downplays, or discounts the radical intensity of what he points to. Ethics is as real and alive as experiencing the wake-up call of a face. How real is the realness of others? One grows into realization of the other's realness, a sobering awakening without end. "I mean to say that a truly human life cannot remain life *satis*-fied in its equality to being . . . that it is awakened by the other, that is to say, it is always getting sobered up, that being is never . . . its own reason for being."

One can make a case that all this happens within being. Where else *can* it happen? To be critical and questioning is part of who we are. To be caring is part of who we are. What is this other than being?

Levinas is a believer, speaks of God as older, other than being. God is absolutely other, and there is no way to rationalize or otherwise shrink such mystery. Nevertheless, there are feeling, thinking steps we can take. As Descartes' God guarantees trust, so that thinking is not in vain, Levinas's God guarantees otherness, key to Levinas's ethics. The absolute, infinite valuation of the otherness or difference of the other, part of our response to her face, requires our effort on the other's behalf.

In *Totality and Infinity*, Levinas invokes our response to the face of the other as a permanent guard against war. Squeezing other or self into packets, totalities, wholes with positive and negative valences justifies war. I am this, you are that—defined, rationalized. I respond to my interests, my images, my identity packets, and if war is in my interest, I shape the situation accordingly—and you do the same. Levinas's difference is perception of each other beyond definitions, totalities, identity sums. The otherness of God runs through us, maintaining a sense of difference that requires respect, care, justice, a difference that cannot, must not be undone. Infinite difference, infinite otherness opens infinity the face mediates. Awakening to the face, to human otherness, awakens resistance to war. Is this transcendence or a pitting of being against being, since we struggle with being, our own beings, to do justice to the other?

Many questions are dangling. If God guarantees absolute otherness, is God vulnerable, since vulnerability is a core part of experiencing the infinity of the other (infinite value, priceless-ness of another)? Since otherness awakens us to caring and the promise of justice, is there a sharing, a same that runs through it? Where is the nearness, the intimacy that nurtures empathy?

We will be frustrated if we look to Levinas for accounts of everyday sharing and mutuality. The "sociality" he points to runs through the everyday but is not exhausted by it. After everyday mutuality runs its course and one is ready for bed, the "insom-nia," the awakening, the call of the other to do justice continues. It is an abiding call, an abiding principle, an abiding reality.

Levinas gives us an appeal, a call, an infinite valuation that trauma cannot cancel. It is more or other than the sum of every-day pleasures and pains. It goes with the golden rule to do good to others, to treat others as ends, thou rather than it, the extrava-gance of putting the other first.

As a psychologist, I wonder where or how putting the other first becomes a guiding star of existence and do not have to look far. Putting the baby first is a start. Taking care of infants re-quires sacrificing, giving, putting the other first. A parent feels the appeal of the infant, its helplessness, vulnerability, need for help—as well as its pleasure in being and doing. To a certain ex-tent, putting the other first is built into the foundation of rela-tionships. It does not mean that all parents put the baby first but that there is a call to do so. Many put the other first in certain ways, at certain times. All life long there is competition, conflict, confluence between me-first, you-first, us-together, and situa-tions call for one inclination more than another, although com-binations are the rule.

Waiting and patience are important for Levinas—to wait on the other, to be patient with the other. Sometimes we do not know what else to do. This waiting and patience is a gift. We rush each other today. Impatience is the rule. We push each other to do this or that, fill each other with advice, like modern Job's comforters. So much of our pushing and rushing is tied to nervous energy, fear, irritability, the need to quickly get on with or on top of things. Levinas's valuation of passivity and waiting may seem strange, but it is a tribute to the other, a caring for difference, giving difference time.

Here, perhaps, is where we get to Levinas's version of intimacy, nearness, the kind he is at pains to communicate, to add. For Levinas, caring for difference is a kind of proximity, nearness. A proximity that is difference, almost deference, in which the other comes first. The other is worth waiting for, worth patience. In-difference takes on new meaning, the opposite of ignoring, brushing off. A very special "in" arises and becomes important. The in or out that protects difference is the core of proximity. Disinterest guards proximity, enters into a form of proximity in which the other's good is infinitely valued.

"The idea of the Infinite must be thought . . . according to the perhaps most profoundly thought thought, that of dis-interestedness, which is a relation without hold on a being, or anticipation of being, but pure patience. This passivity, deference beyond all that is assumed, irreversible de-ference, is time."

Gratuitous, abundant, overflowing, a surplus: these are some words or realities Levinas connects with what is usually envisioned as poverty of self-giving, giving of self to serve the other, devotional realness. The infinite defines time insofar as the latter becomes a waiting, anticipation, "an awaiting that is patience or pure passivity, a pure undergoing," not an impatient taking upon oneself, taking control, not a taking hold of.

No one can take our place in the particular way we put ourselves in the place of the other. It is an obligation we cannot slip away from. It will not let go. "A deference in disquietude and, thus, an awakening, and an awakening as awakening for the neighbor in responsibility for him. This means a responsibility from which one does not slip away: the fact of being irreplaceable in responsibility for the other defines me, as me and as a unique me [*moi*]. That is an awakening in which awakening is not complacent in its state of awakening, and does not fall asleep standing up."

A personal comment: *I* may fall asleep standing up or sitting down. I may try to help, wait on the other, and my eyes close. I drift off, dose. Is this a meaning of Freud's child-is-burning dream? A father is woken by a dream that there is a fire in the next room, where his dead child lies. In the dream his child comes to say that he is burning. And there really *is* a fire, as the man who kept vigil over the body, perhaps reciting psalms all night, this man dosed and tipped the light over, igniting flames. *We* may dose in the face of the other, but the fire of the other's urgency will get to us, wake us again and again. The fire of the call of the other never goes out.

In a me-first age, an age where sacrifice is at once idealized and pathologized, it is easy to escape the import of Levinas's concerns. Here's a toast, a L'Chaim to waiting, patience, responsiveness, hearing, caring. Through Levinas we approach and come near to a caring, devoted, gratuitous, giving, bountiful disinterestedness, close to the face of the moment's appeal. One more quote from Levinas before moving on.

A new attitude . . . the search for a proximity beyond the ideas exchanged, a proximity that lasts even after dialogue has become impossible. Beyond dialogue, a new maturity and earnestness, a new gravity and a new patience, and, if I may express it so, *maturity and patience for insoluble problems*. . . .

Neither violence, nor guile, nor simple diplomacy, nor simple tact, nor pure tolerance, nor even simple sympathy, nor even simple friendship—that attitude before insoluble problems, what can it be, and what can it contribute?

What can it be? The presence of persons before a problem. Attention and vigilance: not to sleep until the end of time, perhaps. The presence of persons who, for once, do not fade away into words, get lost in technical questions, freeze up into institutions or structures. The presence of persons in the full force of their irreplaceable identity, in the full force of their inevitable responsibility. To recognize and name those insoluble substances and keep them from exploding in violence, guile, or politics, to keep watch where conflicts tend to break out, a new religiosity and solidarity—is loving one's neighbor anything other than this? Not the facile, spontaneous élan, but the difficult working on oneself: to go toward the Other where he is truly other, in the radical contradiction of their alterity, that place from which, for an insufficiently mature soul, hatred flows naturally or is deduced with infallible logic. One must abstain from the convenience of "historical rights," "rights of enrootedness," "undeniable principles," and "the inalienable human condition." One must refuse to be caught up in the tangle of abstractions, whose principles are often evident, but whose dialectic, be it ever so rigorous, is murderous and criminal. The presence of persons, proximity between persons: what will come of this new spirituality, that proximity without definite projects, that sort of vigilance without dialogue that, devoid of all definition, all thought, may resemble sleep? To tell the truth, I don't know. But before smiling at *maturity for insoluble problems*, a pathetic formula, actually, let us think, like one of my young students, of St. Exupéry's little prince, who asks the pilot stranded in the desert, who only knows how to draw a boa constricter digesting an elephant, to draw a sheep. And I think what the little prince wants is that proverbial lamb who is as gentle as a lamb. But nothing could be more difficult. None of the sheep he draws pleases the little prince. They are either violent rams with big horns or too old. The little prince disdains the gentleness that only comes with extreme age. So the pilot draws a parallelogram, the box in which the sheep is sleeping, to the little prince's great satisfaction.

I do not know how to draw the solution to insoluble problems. It is still sleeping in the bottom of the box; but a box over which persons who have drawn close to each other keep watch. I have no idea other than the idea of the idea that one should have. The abstract drawing of the parallelogram—cradle of our hopes. I have the idea of a possibility in which the impossible may be sleeping. (Levinas's italics)

To step out of Levinas and back to just plain me, Mike Eigen, I'll never be a saint. Pick up your cross and follow me, says Jesus. Well, we try, as we are given. Some push further, go further, perhaps all the way. Few go as far as we might. We don't dare. We hold back. We survive. We live our own lives.

Some of us—many?—share Wittgenstein's torment, Levinas's call. We hear the call of the other and sense an answer rising to her appeal. In this context, answer means response, answering a call, "Here I am." Here I am is a famous phrase in the Bible. Adam and Abraham say it when God calls, one evasively, one fully. Perhaps we are always between two ways of speaking, moving in both directions.

To live our lives as human, as Ecclesiastes describes, plagued by vanity, benign and malignant deceits, love and companionship, setting hands to work we can do—isn't this enough? Freud's famous association of love and work with health has this ancient book as a predecessor. In comparison with the good sense of Ecclesiastes, its modest advice to scale back, to share and care, cultivate our gardens, Levinas and Wittgenstein have an eye on the impossible. A life dedicated to the other, to doing good. What can this mean? For most, it would mean the end of life, giving oneself up, subjugation, suffocation. What about actualization of self, discovery of potential, a Goethean life? Or individuation, a Jungian life? Aren't religious principles, ideas, experiences evoked by Levinas and Wittgenstein exactly what Nietzsche called servile, crippled, crippling? How can putting the other first help us? Doesn't this last question betray our selfishness? It is as if Levinas and Wittgenstein declare saint-hood a necessity, a privileged and necessary part of self-image.

I fear any meaning I give this will water it down, but I'll do a little watering anyway, as just plain me resituates Levinas and possibly Wittgenstein. They add the saint as a positive ideal—rather, they affirm or reaffirm sainthood as a necessary human direction, a fertile reality. Modern psychology gives us so may parts of selves, and now the saint takes a legitimate place in self-conception as psychic force, template, archetype, tendency. The saint in us saves us from ourselves, lifts us to new possibilities of living, gives the gift of cherishing others. Putting the other first may be the most realistic move of all. We are so used to seeing what can go wrong with this impulse—masochism, en-slavement, constriction, degradation—that we fear illness when generosity moves us. What a safer, kinder, fuller world, if re-spectful, impassioned caring for the other were a vital nerve of living.

Saint as dimension of personality, aspect of self, part of one's potential, part of the good inclination. Wittgenstein warns against a piecemeal approach to spirituality by saying that reli-gious belief or faith, allied with doing good, is not a "dimension" but a way of living. Whatever their differences, Levinas and Wittgenstein affirm that an absolute response is required by an absolute call. Do I merely aesthetically appreciate what they say? Dare I live it? What can it mean to say that I live it sometimes, to some extent? Which is to say, I fall short. Are they right that nothing is more real or more viable?

So many storms when two people meet, often going on nearly invisibly. Clash and interplay of desires and drives jockey-ing for position, quivers of peace-to-peace contact (yes, there are resonant shalom centers), emotional waves coupled with sensa-tions of all sorts, nuances we don't have names for, that, along with hate, love, fear, joy, sadness, hope, despair, and other regulars, we put in the basket of the ineffable awaiting metamorphosis. We are beings made up of filaments.

And the great storm, the thunder, clash, disturbance, turbulence expressed by Levinas and Wittgenstein, the call of the other, the appeal to give of oneself, to make oneself available, to respond, to wait. It may be that guilt plays a larger role in Wittgenstein than in Levinas, although I am not sure of this. Together they legitimate the guilt of sainthood—we are guilty if we are not saints. We are guilty because we are failed saints, and who is not guilty? The great lack we speak of, is not an important part of it a lack in our ability to give?

We are included in this self-giving. No one can give herself like we can. It is *our* self-giving, *our* waiting on the other that counts. No one can do it for us. In this, we are irreplaceable. No one can do for the other what we can. We give ourselves, our unique beings, our self-substance, our abilities, our personalities, and it may be precisely this, exactly this the other waits for and needs. The other waits for and needs—*us*. And in this, no one else will do.

When Keats says "A thing of beauty is a joy forever," he taps into the eternity, the foreverness, the undying value of touching one another now. He perhaps takes us out of guilt to something else. Like the beauty that pervades the face Levinas speaks of. A beauty that lifts us out of ourselves, touches us to the core, brings us to exquisite levels of pain, not just of longing but of caring, wanting to give all. Perhaps, after all, an exquisite guilt seeps into beauty, lightly pervades it. To suffer the joy of beauty, to protect it, to find ways to help it grow. A joy kernel in response to the face, a joyous faith. A need to do the face justice, an ethics of the face.

I suspect as infants we experience beauty as good and goodness as beautiful. The link between truth and beauty Keats alludes to is mediated by implicit goodness through which we care. Seeds of goodness arouse the striving for justice. Why, then, make so much of guilt?

My awareness of evil has had time to ripen. Everyday psychopathy grows more acute (an illusion? isn't it always present?). Guilt recedes as technology blossoms, enabling me-first aspects of psychology to reach new heights for more people. A kind of stampede results. More people achieving more leads to economic acceleration for those with most. A hyperinflated top rises over those below racing faster and faster to find a fair share. Economic mania, fueled by greed and fear and power and its own momentum, pierced by resentment, managed by a you-can-have-it-all propaganda. Economic power mixed with ego and God. Meanwhile, a shadow vision grows of the world population working like slaves for a fraction of one percent of the population, imagining they are doing good for themselves. Is the blossoming of psychopathy a freeing reaction to the slavery of guilt or, more likely, a growth of ability to ignore impediments (including fellow feeling) like guilt? Will guilt soon be old-fashioned? Is it already?

Wouldn't you have to be an idiot to put the other first? Self-interest rules. You know the next guy is out for himself. Where does that leave you if you don't join the race? Are there resources beyond self-interest and guilt to make us want to help each other? The look of a face? The appeal of a plight? Maybe if we ignore it, look the other way, that empathic sensation will pass or lighten and we can carry on.

Do we wish or dare to help only if we can afford to? It *is* possible to go through life ignoring the still, small voice that asks, "Can we afford *not* to?" The paradox of selfish selflessness/selfless selfishness: to fail to do justice to the inner saint is to fail to do justice to ourselves. The saint in ourselves must get its due too. The desire to help poses a challenge to the rest of personality. Do we fit self-interest within a larger helping frame or the reverse, allot what help we can within an encompassing me-first attitude? Do we encompass both tendencies within a larger framework of mutuality? A kind of oscillating me-first, you-first, and much else (partners in feeling out the "wheelbarrow" of relationship). Guilt challenges us, reminds us, requires us to meld strands of personality together in ways we can live with. It asks us to become the sort of persons we would *want* to live with, who not only can look ourselves in the face, but have a face to look at. We are amazing beings who can kid ourselves into justifying almost anything—but justifying is not justice. Did one imagine the desire to help would be so problematic, a heart of the storm?

Storm Sharing

In my introduction, I say I want this book to end on a ledge. The note Chapter 10 ends on is the note I want the book to end on. By writing this, I go past it.

I feel a little like John Coltrane, famous for endless sax solos, asking Miles Davis, a great trumpet man, how he knows when to end. "Just put your horn down, man. Put your horn down," Davis answered. Easier said than done.

Storms keep coming.

I can't stop without a little more on three great literary storms.

First, the biblical flood. Perhaps there was an ancient flood that left an indelible impression. There certainly were floods that impressed the human mind. One can, also, view flood as an archetypal image with archetypal meanings, appearing in fantasy, storytelling, and mythology as part of cultural/somatic heritage and propensity. A flood is an impressive experience, disastrous in fact or potential, not simply thrilling. Making up flood stories creates focus, enabling preparatory thinking to evolve. It is important to think about what can kill or harm so that we can, to the extent we are able, begin to plan ahead. Perhaps there are things we can do to minimize storm's danger, like finding or building better shelters, storing food, some modicum of thermal control with clothes and fuel, tools to aid survival. Imagination fuels urgency and motivation to find better ways to do things.

My particular style of depth psychology includes emotional storm. Stimulus storms, affect storms, primal trauma as flooding. I see the biblical flood portraying what it might feel like to an

infant submerged in affect. Going through an emotional experience fully may be like surviving a flood. "Storm-tossed but not
submerged" describes Noah's ark. But in real life, we are at various
stages of submergence, sometimes drowning. In my work, I
meet people who have drowned. They have died and come back
or persist in death, living underwater, submerged, speaking from
beyond their graves in the sea. Voices from graves. Is it difficult to
take in that living in despair is not so unusual?

Let us say that Noah's flood is something we all go through—
some of us now and then, some more often, some nearly all
the time. To be in the flood, to go through the flood, to come
through it—an intermittent rhythm, a dynamic structure of experience. Part of every rise and fall of affect, as natural as breath
or heartbeat, subject to arrest or attack. Flood and suffocation,
too much *and* too little: emotional flooding involves dramas of
intensity.

We come through with more and less success, stiffening
against the affect we need to endure and try to process. Later in
life, after chronic stiffening and self-gripping take their toll, we
wonder why we get the somatic pains and conditions that arise.
They are not just in our head. They are everywhere.

The Bible gives some glimpse of what it is like to go through
a state undefensively, fully. From storm to rainbow. An idealization partly, but also an echo of what happens often in fact. Usually, we partly go through partial storms, bits of storms. Stiffening and self-bracing somewhat, somewhat wading in. We brace
against our own processes as we are drawn to them. We shut
out, we let in. We taste ourselves and desire more and, as we
close, begin to gather ourselves for the next opening. It is difficult to let ourselves feel feelings, afraid of the flood. Afraid the
intensity will be too much, afraid of meanings it might bring.
Mind often goes haywire making meanings for feelings.

The biblical framework of meaning for affect is important in
its own right, but the fact of undergoing emotional storm is not

limited to a particular set of meanings. The storm with many faces is a constant. Affect that rises, peaks, falls can have many meanings.

In the biblical flood story, God grieves and repents of creating human beings because of the latter's evil, particularly violence. Human inhumanity shocks, hurts, infuriates God, traumatized by creation's lack of caring responsiveness. His reaction is a perfect example of an important response to pain: His urge is to blot it out. And how will He blot it out? By destroying everything, or almost everything. The Bible gives the show away near the outset: destruction as a way of blotting out pain, difference, difficulty, evil. Destruction to destroy destruction.

To blot out. A doubleness in emotional storm. The use of storm to blot out storm, to blot out being, to blot out states of being. To turn ourselves off, *not to be* in the face of the impossibility of solving life's problems, the great problem of living together, problems of society and psyche. The Bible's language is filled with emotional color, conveying life's impact, pain in one's heart, grief of evil, ugliness of destruction. A chilling, reverberating reflex: Destruction triggers destruction. The howl Allen Ginsberg discovers goes back a long, long way and starts anew with every infant's scream, expressing and blotting out agony. In the Bible story grace comes through, flood subsides, life is fresh, a new day, a new song—for moments.

What about Jonah's great storm? We respond to it because of the emotions it conveys, feelings we know too well:

I called out of my affliction to the Lord and He answered me,
Out of the belly of the netherworld cried I
And Thou heardest my voice.
For Thou didst cast me into the depth, the heart of the seas,
And the flood was around me.

All thy waves and billows
Passed over me.
I went to the bottom of the earth.
Her bars closed over me forever;
Yet Thou brought my life from the pit,
O Lord my God.

Who doesn't know what this means? Who lacks this distress? Has any human infant escaped it?

Why do so many pretend this psychic reality does not exist? Why do many seek to nullify or exploit it? The price paid for making believe this emotional nucleus does not exist or for misusing it is chilling.

A prophet runs from storm to storm, storms of meeting, storms of hiding. There is no place to hide if one is hiding from oneself and God. Prophets hear an anguished cry that teaches we must help each other. At least try to.

Jonah comes through with a grudge. He hopes Nineveh will be destroyed to fulfill his prophecy, but fears God will save it and he will look bad, more worried about ego than helping. He feels screwed if he tries to help, screwed if he doesn't, an incomplete going through. We abort rebirths and transformational passages one way or another, always some skew, contraction. But Jonah did what he had to do. He shouldered the burden, participated in the mystery. He mirrors a challenge, the need to open a little more, to go through things better, to learn more about helping or failing to, to move toward a richer blend of trust and circumspection.

As in Job, God has the last word. "What are you mad about?" he asks. "All those people in the city. They needed a little help, a wake-up call. Kill them all? They don't know their right hand from their left!"

One has to give the writer of this gem credit for adding a comedic, all-too-human touch: "I shouldn't have pity on this great city, all those people who don't know what they're doing? And also much cattle?" At least take pity on the cattle!

For the moment, at least, the spotlight is on our unforgiving nature. Even so, a happy enough ending—for a moment. A few prophets later, Nahum, and Nineveh is destroyed.

One last literary storm (unfair, of course, since art and literature are packed with them). The storm in *King Lear* is a peak dramatization of tormented consciousness. I'm tempted to say that it says it all, if not for the fact there is always more to say. Rage, folly, vanity, madness, deceit, treachery, grief, selfishness, faith—seamlessly compounded. A scream runs through it, and Lear explicitly speaks of the baby crying at birth, a cry that gathers momentum all life long, melding with horrors unimagined in the womb. The whole play is an emotional storm with deepening layers of pain.

Human vanity and anguish are laid bare, psychic insides eviscerated. The king wants a show of his favorite child's love and ends up with her death. The loss of power pales next to loss of mind, loss of child. We discover what values most as we lose it. In Lear, losses are irreversible except for one.

Madness and sanity come and go, reverse, pilfer, infiltrate each other. There is no clear line. What seems sane is mad, what seems mad is madder, pocked with unbearable moments of illumination. Normal life feels superficial, trivial, as emotional depths wedded to delusional poses and desires drop like rotting skin off an onion.

Is the ghastly suffering that runs through this play too much for life? Is life speaking to us, letting us in on what life feels like to be life? Life is the main character of this play and it reaches out to us, its products, its partners, for help.

Perhaps not help, that may be too much to ask—although I believe I hear this desire coming through loud and clear. Perhaps Life will be satisfied with only a responsive ear, an ear that cares, that registers the psychic facts, the situation: what Life feels like to be alive, what we dare to do with such sensitivity.

At the center of life in this play is the tie that keeps life going, a parent-child tie, a warped love as true as it is delusional, a connective tissue, testimony to our closeness, a mad bond that breaks hearts, yet chillingly shines as death eclipses it. It lives through death, barely. Loss is its soil and promise—so much failed promise, in which light flickers.

What we express in literature is the howl, the pain, the agony that is part of aliveness. Nothing cures this scream, this hurting. It doesn't need a cure. It needs a wider range of responsiveness.

A perennial danger is falling into small response sectors, for example, hard, burning, relentless hate in response to injury and injustice, whereby hate has momentum of its own, perpetuating itself even as outside conditions change. Hate that feeds on itself does not care much for the life of individuals and is easy prey to exploitation by a group's will to power. To open the range and quality of responsiveness is humanity's challenge.

There is a deep sense of fear and loss attached to refusing to be dominated by age-old links between violence and fertilization. It is a response range we don't know much about because some form of violence eventually erupts. Violence is part of control—social, moral economic, or thought control—an ingredient in the push for life and an ingredient in suppression. We lack faith in dialogue for good reason. Yet we are at a crossroads, an extended, painful crisis, in which we must learn something about what makes dialogue fertile. If it is true that technology spreads hate faster than dialogue, we quickly reach a point where attempts to communicate are necessarily inflammatory. Storms spread nearly instantaneously, seemingly without barriers, through veins of electronic transmission, forming new links between calculation and explosiveness.

Destructiveness, dominance, self-assertion seem to be part of the life drive, a drive for more life. The will to power exploits speech and tools (computers, planes, image-generators) as well as passions. We fear turning against our vitality when we talk things out. We need storm centers to feel real. Does this mean we need to injure and be injured in order to be real? Is our hunger for intensity a hunger for destruction? Is the mother of all orgasms achieved by destructive, triumphant will?

What will it take to learn how to use speech, the mother of all weapons, effectively, to place speech on the side of survival? Not only survival, *quality* of survival. I do not think that speech outside the storm is enough. We have tried that. We have ideologies of control reaching back to antiquity. Control and balance—the golden mean, wedding of opposites, rationality over passions. It has worked to some extent, but not well enough. We must do more, something not quite the same. Over-under or in-the-middle models help to a point, but it is time to go beyond them. Even if it is not always true that control is explosion postponed, it has been true enough, often too true.

We need to learn to speak inside the storm. To hear storm's voice. The Bible speaks of God's voice coming from inside a whirlwind or other storms. I think that is a hint we need to pick up on. The voice in the whirlwind is not just God's. How to speak from inside affectivity, to let affect speak, to be the affect speaking for a time. Not totally, always or absolutely—that would be as impossible as it is undesirable. We are a mixture of distance-immersion, contact-disengagement, connection-disconnection. But it makes a difference whether we try to realize an ideology of detachment or one that includes and values speaking within the whirlwind, doing justice to emotional storm, an ideology of con-tact. I might add respectful, caring contact—contact that cares for experience. Contact that cares for sensing what is happening to us.

How is it possible to stay respectful and caring in a storm? How to respect and care for storm, our stormy states, emotional storms? A receptive sensing and speaking from the storm center that goes with expressive reaching out? This is just the capacity I am hoping to call attention to, to help birth and develop. A capacity we need to discover and nourish. It is, after all, something of what we mean when we say we value speaking heart to heart.

NOTES & REFERENCES

Introduction: Inside the Storm

p. 2: "fierce thread": Eugenio Montale (1965), *Selected Poems*, New York: New Directions, "Motet XV"; "Your sweetness itself is a storm . . .": "Dora Markus." Love's unrest is at once delicate and violent:

> Your unrest reminds me
> of those great birds of passage
> who brain themselves against beacons
> during evening storms; ("Dora Markus")

pp. 2–3: In these paragraphs I cull images associated with emotional storm in Montale's poems. Social, physical, emotional storms blend. In love and creativity, emotional storm is privileged. The coupling of eyelashes and emotional storm, thrills, delicate shivers that decimate one—eyelashes that lash one through and through, like lightning, that blind and bind ("Lungomare," "The Eel," "The Strands of Hair," "The Storm"). Or a lover's absence, "the empty breaker shatters." ("A Letter Not Written"). One of Montale's best books is *The Storm and Other Poems* (1978), trans. Charles Wright, Oberlin, Ohio: Oberlin College Press. Emotional storm, delicate and fierce permeates it. In general, emotional storm is one of poetry's great obsessions, an incessant subject. Poetry is a privileged way of focusing, attending to, expressing emotional perturbation. Texture, color, aliveness of feeling are among its central concerns, taking life's temperature, pulse, an attempt at emotional digestion, news from the edge of the psychic universe. Poetry is often a considered storm itself, made of fresh impacts, not just reflecting but originating feelings.

p. 3: "siren of sleety seas," "to lash upcurrent," "of the flood, sunk deep . . . ," "more inner always . . . ," "explosion of splendor . . . : Montale, "The Eel."

pp. 3–4: "Springtime soul . . .": ibid., translated by Jane Toby, personal communication.

p. 4: "edens of fertility," "brief rainbow . . .": ibid.

p. 5: "When two personalities meet, an emotional storm is created": W. R. Bion, "Making the Best of a Bad Job," in *Clinical Seminars and Other Works* (1994), London: Karnac Books, p. 321.

p. 7: The Confucius/Lao Tzu tension refers to Lao Tzu's (*Tao Te Ching*) emphasis on spontaneous rather than ritual organization, somewhat parallel to the grace vs. law tension in Western religion. Such distinctions are not as polarized as they may seem, since they complement, feed, depend on each other and likely flow from a common source.

p. 7: For Freud on our transference-stained ego, see Group Psychology and the Analysis of the Ego (1921), *Standard Edition*, 18:65–143. I'm using Freud's terms for structures and functions a little like a painter uses color, part of an expressive gesture to touch something real.

p. 14: Paul Krugman (2003), *The Great Unravelling*, New York: W. W. Norton & Company; Walter A. McDougall (2004), *Freedom Just Around the Corner: A New American History, 1585–1828*, New York: Harper Collins.

Chapter 1. Emotional Storms

p. 17: "When two people meet, an emotional storm is created": Bion, "Making the Best of a Bad Job," p. 321.

p. 17: Bion's entry on Martin Buber is in *Cogitations* (1992), London: Karnac Books, p. 371. It is dated August 8, 1978.

p. 17: "All real living is meeting": Martin Buber, *I and Thou* (1957), New York: Charles Scribner's Sons, p. 11.

p. 17: A representative text by John Bowlby is *Separation Anxiety and Anger* (1976), New York: Basic Books.

p. 18: See Michael Eigen (2004), *The Sensitive Self*, Middletown, Conn.: Wesleyan University Press, chap. 2, "A Basic Rhythm." See also, Eigen (1992), *Coming Through the Whirlwind*, Wilmette, Ill.: Chiron Publications, for discussions of different kinds of rebirth, and Eigen (1995), *Reshaping the Self*, Madison, Conn: Psychosocial Press, for meanings of renewal.

pp. 19–20: Sensitivity-insensitivity: a central theme in *The Sensitive Self*.

p. 21: "the feel of another": For one author's attempt to delineate steps in building an appreciative sense of the other, see H. Covitz (1998), *Oedipal Paradigms in Transition*, New York: Peter Lang Publishing, chap. 9.

p. 23: baby as an "annihilating force": W. R. Bion (1991), *A Memoir of the Future*, ed. Francesca Bion, London: Karnac Books, p. 61 ("the growing annihilating force, the 'helpless infant'").

p. 25: "life he dares not feel": My patient's aborted baby came to symbolize unlived life, neglected areas of living. In his case, control substituted for experiencing. A double annihilation was at work. The crevice of power he nurtured feared annihilation by a fuller life, while his egocentric position killed off fuller living. Some people do better not having children or a lasting relationship. Perhaps my patient is one of them. At present, he insists he wants a family but does not know how to get from here to there. Maybe he will discover he is wrong and that his style of life suits him. But, for now, a wish for family presses him with experiential deficiency.

As Freud's *Totem and Taboo* father acquired increased significance after his murder by his sons, so my patient's aborted baby grew in inner significance, bringing my patient up against the life he failed to live. In both cases, a mixture of destruction, lack and loss challenge personality, tantalizing and frightening it with growth possibilities. (Freud [1913], "Totem and Taboo," *Standard Edition* 13:1–162)

p. 25: "All that they could do . . .": Bion, *A Memoir of the Future*, p. 47; ". . . worship it to death": ibid. Jesus and baby here have to do with the aliveness of life and new possibilities of growth. Bion sometimes calls creativity or a new idea, feeling, or action the Messiah or Genius part of personality in contrast with the conservative or Establishment tendency (e.g., *Attention and Interpretation* [1970], London: Tavistock Publications, chap. 6, "The Mystic and the Group"). The alive navel of experience often evokes smothering responses, attempts to tidy it or make it "safe." In aborting his baby, my patient kills life before it can kill him. He fears too much aliveness will kill him. Baby aliveness delights us but threatens systems we have built up to regulate aliveness. As in my second example, one can also "love" a baby to death.

p. 26: "Daimon": James Hillman (1996), *The Soul's Code: In Search of Character and Calling*, New York: Random House; Jesus as Imagination: William Blake, *Milton*, Plate 3:4–5. Blake on the Poetic Genius: "All Religions Are One."

Chapter 2. More Emotional Storms

p. 29: "When two people meet . . .": Bion, Making the Best of a Bad Job, p. 321; "All real living . . .": Buber, *I and Thou*, p. 11; Buber as "much closer . . .": Bion, *Cogitations*, p. 371.

p. 30: "an open-ended reality in which there is no termination": Bion, *Cogitations*, p. 371,

p. 30: "A man (M) locates going dead . . .": See also Eigen (1996), *Psychic Deadness*, London: Karnac Books, 2004, chap. 12.

p. 31: God's rage: Eigen (2002), *Rage*, Middletown, Conn.: Wesleyan University Press, particularly the sections "Golden Calf," "Pinchas," "Pinchas Afterwaves," and "God's Personality."

p. 36: For recent work on mother-baby interplay, see B. Beebe and F. M. Lachmann (2002), *Infant Research and Adult Treatment: Co-Constructing Interactions*, Hillsdale, N.J.: Analytic Press.

p. 36: "helpless infant" as a "growing annihilating force": Bion, *A Memoir of the Future*, p. 61; "an experience that is emotional and nothing else": Bion, *Cogitations*, p. 135; the dream's "origin is an emotional experience": ibid.

p. 37: Shifts between me-you around an emotional nucleus, link, threat suggests an underlying permeability, contagion, a basic capacity to absorb each other's emotional pressures, each other's feelings. It is this contagion we try to hide, act superior to, wall off. Psychotics, borderlines, obsessives, hysterics, phobics, panic disorders blow our cover.

p. 37: For Bion's use of the big-bang image, see *Attention and Interpretation*, chap. 2; Eigen (1998), *The Psychoanalytic Mystic*, London: Free Association Books, chap. 3.

p. 39: "The tyrannosaurus . . .": Bion, *A Memoir of the Future*, pp. 60–61, 83–84; "superior organ . . .": ibid., p. 60; "While his gaze physiological . . .": ibid., p. 61.

p. 40: shalom: Hebrew word for peace.

p. 40: A woman coming alive for the first time—can you imagine seeking payment from an insurance company for birth of psychic aliveness?

p. 41: ". . . an inborn mechanism for self-disposal": Bion, *A Memoir of the Future*, p. 60; ". . . the quality which is to lead to its own destruction": ibid., pp. 60–61.

p. 43: ". . . there is nothing to be done except . . .": ibid., p. 61. See Levinas on waiting in Chapter 10. For examples of failure to wait, failure of patience, see *Psychic Deadness*, chap. 16 "Disaster Anxiety."

p. 44: Shakespeare, *The Tempest*. The storm that leads to healing aims to right a wrong and expresses a wish for emotional life in its fullness without ill effects. See the note for p. 220 below.

p. 44: H. Werner (1970), *Comparative Psychology of Mental Development*, New York: International Universities Press. For my critique of the notion of "undifferentiation" and development of an alternative formulation, see *The Electrified Tightrope* (1993), ed. A. Phillips, London: Karnac Books, 2004, chaps. 6, 11, and 14; *The Psychoanalytic Mystic*, chap. 2; *The Psychotic Core* (1986), London: Karnac Books, 2004, chap. 4.

p. 45: K. Goldstein, (1939/1963), *The Organism: A Holistic Approach to Biology*, New York: The American Book Co.

Chapter 3. Smile and Scream

p. 50: Psalms 30:6. "In the evening, one retires weeping / but in the morning there is a cry of joy."

p. 50: "defining moment . . .": For the experience of the face, see Eigen, *The Electrified Tightrope*, pp. 49–60.

p. 51: W. R. Bion (1982), *The Long Week-End: 1987–1919*, Abingdon: Fleetwood Press; Eigen, *The Psychoanalytic Mystic*, pp. 61–79.

p. 52: ". . . deformations personality undergoes": See *The Sensitive Self*, chap. 4, and Eigen (2002), *Damaged Bonds*, London: Karnac Books, chap. 2.

p. 52: H. Guntrip (1975), "My Experience of Analysis with Fairbairn and Winnicott, *International Review of Psycho-Analysis* 2:145–56; Eigen, *The Electrified Tightrope*, pp. 139–46.

p. 53: "the wild ox": In my teens, I saw a Sumerian proverb at a University of Pennsylvania archaeological exhibit that went something like, "I escape the wild ox only to be confronted by the wild boar."

p. 53: Going dead in response to rage: See above, Chapter 2, p. 30, and my *Psychic Deadness*, chap. 12; for harm done by rage, see *Rage*.

p. 54: ". . . mimicking death and renewal": E. Shure (1961), *The Great Initiates*, Blauvelt, N.Y.: Steinerbooks; "Sensitive to sensitivity": *The Sensitive Self*; "depression and group pressure": S. Freud (1930), "Civilization and Its Discontents," *Standard Edition* 21:59–145.

p. 57: "the marasmic infant": I am thinking of research that depicts infants losing responsiveness when responsive others are absent long enough or at critical periods. For example, R. Spitz (1965), *The First Year of Life*, New York: International Universities Press, chap. 14.

p. 58: Personality traumatized as it begins to form: D. W. Winnicott (1989), *Psychoanalytic Explorations*, ed. C. Winnicott, R. Shepherd, and M. Davis. Cambridge: Harvard University Press, pp. 119–29; *The Sensitive Self*, chap. 2. For hallucination and damaged emotional processing, see *Damaged Bonds*, chaps. 1–4. For recovery after being wounded in sessions, see my *Toxic Nourishment* (1999), London: Karnac Books, chaps. 5, 9, and 10.

p. 61: O is Bion's sign for unknowable reality. In this context, faith is not associated with a particular religion or religious dogma, but a fertile attitude that grows through challenges of living (see the third note for p. 219 below). My book *Toxic Nourishment* depicts crises of faith as a crucial dimension in therapy sessions. For writings on Winnicott, Bion and faith see *The Electrified Tightrope*, chaps. 11 and 17, and Eigen (2001), *Ecstasy*, Middletown, Conn.: Wesleyan University Press. Bion (1970), *Attention and Interpretation*, chap. 2.

Chapter 4. No Amount of Suffering

p. 62: S. Freud (1900), "The Interpretation of Dreams," *Standard Edition*, 4/5:1–361; Eigen, *Psychic Deadness*, chap. 1.

pp. 67–68: Flannery O'Connor (1971), *The Complete Stories*, New York: Farrar, Straus & Giroux; Eigen, *The Psychoanalytic Mystic*, chap. 6.

p. 68: For the juridical Satan, see R. S. Kluger (1967), *Satan in the Old Testament*, Evanston, Ill.: Northwestern University Press; also M. C. Nelson and M. Eigen, eds. (1983), *Evil: Self and Culture*, New York: Human Sciences Press. For the vital Satan, see William Blake, *The Marriage of Heaven and Hell*.

p. 69: "force that continues . . .": W. R. Bion (1965), *Transformations*, London: Heinemann, p. 101; "force against recovery": S. Freud (1937), "Analysis Terminable and Interminable," *Standard Edition*, 23:216–53; "destructive force within"" M. Klein (1946), "Notes on Some Schizoid Mechanisms," in *Developments in Psychoanalysis*, ed. M. Klein, P. Heinemann, S. Isaacs, and J. Riviere, London: Hogarth, 1952, pp. 292–320; see Eigen, *Psychic Deadness*, chaps. 1–5.

p. 69: "deranged id, monstrous ego": I use terms like "id" and "ego" expressively, dramatically, and because they retain value for ease of communication. I do not mean to reify them. Feel free to translate my meaning into more congenial conceptual schemes, hopefully without losing the intuitive sense I try to evoke.

p. 70: I have written on rage and terror in a series of recent works: *Toxic Nourishment*, *Damaged Bonds*, *Ecstasy*, and *Rage*. For catastrophe as link, see *The Psychoanalytic Mystic*, chaps. 3–6, and *Psychic Deadness*, chaps. 1, 2, 4–6, 12, and 16. Bion develops the sense of catastrophe throughout his work, e.g., *Transformations*, *Attention and Interpretation*, and *A Memoir of the Future*.

p. 71: Unfathomable destructive force: Freud, "Analysis Terminable and Interminable, pp. 240–47.

p. 72: "idealization of helpers": Freud, "Group Psychology and the Analysis of the Ego."

p. 72: Melanie Klein's formulations: "Notes on Some Schizoid Mechanisms," and Klein (1957), *Envy and Gratitude*, London: Tavistock; Eigen, *Psychic Deadness*, chaps. 1–3.

p. 73: Wounds to sensitivity. See *The Sensitive Self*.

p. 74: "Health may be more easily associated with being passive, vis-à-vis ultimate good and evil, rather than with being active" (Bion, *Transformations*, p. 149). See also the discussion of Levinas on passivity and waiting in Chapter 10.

p. 74: Catastrophe in Bion's picture of the psyche: See Bion, *Attention and Interpretation*, chap. 2; Eigen, *The Psychoanalytic Mystic*, chap. 3.

p. 75: Rilke, *Duino Elegies*.

p. 76: "Alpha function" is Bion's term for whatever work is done to begin digesting life's impact on us, our impact on ourselves. It overlaps with "primary process" and "dreamwork," which help initiate the processing of affect. He said he chose such a term to keep things open, to remind us we don't know very much about how we digest experience and make life real. In one talk he called alpha something like a nest where birds of meaning might alight. *Bion in New York and São Paulo* (1980), ed. Francesca Bion, Perthshire: Clunie Press, p. 73. Eigen, *Damaged Bonds*, chaps. 1–4, and *The Sensitive Self*, chaps. 2–4.

p. 77: Medicating humanity for human nature: See *Rage*, pp. 170–79.

Chapter 5. Somatic Storms

p. 81: An intimacy runs through language and somatic, feeling states. The defeated man who loses weight, for example: defeat eats at him; indeed, defeat threatens to devour him. It is one of those odd accidents of language that "eat" is part of "defeat." Etymologically, the word has more to do with nullifying a possible feat. The "eat" did not come about from anything to do with food. But there it is, whatever its origin. One can take the ball and run with it, leaving scholarship behind. After all, eating is one of our first great feats.

pp. 82–83: Stacey's mother's toxic love: See *Toxic Nourishment* and *Damaged Bonds*. It is not as uncommon as one might think to eke out what nourishment one can from emotional toxins, thereby poisoning oneself while drawing nourishment.

p. 83: I think of David Bohm's implicate order where all is connected, what affects one part of the world-field ripples through all parts, if we can speak of parts (in Judaism, God is One, a vision implicitly rippling through Bohm's implicate order). In the explicate order, we perceive separateness, causality, time-space distinctions. We lose sight of the fact that the explicate order grows out of and is part of a deeper, encompassing field, the implicate order. In a way, as Freud's I grows out of and remains part of It or, perhaps, as I-it enfold each other. David Bohm (1983), *Wholeness and the Implicate Order*, London: Ark Paperbacks.

pp. 88–89: The mix of love and disgust that Amanda felt for her father reminds me of Freud's Dora case. For Freud, disgust signaled desire. Freud believed Dora was aroused by the advances of her father's friend and was criticized for not crediting Dora's disgust and anger as realistic. Freud saw the connection between sex, disgust, and revulsion. With Dora, his emphasis was the latter two as defense against the former, a primacy of desire, of love. It takes but a slight adjustment of sight to see fusions of desire, disgust, and anger as part of trauma, adult misbehavior. Freud's writings indicate he knew about environmental trauma, the push of desire, and their interactions. That he early emphasized the work of desire suggests a conviction that the individual contributes to the shape of his or her life. A dilemma for the person is that her makeup includes generic, anonymous urges, which she may embrace, recoil from, and ponder. S. Freud (1905), "Fragment of an Analysis of a Case of Hysteria, *Standard Edition*, 7:2–122.

To add complexity, Freud saw disgust as part of an evolutionary advance, associated with the upright posture, emphasis of the higher over the lower. Not only disgust with smelly anality, but with genital pleasures, associated with fear of excitement. Disgust becomes a way of regulating libidinal stimulation, protecting against flooding in the movement toward thought. "Civilization and Its Discontents," p. 100n.

For Amanda, things were complicated. Love *and* disgust, fear, desire, dread, a sense of violation, fascination, caring. Life is packed, dense with feelings a rational attitude would like to unpack, divide, control. Freud did us a favor to paint libido, fury, disgust with the same brush. But more than one painting emerges.

p. 89: *Fort-da* refers to Freud's account of a child throwing an object to the floor and wanting it returned, symbolizing the leaving-returning mother. Lacan emphasized the triumphant thrill the child felt imagining control over the mother's departure, as if we were masters over lack. Now you see it, now you don't—the Russian roulette of life—here embodied by Amanda's father's penis, the snake in the hole, tempter, begetter of trauma, traumatic excitement, disgust, anger, fascination, interest, self-protectiveness, the need to show oneself and hide. S. Freud (1920), "Beyond the Pleasure Principle," *Standard Edition*, 18:15–17. J. Lacan (1976), *The Four Fundamental Concepts of Psycho-Analysis*, trans. A. Sheridan, New York: Norton, pp. 62, 239.

p. 89: Amanda felt her father was not around enough. She felt de-
serted, emptied by his absence. By contrast, his dancing with
her was all the warmer, fuller, happier. The full-empty contrast
parallels the now you see it, now you don't penis. The latter a
pars pro toto repeating and signifying, with special impact, the
gone-here relation with father as a whole. Seeing him as inadequate was, partly, her way of translating the fact that she could
not control him. As the common phrase says, to have someone
coming and going is to dangle, tantalize, puppetize the other,
mix the other up, use confusion as a mode of control. Seeing
her father as inadequate helped stabilize Amanda. To see the
other as less is to gain some power back. Freud spoke of man's
contempt for women as granting an illusory sense of mastery,
being on top of the powerful mother. Amanda displays a kind
of feminine counterpart, topping injury that father inflicts.
Of course, this is not to imply that parents are up to being
parents.

pp. 89–90: Amanda used her head in a new way, a new head. Did
defensive, partial imaginary castration of father lead from lower
to higher head? A kind of castration and opening. To see fatal
flaws, lies one lives, to experience truth about lies that bind a
life—will seeing be cruel, compassionate, matter of fact? What
conflicting tones, attitudes, spirits define Amanda's struggle?

p. 92: Susan Deri gave an example of a man she helped, to a
point where he was able to fall in love and marry and find
happiness—only to die of a heart attack on his honeymoon,
after having sex for the first time. In *Bion in New York and
São Paulo*, pp. 69–70. Also, *Psychic Deadness*, pp. 225–26.

p. 93: "Probably the greatest suffering. . .": D. W. Winnicott (1988),
Human Nature, New York: Shocken Books, p. 80.

p. 94: In Blake all capacities contribute to creativity, vision, poetic
genius. Tennyson: "Till the war drum throbbed no longer and
the battle flags were furled / In the Parliament of man, the Fed-
eration of the world." "Locksley Hall," l. 27.

Chapter 6. Dream Images

p. 96: My old lady moving in all directions is a little like Ezekiel's angels, who moved straight ahead on wheels wherever the spirit moved them. Ezekiel 1.

p. 98: Egyptian circumcision: S. Freud (1939), "Moses and Monotheism," *Standard Edition*, 22:26–30. A few loose associations: circumcision, a kind of crazy pregnancy. Broad parallel: cliterectomy, clitoris envy. *Pars pro toto* (substitute part for the whole). Cut off part of oneself, so one may live. So one's children may live. Circumcision instead of infanticide. It is a custom as the Days of Awe approach (Rosh Hashanah, Jewish New Year, and Yom Kippur, Day of Atonement), to wave a chicken around one's head and kill it—may it take our place. So many ways to control sin, regulate excitement, subdue emotional floods, attempt to clean the psychic landscape.

p. 98: I write about my grandmother in *Ecstasy*, pp. 19–20.

p. 101: *Shabbos*: Yiddish for Sabbath.

p. 101: Evolution of sensitivity-insensitivity: See *The Sensitive Self*.

p. 103: Little girl thrown to her death, popping up unhurt: I think of a dream I had many years ago of watching my parents murdering each other in bed but it turns out they are jumping rope in sexual intercourse position. Sex as play, not murder. For a basic faith structure in the injury-recovery rhythm, see *The Sensitive Self*, chap. 2. My girl-alive dream affirms active girl energy enlivening my psyche. Active female energy survives cultural as well as familial trauma.

p. 107: Lacan, *The Four Fundamental Concepts of Psycho-Analysis*, e.g., pp. 143, 145. The transference makes present the closing of the unconscious, "which is the act of missing the right meeting just at the right moment."

pp. 106–7: Disaster anxiety as part of the background of experiencing: See *Psychic Deadness*, chap. 16, and *The Psychoanalytic Mystic*, chap. 3.

p. 109: To grow or not to grow, a theme in Lewis Carroll's *Alice's*

Adventures in Wonderland and *Through the Looking Glass*. Alice deals with size changes, strangers in strange universes, irritating mysteries, as she moves from shock to shock. Wonder borders on nightmare. Indeed, wonder and nightmare permeate each other. In my girl-alive dream, shock reveals possibility.

Falling down dead and arising is part of a tricky sequence in Alejandro Jodorowsky's movie *El Topo*. El Topo, on an enlightenment journey, faces masters of the desert, one of whom is a perfect shot. In a pistol dual, the master appears to shoot El Topo in the heart, and El Topo falls to the ground. Moments later he is laughing, arises, shoots the master dead. He takes a little metal plate, just big enough to deflect a bullet, from his chest pocket saying, "It's not good to be too perfect." My psyche is pretty tricky—my dream is surprising. Nevertheless, I don't feel the essential energy of my alive girl is tricky. I feel she is just the is-ness of living, implicit buoyancy, self-assertion, simple enjoyment of being at no one's expense. A good spirit.

p. 110: "Helplessness, rage, control meld": See *Rage*.

p. 111: For a critique of a psychotic element in all-or-nothing thinking, see *The Sensitive Self*, chap. 4.

p. 116: Freud's writings on Daniel Paul Schreber: "Psycho-Analytic Notes on an Autobiographical Account of a Case of Paranoia" (1911), *Standard Edition*, 12. Eigen, *The Psychotic Core*, chap. 7.

p. 116: A young man who thought he was a woman had a sex change operation only to discover later that he was a gay man, not a woman. *Psychic Deadness*, chap. 14.

p. 116: Bion, *A Memoir of the Future*, p. 14.

p. 118: Walt Whitman, the Upanishads, Chassidus (a form of Jewish mysticism, soul's connection with God)—all in their own ways affirm the more of life, the life of life. In Ralph Waldo Emerson, a mysterious power. In William Blake, energy, imagination. The spirit of life—words still growing in meaning. See *Ecstasy*.

Chapter 7. Killers in Dreams

p. 120: To go on annihilating nothing: For Bion's "force that continues after . . . it destroys existence, time, and space," see *Transformations*, p. 101, and *Psychic Deadness*, chaps. 1, 3, and 4.

p. 120: Flannery O'Connor's destroyers: Examples are Pointer in "Good Country People," the Misfit in "A Good Man Is Hard to Find," and Shiftlet in "The Life You Save May Be Your Own." *The Complete Stories* (1971), New York: Farrar, Straus and Giroux. For a comparison of destruction in O'Connor, Bion, and Winnicott, see *The Psychoanalytic Mystic*, chap. 6.

p. 120: Barbed wire: O'Connor's Hazel Motes in *Wise Blood* wears barbed wire under his shirt. As he dies, he is gifted with disappearing into a vanishing point of light.

p. 121: Leila is Sara in *The Sensitive Self*, chap. 6.

p. 123: Doing *it* to herself or others doing *it* to her. *It* = the bad stuff, illness, misery, suffering, the massive negative in life.

p. 124: Freud, "Beyond the Pleasure Principle," p. 18; Eigen, *Psychic Deadness*, chaps. 1 and 2.

p. 124: That every psychic act is made up of dual currents: "Only by the concurrent or mutually opposing action of the two primal instincts—Eros and the death drive—never by one or the other alone, can we explain the rich multiplicity of the phenomena of life." "Analysis Terminable and Interminable," p. 243.

pp. 124–25: Freud posited a fixed amount of psychic energy in each individual, with forces working for and against the use and availability of that energy. People varied in constitutional vitality, weaker or stronger. Psychasthenia (low psychic energy) could be innate but also involve antilibidinal forces (e.g., repression). In his early writings, he took the notion of sexual weakness and lack of satisfaction quite literally, associating this lack with anxiety. His work grew in complexity, resituating but rarely abandoning a position once taken. I've traced the structure of his picture of normative or idealized erotic vitality in *The Electrified Tightrope*, chap. 9. For the movement of his thought toward the death instinct, see *Psychic Deadness*, chaps. 1 and 2, where I delineate aspects of his special sensitivity, including sensitivity to mood, affect tone, changing energy states, and ebbs and flows of aliveness

p. 125: Plato, *Phaedrus*; H. L. Bergson (1998), *Creative Evolution*, trans. A. Mitchell, New York: Dover Publications. Freud compares his life and death drives to the love and strife of Empedocles in "Analysis Terminable and Interminable," pp. 245–47.

p. 126: Freud's concern with neurotic weakness as a by-product of civilization overlaps with biblical concern for the weak, those in danger of being run over by the powerful. Freud focuses on dynamic details of weakness. His writings are important not only for his "solutions," but for valorizing human weakness as an important area to study. Even so, many practitioners evidenced contempt for weakness, contrary to the therapeutic attitude that was unfolding. Workers as great as Jung and Binswanger deprecated weakness and negativism they found in patients. Winnicott is as important for his kindly yet percipient attitude toward dependency as for his therapeutic formulations. His "feel" and approach open new possibilities of experiencing. (Re Binswanger, see *The Psychotic Core*, p. 140; on Jung and Winnicott, see *The Psychoanalytic Mystic*, pp. 191–92).

p. 126: vision of maximum vitality: For an account of Freud's "purist," "normative" vision of genital vitality, see *The Electrified Tightrope*, chap. 9.

p. 126: Thomas Mann, *Death in Venice*; Elizabeth Sewell talk in New York City, 1960s.

p. 127: S. Freud (1914), "The *Moses* of Michelangelo," *Standard Edition*, 13.

pp. 127–29: See my *Rage*.

p. 130: J. Breuer and S. Freud (1893–95), "Studies on Hysteria," *Standard Edition*, 2; Freud, "The Interpretation of Dreams."

p. 131: conflict between self and species preservation: S. Freud (1940), "An Outline of Psycho-Analysis," *Standard Edition*, 23:148; urge to exist as threatening: Bion, *Clinical Seminars and Other Works*, p. 169.

p. 131: Freud's ego as hallucinatory organ: Eigen, *The Psychotic Core*, chaps. 1 and 2. Freud's ego in relation to authority, culture, art: "Group Psychology and the Analysis of the Ego," and (1908) "Creative Writers and Day-Dreaming," *Standard Edition*, 9.

p. 132: For strong descriptions of ego destructive superego activity, see Bion (1967), *Second Thoughts*, London: William Heinemann. These are descriptions of a mad superego co-opting psychic capacities, creating more madness. They appear in Bion's depictions of psychosis but pertain to mad dimensions in human life. My use of terms like "life drive" and "death drive" is meant expressively, informally. I've heard many people spontaneously use words like "life force" or "death force" and sensed what they meant, even though signifiers of life or death vary with contexts, groups, individuals.

pp. 132–33: S. Ferenczi (1995), *The Clinical Diary of Sandor Ferenczi*, ed. J. Dupont, trans. M. Balint and N. Z. Jackson, Cambridge: Harvard University Press; (1953), *The Selected Papers of Sandor Ferenczi*, vol. 2, ed. John Rickman, trans. J. I. Suttie, New York: Basic Books. For a depiction of love in "Ferenczian" therapy, see a work by one of his students: Izette De Forest (1984), *The Leaven of Love*, Cambridge, Mass.: Da Capo Press.

p. 133: Ferenczi's writings on mother offsetting the death drive and mutual responsiveness between individuals, analyst and patient, mother and baby set off waves of explorations of our permeability to one another, seen in infant research today as well as therapy interactions. See Chapter 3 above, chap. 2 of *The Sensitive Self*, and the preface to *Coming Through the Whirlwind*.

p. 134: Freud, "Beyond the Pleasure Principle."

p. 136: "Abraham's psychotic command . . .": This paragraph is a starting point for meditations developed below in Chapter 9, "The Binding" (see the note for pp. 168–69). I also write on the sanity-madness of Abraham and Isaac in *The Psychoanalytic Mystic*, pp. 86–88. For God's magnified anger and the right to kill, see *Rage*. For the powerful rhythm in psychic life based on relief after fright, see above, Chapters 3 and 4; *The Sensitive Self*, chap. 2; *The Psychoanalytic Mystic*, chap. 3; Coming Through the Whirlwind, chap. 2.

p. 139: Maximum-minimum tension, emotion: Bion, *Attention and Interpretation*, chap. 2; Eigen, *The Psychoanalytic Mystic*, p. 63, and *Toxic Nourishment*, chap. 8.

p. 140: Freud, rage, murder, religion: Freud, "The *Moses* of Michelangelo," and "Totem and Taboo"; Eigen, *Rage,* and Chapter 9 above. For ecstatic destruction, see Eigen, *Ecstasy.*

p. 140: Hagar and Ishmael: Genesis 8–21; Sarah's laughter: Genesis 21:6; Lot: Genesis 13–14. Meldings, reversals, antagonisms of affects and souls are incorporated in Abraham's life.

p. 141: Bion's murdering into life: *Cogitations*, p. 104. Speaking of a psychotic experience, he writes, "At the point when his blood will be fully restored to his circulatory system he will experience being murdered. And then he will be all right." For development of this movement, see above, Chapter 3, and *The Sensitive Self,* chaps. 2 and 10.

p. 141: infinite destructive force: Bion, *Transformations*, p. 101; Eigen, *Psychic Deadness*, introduction, chaps. 1, 2, and 4.

pp. 141–42: Destruction of dreamwork and the need to dream destruction in order to process destructive affective attitudes: see Eigen, *Damaged Bonds*, chaps. 1–4, and Bion, *Cogitations*, pp. 1–120.

p. 144: "A thing of beauty . . .": Keats, "Endymion."

p. 146: An early attempt by Freud to relate neural function to psychology, *Project for a Scientific Psychology. The Origins of Psycho-Analysis: Letters to Wilhelm Fliess, Drafts and Notes, 1887–1902* (1954), ed. M. Bonaparte, A. Freud, and E. Kris, trans. E. Mosbacher and J. Strachey, New York: Basic Books, pp. 347–445. For a description of brain functioning (including a nineteenth-century diagram of the brain) when Freud was a student in gymnasium, see H. McCurdy (1961), *The Personal World*, New York: Harcourt, Brace & World, pp. 222–30.

p. 148: the ego dividing itself: "The psychological novel in general probably owes its peculiarities to the tendency of modern writers to split up their ego by self-observation into many component-egos, and in this way to personify the conflicting trends in their own mental life in many heroes." Freud, "The Poet and Day-Dreaming," in *On Creativity and the Unconscious* (1958), ed. B. Nelson, trans. C. M. J. Hubback, New York: Harper & Row, p. 51. See also, Freud, "Creative Writers and Day-Dreaming," p. 130.

p. 149: Bion uses the term "vertex" so as not to allow vision to substitute for other approaches to experiencing. One may approach ("see," feel, taste, live) experience via digestion, reproduction, respiration, nerves, heartbeat—the world being different depending on where and how and through what medium you dip in (*Transformations*, pp. 89–91). Marion Milner: "I could now see that the idea went back once more to . . . my amused surprise that a beginning of a mystic's training could be to become aware of one's own toe from the inside." *The Suppressed Madness of Sane Men* (1987), London: Tavistock Publications, p. 263.

p. 149: guilt as an important part of sensitivity. See Chapter 10.

pp. 149–50: "life destroying superego": Bion, *Second Thoughts* and *Transformations*. Eigen, *Psychic Deadness*, chaps. 1, 2, 4, and 5; "immoral conscience": Eigen, ibid., chap. 8; *Toxic Nourishment*, chap. 8.

p. 151: Taking in objects or presences: Aristotle seemed to say that the psycho-organism was, in some sense, transformed by what it perceived or thought. To think X or about X, the thinking capacity molded itself to the object thought, became isomorphic with it. In perception, the senses molded to and became like the object perceived (*De Anima* ii 5, 418a3–4). This certainly is a tribute to our permeability and adaptability. To extend this, for a moment, to an area that concerns many psychoanalysts: If we take in good or bad objects, do we become better or worse, good or bad? Is our introjective capacity shaped by what it introjects? Perhaps, to some extent. But something in us opposes what we take in, partly defining ourselves in opposition. But this opposition changes the shape or form of our beings, the feel of ourselves, as we *are* touched by what we introject and identify with. We have not yet unpacked the meaning of Aristotle's idea that we mold to the object thought, felt, sensed, taking its likeness. Nor do we understand the processes whereby our sense of self changes (our shape changes) with impacts from our psychocultural landscape. Bion posited the open term, "alpha function," to alert us to the fact that we have a lot to learn about processing feelings, impacts. (See, e.g., Bion, *Cogitations*, pp. 53, 55, 70–71, 96, 110, 135, 141, 184). It is a subject that appears in many places in his oeuvre.

p. 152: Lacan, *The Four Fundamental Concepts of Psycho-Analysis*, pp. 234–37, 251–56. Eigen, *The Psychoanalytic Mystic*, chaps. 8 and 9.

p. 153: Bion's destructive force: See the second note for p. 141 above.

Chapter 8. Training Wheels

p. 159: guilt that outlasts our attempts to get rid of it: See below, Chapter 10.

p. 160: To evoke a sense of the duality of the analyst's position, at once feeling and mindful, Bion recalls a motto Freud saw in Paris and translated as "storm-tossed but not submerged." *Bion in New York and São Paulo*, p. 77. The analyst is supposed to stay in the emotional storm and go on thinking, imagining, feeling. At times, furtherance of life requires action faster than thought and the gut mind takes over. Bion notes that the state of being he envisions, an ability to be in the storm and think about it, is a capacity he has not reliably achieved, but psychoanalysis attempts to develop it. (*Cogitations*, p. 365). See p. 214 below and the note for it.

p. 164: Eva hit on the practice of breathing into or through feelings. Feelings affect breathing and vice versa. For an account of breathing and identity, see *The Electrified Tightrope*, chap. 5.

p. 165: In Genesis 29:14–24, Rachel sells Leah a night with Jacob for mandrakes. Therefore, it is said that Leah was hotter for Jacob than was Rachel. Rachel displays a selfish, self-absorbed streak more than once. It is a high thing to sleep with a holy man, which Leah desired more than Rachel. Rachel desired mandrakes more than she desired Jacob. Nevertheless, Jacob loved her more, although Leah bore him more children. Jacob ended up fathering children not only with Leah, but also with her handmaids, as was customary. The story suggests ins and outs of realistic and romantic love. Each person in the story had to bear core frustrations. Rachel finally died in childbirth.

"Drosh" refers to *midrosh*, tales, commentaries, imaginative elaborations on biblical stories, amplifying spiritual and psychological threads.

p. 166: Eva's husband hovering in her dream, leaving but waiting: Sounds like something I do, hover and wait, while mixed tendencies get their moments and move along. A more flexible attitude that gives a person time, something that gradually becomes part of Eva's life. For waiting, patience, see above and below, pp. 42–43, 74, 204–8, 210, 250–51.

p. 166: turning self or others into things: In reality, I-Thou and I-It intermix. We do turn each other into things and are things for ourselves as well. But the realness of our lives also stands out and asks us to respond more fully, more truly. Heart of stone, heart of flesh.

p. 167: Possibility of emotional disaster: *Psychic Deadness*, chap. 16.

Chapter 9. The Binding

p. 168: Abraham and Isaac: Genesis 22; Abraham and Ishmael: *Quran*, 37:99–111. In *Al-Quran*, Abraham dreams of sacrificing Ishmael, tells the latter, and they proceed to demonstrate their faith to heaven's satisfaction. No mention is made of Hagar and Sarah. In Genesis, Sarah sends Hagar and Ishmael into the desert, protecting Isaac's heritage. God hears Ishmael's cry and blesses him. Descendents of Ishmael and Isaac are at war today, a testimony to how virulent family tensions can be. Many holy stories express tensions we never stop facing, dramas of affective attitudes whirring in storm centers.

pp. 168–69: "Crazy God tests crazy Abraham's faith": This paragraph overlaps with "Abraham's psychotic command . . ." in Chapter 7 above, p. 136 (see the note for that page and see the Introduction, pp. 12–13). The present chapter elaborates on the theme of mad commands, beginning with the command (compulsion, desire) to murder one's child. To some extent such commands are part of power structures and strivings, part of competition and rivalry. Yet they exert force in mad ways. It's hard to resist connecting meanings of "mad" as angry and crazy. In the *akedah*, the focus is on madness and faith, but it is easy to trace mad faith in venomous and lethal battles for worldly power (it is already present in the pairings Sarah-Hagar, Isaac-Ishmael). Perhaps you are reading a writer who is overly sensitive to madness, a somewhat mad writer who sees madness everywhere. One needs to learn to use madness in order to *modify* it. Ending it is a futile goal. Because madness is normative doesn't make it less mad. To some extent, one fights madness with madness, fire with fire. *Our* search is for alternate ways of relating to madness. Intense vision underlines intense realities, and without the former the affective force needed to face destructive tendencies will be ineffectual.

p. 169: Freud, "Totem and Taboo," suggests that guilt over murderous feelings by sons for fathers intensifies brotherly bonds. How to express and organize mixes of murderous and loving feelings is one of Freud's nuclear themes. Reverie: It is usual to think murder creates or leads to guilt. But I suspect there are instances wherein murder attempts to bring guilt that is already there into focus, to provide a home for inexplicable guilt. Murder makes it possible to feel the bond one is symbolically annihilating. The more inaccessible the guilt, the more extreme the action. Murder, too, is a helplessness before guilt one cannot solve, even an attempt to annihilate guilt. The double need, to intensify and annihilate guilt, is solved in one blow. Such explosions may not solve anything in the long run, but they cement bonds in the face of doubt and uncertainty.

p. 169: Feelings that break free of suffocating bonds may disperse and become virulent. But those that remain tied and packaged can be virulent too. See *Damaged Bonds* and *Toxic Nourishment*.

pp. 169–70: For links between parental death wishes and childhood depression, see D. Bloch (1984), *"So the Witch Won't Eat Me": Fantasy and the Child's Fear of Infanticide*, New York: Grove Press.

p. 170: K. Abraham (1973), *Selected Papers*, London: Hogarth Press, p. 4; H. Loewald (1980), *Papers in Psychoanalysis*, New Haven: Yale University Press, pp. 367–404.

p. 171: All this talk about death and destruction, as if it were foreign to life when nothing is closer, except, some say, love. Something missing, something wrong—what is more normal? Bad things happening, part of reality. Nevertheless, we do not like bad things happening to *us*, and we fight them or try, some way, to stop or solve them. Many dislike bad things happening to anyone anywhere, and we conceive the felt idea of being in this together.

Some point to destruction as enrichment. Would Shakespeare be Shakespeare without death, destruction, corruption, deformation, poisonous spirit, political and personal sickness? War cross-pollinates, brings peoples together, spreads and opens influences. Yet some of us say that there must be a better way, without knowing whether there is or how to go about it. Psychoanalysis tries to find better ways for individuals, with greater and less success. What social organs exist to find better ways for societies, without people tearing each other apart? Even when they begin to exist, are there ways to protect them from exploitation? I used to think our society was giving it a go, but it is sobering to realize that separation of powers is subject to "laws" of dominance, and that in a "free" society, elections are subject to seizure.

p. 171: One of the nuclear themes in Jewish narrative is reversed in the blood libel. A point of the *akedah* is the swerve away from human sacrifice, a source of Jewish pride. There is precision of destructive logic, accusing Jews of drinking blood of children (Christian or Muslim) in rituals. The blood libel tries to degrade the foundations of Jewish faith, partly expressing a desire to quash Jewish pride. How destructive circles begin are difficult to trace, but once started, people inside and outside the circle suffer.

p. 172: For a synopsis of major rationalizations of the *akedah*, see *Encyclopaedia Judaica* (1972), Jerusalem: Keter Publishing House, 2:479–87. Even mystical systems create their own kind of rationality out of experiences they point to.

p. 172: S. Kierkegaard (1954), *Fear and Trembling*, Princeton, N.J.: Princeton University Press. The link between joy and trembling is in Psalms (e.g., "Serve God with fear and rejoice with trembling," near the end of Psalm 2).

p. 174: Freud "The *Moses* of Michelangelo." Freud's depiction of Moses holding back rage grows from his response to Michelangelo's statue of Moses in the church of San Pietro in Vincoli. See, too, Y. H. Yerushalmi (1991), *Freud's Moses*, New Haven: Yale University Press. See also Chapter 7 above, pp. 127–28, 140.

p. 175: Eigen, *Rage*.

p. 176: In Exodus 2, the newborn Moses is found in a basket on a riverbank and becomes the adopted son of an Egyptian princess. Moses is saved from destruction by a blend of strategy and good heartedness. In this story, Pharaoh mediates destructiveness and hard-heartedness that recoils against the Hebrews and himself. That many Hebrew male babies perished and Moses was saved symbolizes faith withstanding destructive currents. The Bible often refers to something small, a good seed, a remnant, a thread coming through massive destruction. The fact that some date Isaac's age as thirty-five at the time of the *akedah* and that Abraham had reached one hundred, suggests dramas between faith and destruction mark all phases of life.

p. 176: Freud uses the image of binding for channeling libidinal and destructive energies (see pp. 13, 174–75 above). I wouldn't be surprised to learn that the *akedah* played a subterranean, background role. The term *akedah* appears once in the Bible, in the Abraham-Isaac story, yet is a foundational image binding Abraham's children to God. God's blade to our heart cuts through layers of the insensible until sensitivity can be borne. Freud was very interested in the fate of sensitivity and the fact that we are so subject to psychological wounds.

I would also not be surprised to learn that mystical Judaism's emphasis on good vs. evil inclinations played a background role in Freud's focus on tensions between love and destruction. This interest took a new turn in "Beyond the Pleasure Principle," partly summarized in "Analysis Terminable and Interminable." See Eigen, *Psychic Deadness*, chaps. 1 and 2, and D. Bakan (1975), *Sigmund Freud and the Jewish Mystical Tradition*, New York: Beacon Press.

The commandment (Deuteronomy 6) to love God with all one's heart, soul, and might is often mystically interpreted to mean loving God with one's good and evil inclinations, right and left heart chambers, so that destructive energies, so necessary to life, are placed in greater service.

pp. 177–78: Sodom and Gomorrah: Genesis 18–20. Abraham and Moses differ from Noah in that the former two try to talk God down, turn Him away from destruction, while Noah went about saving himself and those close to him.

pp. 177–78: Joshua and Caleb are surviving good seeds, the only two of the original group who left Egypt to wander in the wilderness, and forty years later, entered the promised land.

p. 178: Many people would be loathe to shit in public but have few scruples about shitting feelings into their fellows near and far. Evacuating feelings rather than developing a capacity for responsive dialogue is common.

p. 179: Freud's life and death drives as components of psychic acts: See the second note for p. 124 on p. 234. For descriptions of coming through psychic annihilation, see Eigen, *The Sensitive Self*, chap. 2.

p. 180: See *Toxic Nourishment* for fusions of emotional nourish-

ment and toxins and *Damaged Bonds* for damage inflicted by
necessary bonds.

Chapter 10. Guilt

p. 182: For Lady Macbeth breast became death-giving rather than
life-giving. She strove to undo and reverse her femininity:
>   unsex me here
>   And fill me from the crown to the toe top full
>   Of direst cruelty . . .
>   Come to my woman's breasts
>   And take my milk for gall . . ." (*Macbeth* I.v.38)

p. 184: In *Rage* (e.g., pp. 9–10), I describe black, red, and white
flashes at the onset of many moments of rage. Red also is associated with sexual heat. By contrasting rainbow with black and
red I try to suggest how reduced, albeit intense, a world the heat
of power and ice of cruelty can become. "To see red," is colloquial for rage. Its association is with blood (life, soul): "blood
boils," "bloody murder." It straddles passions, as in "hot-
blooded." Black is associated not only with evil but also with
blindness and incomprehension ("being in the dark"). This hostile reduction of red, black and white feeds on creative counterparts, since the same colors are associated with mystical experience and creativity.

p. 184: It is possible that personal encounter took the form of com-
mandments, that encounter was informed by godly demands
and directives. Godly auditory commands are issued in psychosis and characterize aspects of early language usage (Eigen,
The Psychotic Core; J. Jaynes [2000], *Origin of Consciousness in the
Breakdown of the Bicameral Mind*, Boston: Houghton Mifflin
Company, pp. 48–144, 404–46). However, it is unlikely that the
command aspect of encounter exhausts primordial experience.
Affect swirls are important in themselves and take many forms.
Terror, fear, awe, love undergo many spontaneous as well as rit-
ual organizations. The command to love God with all one's
heart and soul and might is not merely an order. It expresses

immediate experience of abundance, something dear, precious, central. As always, experience is mixed, and there are threads to pull.

p. 185: The Hebrew word *Hashem* literally means "The Name," referring to the unspeakable name of God. It is a kind of Jewish colloquial, informal way of talking about God, sometimes carrying a muted sense of endearment and intimacy.

p. 186: Melanie Klein associates fear with the "paranoid-schizoid" position, which works by projection, and guilt with the "depressive position," which involves greater tolerance for ambivalence, more inner complexity. Developmentally, one moves from the former to the latter, although both exert force throughout life. In the former, hate is projected; in the latter, tension between love and hate is less disowned. The desire to make reparation is, partly, an attempt to relieve guilt over hating connected with loving. Judaism distinguishes between fear and love of God. The latter goes through various stages beginning with guilt but rising to love for its own sake, intrinsic love. It is recognized that fear and guilt are important in modulating behavior while the personality ripens toward deeper, fuller levels of loving. If love is not enough, there is guilt; if guilt fails, there is fear. There is often a great gap between theory and practice. Nevertheless, states that find their ways into formulations are real, although formulaic treatment of them can close off further development. (Klein, "Notes on Some Schizoid Mechanisms; see *The Sensitive Self*, chap. 1; *Psychic Deadness*, chaps. 2 and 3).

p. 187: The serpent could walk until Adam and Eve fell for his temptation. For the lies he told, he had to lie down, crawl, eat dust, bite the heel of man, expose man as a heel. Somehow it did not feel right or complete to make the first tempter male, so stories arose of an even earlier temptress, Lillith, who as a powerful demon torments us still.

p. 188: "The idea of cause . . ." and "I am guilty of . . .": Bion, *Cogitations*, p. 121.

p. 189: "caused it and . . ." and "denial that the guilt . .": ibid.

p. 190: "In 'space,' does the infant . . .": ibid.

p. 190: I am referring to the use of causality as premature closure and barrier to experiencing, especially with regard to emotional perception. One could also focus on moral causal thinking (you're to blame, I'm to blame) as a way of prematurely substituting primitive causality for maturation of an adequate ethical sense. Earlier I spoke about emotional navels acquiring heads and tails, subjects-objects and some kind of affective link or narrative (pp. 39, 45, 48). As important as these meaning structures are, they are not the whole tale.

p. 191: J. Heaton (1999), *Introducing Wittgenstein*, illus. J. Groves, London: Icon Books, pp. 128–29. I do not know if Wittgenstein compared thought to a rhizome. If he did, I do not know where. Although Heaton does not mention Deleuze, his material seems to be based on G. Deleuze and F. Guattari (1987), *A Thousand Plateaus*, trans. B. Massumi, Minneapolis: University of Minnesota Press, "Introduction: Rhizome," pp. 3–25. Wittgenstein is not mentioned in the latter text.

p. 191: Freud, "The Interpretation of Dreams," 5:525

p. 191: "A rhizome has no beginning or end . . .": Deleuze and Guattari, *A Thousand Plauteaus*, p. 25.

p. 192: "the calm bottom of the sea . . .": L. Wittgenstein (1984), *Culture and Value*, ed. G. H. von Wright in collaboration with H. Nyman, trans. by P. Winch, Chicago: University of Chicago Press, p. 53; "absolute guilt": See W. H. Brenner (2001), "Creation, Causality and Freedom of the Will," in *Wittgenstein and Philosophy of Religion*, ed. R. L. Arrington and M. Addis, London and New York: Routledge, p. 57; "shudder of disgust": Wittgenstein, *Culture and Value*, p. 83.

p. 192–93: "only religion would . . .": Wittgenstein, *Culture and Value*, p. 48; "Sound doctrines are all useless . . .": ibid., p. 53; "'Wisdom is gray.' Life on the other hand . . .": ibid., p. 63; "Life can educate one . . .": ibid., p. 86.

p. 196: Perhaps even beyond guilt, Levinas and Wittgenstein are exercised by the lived infinite, something given to life that is more than life. Life more than life can bear, life that asks itself to change, that asks a person to become a better person.

p. 197: F. O'Connor (1952), *Wise Blood*, New York: Harcourt, Brace & Co.

pp. 197–98: "but a description of an actual . . .": Wittgenstein, *Culture and Value*, p. 28; "*Here you have a narrative . . .*": ibid., p. 32; "And faith is faith . . .": ibid., p. 33; "historical proof . . . is irrelevant . . .": ibid., p. 32.

p. 198: "Wisdom is passionless . . .": ibid., p. 53; "The Christian religion is only . . .": ibid., p. 46.

p. 199: In the first hundred pages of *Cogitations*, Bion writes of difficulties involved in letting others in and the importance of dreamwork in processing feelings. If dreamwork is damaged, what others give us cannot be processed and we suffer emotional starvation. For damaged dreamwork, see *Damaged Bonds*, chaps. 1–4. For faith as opening, see *The Psychoanalytic Mystic* and *The Electrified Tightrope*.

pp. 199–200: "has the right to pity . . .": Wittgenstein, *Culture and Value*, p. 46; "can come about only . . .": ibid., p. 33.

p. 200: "Before losing consciousness . . .": N. Malcolm (1984), *Ludwig Wittgenstein*, Oxford: Oxford University Press, p. 81.

p. 201: "to put oneself in the place of the other": E. Levinas (1998), *Of God Who Comes to Mind*, trans B. Bergo, Stanford: Stanford University Press, p. 11.

p. 202: "It is not because the Other . . .": ibid., p. 13.

pp. 202–3: On p. 185 above, I wrote of my childhood quandary over the beautiful Hebrew song about returning to the days of the ancient temple and the way I eventually came to understand the sense of return as a turning to God. Levinas provides another meaning that is startling, searching, and profound. He writes of God and ethics as before being, other than being. A permanent questioning of being. So that in returning, one is refinding or making a journey of discovery relating to the ethical roots of *human* experiencing, based on the *humanity* of humans, summarized most intensely in the appeal of the face.

p. 202–3: "By being, by persisting in being . . .": Levinas (1985), *Ethics and Infinity: Conversations with Phillippe Nemo*, trans. R. A. Cohen, Pittsburgh: Duquesne University Press, p. 120; "the explosion of the human": ibid., p. 121; "I mean to say that a truly human life . . .": ibid., p. 122.

p. 203: "*satis*-fied": a strange, idiosyncractic breakup of the word "satisfied," with emphasis on *satis?* The word "satisfy" has to do with enjoyment and pleasure (in common language, often sexual pleasure: to satisfy your partner, to be satisfied), debt, guilt, and sin. In terms of satisfying obligations, meanings range from simple, everyday legal, business, and personal transactions to Christ's satisfaction of humankind's debt of sin. *Satis* means "enough." I suspect Levinas is suggesting that satisfaction in any realm, from natural or social pleasures to cleansing of sin, cannot satisfy the call from the other. Enough is not enough. The call from the other is infinite and sets up a life of infinite approach. One can never do enough, but that does not detract from the infinite call, a personal call. What makes this different, an addition or supplement to Kant's ethical sense—to treat others as ends in themselves, his variant on the golden rule—is the personal root: respect and care for others grows out of immediate experience of the face, a response to human, affective presence. It is not enough to be: what kind of life we lead, what kind of person we become is at stake. Affective quality, tone, spirit, attitude *is* part of ethics. It is not enough to go through the motions or reduce the other's appeal to something that can be satisfied.

p. 203: Levinas (1969), *Totality and Infinity*, trans. A. Lingis, Pittsburgh: Duquesne University Press.

pp. 205–6: "The idea of the Infinite must . . .": Levinas (1987), *Time and the Other*, trans. R. A. Cohen, Pittsburgh: Duquesne University Press, p. 135; "an awaiting that is patience . . .": Levinas (1993), *God, Death and Time*, trans. Betina Bergo, Stanford: Stanford University Press, 2000, p. 29; "A deference in disquietude . . . ": ibid., pp. 26–27.

I am struck by a confluence or overlap between Levinas and Bion concerning the importance of waiting, patience, passivity, faith. For Bion, faith, contrasted with other attitudes, is openness par excellence. He equates it with the psychoanalytic attitude, a call to be without expectation, memory, desire, and understanding (an amplification of Freud's free-floating attention). An impossible call, to be sure, but no less valuable for that. It expresses an ideal, an aspiration, a struggle to be as open as possible to the impact of experience, sensitive to the drama of impact and response. One who joins this struggle encounters transformative possibilities otherwise missed. Not exactly the other first, the primacy of the saint, as in Levinas and Wittgenstein, but a close kin.

Bion values waiting and patience, which are essential in Levinas. If in Levinas, one waits on the other, in Bion one waits on processing of impacts, transformation of impacts, a highly complex response process involving dreamwork digesting affects. One *always* has a feeling response to others. Much unconscious as well as conscious responding goes on. To let the other in and do the necessary feeling work takes time. One cannot do the other or one's response justice without time. Waiting and patience are necessary for psychic digestion.

Bion goes further and points out that passivity can be associated with health when confronted with insoluble splits. In certain circumstances, activity makes things worse, especially in situations in which anything you do is wrong. The value placed on being passive in the face of impossibility or wrong possibilities is far-reaching, particularly if it is a passiveness that makes room for further, unknown development (a theme close to Levinas). For Bion on faith, waiting, patience, passivity, see *Transformations* and *Attention and Interpretation.* For my writings on these themes in Bion, see *The Electrified Tightrope*, chaps. 11 and 17, and *The Psychoanalytic Mystic*, chaps. 3 and 4. A key difference between Levinas and Bion is the latter's emphasis on the mystic rather than the saint. Although the mystic and the saint often are in conflict, it is my belief that they feed each other, providing veins of nourishment human beings need. See the note for p. 43 above.

p. 206: For Lacan's comments on the child-is-burning dream, see *The Four Fundamental Concepts of Psycho-Analysis*, pp. 33–34, 44–45, 57–60. Also, see my *Ecstasy*, pp. 37–38, and *The Sensitive Self*, pp. 55–56. It is a Jewish custom not to leave the body of the deceased, but to keep vigil, reciting psalms.

pp. 206–8: "a new attitude . . .": Levinas (1999), *Alterity and Transcendence*, trans. M. B. Smith, New York: Columbia University Press, pp. 87–89. This quotation is from a talk given in 1967 to a society for Judeo-Christian fellowship, with an eye to much more.

p. 209: In criticizing Levinas, C. Fred Alford points to the human values of Greek literature, shared grief in the face of basic agonies, and the growth of mutuality depicted as an elemental capacity in current developmental literature (Alford [2002], *Levinas, the Frankfurt School of Psychoanalysis*, Middletown, Conn.: Wesleyan University Press). Alford is not wrong, I feel, but misses the reality of crucial threads that Levinas and Wittgenstein touch in their special ways. It is easy to downplay, dismiss, or denigrate (pathologize) the call Levinas and Wittgenstein find so real. But, once experienced, it does not let go, and one's life gradually reorganizes around it or, at least, attempts to include it in a more central way. It is as if (and more than "as if") one's life, one's being recognizes a pole of existence that brings a real realness.

p. 210: "A thing of beauty . . .": Keats, "Endymion."

p. 210: Keats, "Beauty is truth, truth beauty . . .": "Ode on a Graecian Urn." There is much in Keats that one might call a "dialectic" between the pain of life ennobled by poetic suffering and the painless lovers on the urn whose blood will not be spilled. Poetry by no means leads one down a simple path.

p. 212: The "wheelbarrow" of relationship refers to the image of mutual sensing developed earlier in this chapter on pp. 195–96.

Afterword: Storm Sharing

p. 213: biblical flood: Genesis 6–9.

p. 214: "Storm-tossed but not submerged": Bion's rendering of a motto that impressed Freud in Paris: "Fluctuat nec murgitur." Bion, *Bion in New York and São Paulo*, p. 77. See the note for p. 160 above.

p. 215: God grieves, repents of creating man, decides (almost) to blot it all out: "And the Lord saw that the wickedness of man was great in the earth, and that every imagination of the thoughts of his heart was only evil continually. And it repented the Lord that He had made man on the earth, and it grieved Him at His heart. And the Lord said: 'I will blot out man from the face of the earth; both man, and beast, and creeping thing, and fowl of the air; for it repenteth Me that I have made them.'" (Genesis 6:5–7). Modeled after *The Soncino Chumash* (1947), ed. A. Cohen, London: The Soncino Press, pp. 26–27.

p. 215: A. Ginsberg (1972), *Howl and Other Poems*, San Francisco: City Lights.

pp. 215–16: "I called out . . .": Jonah 2:3–7. My translation loosely based on *The Twelve Prophets* (1961), ed. A. Cohen, London: The Soncino Press, pp. 143–44.

p. 216: See *Coming Through the Whirlwind*, chap. 1, for ways of coming through different kinds of rebirth.

p. 217: Lear's cry: "Howl, howl, howl, howl!"—the agonized gasp, outburst of the pulverized heart, holding dead Cordelia in his arms. (V.3) What a ghastly transformation of the baby's wail upon entering life! (IV.5) A cry which, in this speech, culminates in "Kill, kill, kill, kill, kill" (IV.5.185). Other words repeated by Lear in this way include "never" and "now." The link between absolute agony and murder is deep indeed, as is the double annihilation, turning never into now, now into never. In Lear, pain and madness feed each other. For the sense of totality in psychotic thinking, see *The Sensitive Self*, chap. 4.

p. 218: See *Damaged Bonds* and *Toxic Nourishment* for blends of madness that make up bonds of love and hate and other attachments that nourish and plague the human condition.

p. 219: Destructive intensity, destructive orgasms, triumphant will: Images of concentration camp victims—something I never witnessed firsthand—seared my consciousness in an ultimate way when I was a child. Here was a final outcome, an end point of human inhumanity, a terminus that marked a nadir of responsiveness, a high point of evil imagining. Human beings are great at torture, degradation, spoilage. Almost as if we need horrifying images to satisfy our imagination. How to turn life into a horrifying image and turn a horrifying image into life. The adventure continues.

p. 219: We lack faith in dialogue: The extended anguish I depict here is the long-term struggle between violence and dialogue as alternative or interweaving problem-solving approaches. It would be wrong to think we know much about either.

p. 219: Above, below, inside the storm: Bion often likened psychoanalysis to his war experiences and the need to keep a clear head in the middle of emotional tumult (e.g., *Cogitations*, p. 365). Freud wrote of a detached watcher outside the psychotic storm ("An Outline of Psychoanalysis," pp. 201–2 [see *The Psychotic Core*, chap. 1]). John Ruskin distinguishes poets who maintain themselves in strong emotional fields and those who give themselves over to emotional swirls, risking deformation (e.g., Dante vs. Keats); see *Modern Painters*, vol. 3, chap. 12, "Of the Pathetic Fallacy."

What I have in mind is a little more akin to, not identical with, autonomic intelligence, when quick psychosomatic response seems of a piece and meets the situation at hand. It is not a matter of being in command or giving in. Bion's concept of transformations in O comes closer to what I mean by affective sensing/speaking. He distinguishes between K-transformations relating to knowledge, knowing about, and O-transformations involving being, the thing itself (*Attention and Interpretation*, chaps. 3–5 and 9; Eigen, *The Psychoanalytic Mystic*, chaps. 3, 4, and 6). My book *Ecstasy*, for example, is a sustained attempt to live and express O-transformations—in the context of the present work, to speak from storm, to be storm speaking, to let storm speak. The particular accent or psychospiritual "body English" I am after is not only to know about (no mean achievement) but to do some O'ing.

p. 220: Speaking from the storm center: William Blake somewhere wrote of heaven as war in which all voices have their maximum say and all benefit. A variation on this theme is Shakespeare's *The Tempest* (see also p. 44 above and the first note for it) in which a magical storm affects travelers, injuring none, after which, through twists and turns, things sort themselves out. I take this storm to be a goal of sorts, in which we evolve to where we can undergo affects in ways that help, not injure. Perhaps emotional richness requires injury. We will see. No need to decide now—definitive answers are beyond what we can do. We can, however, keep working, thinking, inquiring, feeling, speaking.

About the author:

MICHAEL EIGEN is a psychologist and psychoanalyst. He is
Associate Clinical Professor of Psychology in the Postdoctoral
Program in Psychotherapy and Psychoanalysis at New York University.
His numerous books include *The Sensitive Self* (2004), *Rage* (2002),
Ecstasy (2001), *Damaged Bonds* (2001), *Toxic Nourishment* (1999), *The
Psychoanalytic Mystic* (1998), *Psychic Deadness* (1996), and *The Psychotic
Core* (1986). Eigen is also a Senior Member at the National Psychological
Association for Psychoanalysis, where he is currently the editor of *The
Psychoanalytic Review.*

CPSIA information can be obtained
at www.ICGtesting.com
Printed in the USA
LVHW101508100522
718413LV00004B/94